Intergenerational Relationships: Conversations on Practice and Research Across Cultures

Intergenerational Relationships: Conversations on Practice and Research Across Cultures has been co-published simultaneously as *Journal of Intergenerational Relationships*, Volume 2, Numbers 3/4 2004.

D1564997

Intergenerational Relationships: Conversations on Practice and Research Across Cultures

Elizabeth Larkin
Dov Friedlander
Sally Newman
Richard Goff
Editors

Intergenerational Relationships: Conversations on Practice and Research Across Cultures has been co-published simultaneously as *Journal of Intergenerational Relationships*, Volume 2, Numbers 3/4 2004.

The Haworth Press, Inc.

New York • London • Victoria (AU)
www.HaworthPress.com

Intergenerational Relationships: Conversations on Practice and Research Across Cultures has been co-published simultaneously as *Journal of Intergenerational Relationships*, Volume 2, Numbers 3/4 2004.

The Haworth Press, Inc., 10 Alice Street, Binghamton, NY 13904-1580 USA

Cover design by Lora Wiggins

Library of Congress Cataloging-in-Publication Data

Intergenerational relationships : conversations on practice and research across cultures / Elizabeth Larkin ... [et al.], editors.
    p. cm.
    "Co-published simultaneously as Journal of intergenerational relationships, volume 2, number 3/4 2004."
    Papers presented at a colloquium on "Enhancing Global Social Change through Intergenerational Initiatives," held Oct. 19-20, 2003 at the University of Pittsburgh.
    Includes bibliographical references and index.
    ISBN 0-7890-2625-2 (hard cover : alk. paper) – ISBN 0-7890-2626-0 (soft cover : alk. paper)
    1. Intergenerational relations–Congresses. 2. Intergenerational relations–Cross-cultural studies–Congresses. I. Larkin, Elizabeth. II. Journal of intergenerational relationships.
HM726.I47 2004
305.2–dc22
2004022791

Indexing, Abstracting & Website/Internet Coverage

This section provides you with a list of major indexing & abstracting services and other tools for bibliographic access. That is to say, each service began covering this periodical during the year noted in the right column. Most Websites which are listed below have indicated that they will either post, disseminate, compile, archive, cite or alert their own Website users with research-based content from this work. (This list is as current as the copyright date of this publication.)

Abstracting, Website/Indexing Coverage . . . . Year When Coverage Began

- *AgeInfo CD-Rom <http://www.cpa.org.uk>* **2003**
- *AgeLine Database <http://research.aarp.org/ageline>* **2003**
- *CAB ABSTRACTS c/o CAB International/CAB ACCESS . . .*
    available in print, diskettes updated weekly, and on Internet.
    Providing full bibliographic listings, author affiliation,
    augmented keyword searching <http://www.cabi.org> **2003**
- *CAB HEALTH c/o CAB International/CAB ACCESS . . .*
    available in print, diskettes updated weekly, and on Internet.
    Providing full bibliographic listings, author affiliation,
    augmented keyword searching <http://www.cabi.org> **2003**
- *CareData: The database supporting social care management*
    and practice <http://www.elsc.org.uk/caredata/caredata.htm> . . . **2003**
- *Child Development Abstracts <http://www.tandf.co.uk>* **2003**
- *CINAHL (Cumulative Index to Nursing & Allied Health*
    Literature), in print, EBSCO, and SilverPlatter, DataStar,
    and PaperChase. (Support materials include Subject Heading
    List, Database Search Guide, and instructional video)
    <http://www.cinahl.com> **2004**
- *Contents Pages in Education* **2004**
- *e-psyche, LLC <http://www.e-psyche.net>* **2003**
- *EBSCOhost Electronic Journals Service (EJS)*
    <http://ejournals.com> **2003**

(continued)

- *Educational Research Abstracts (ERA) (online database)*
  <http://www.tandf.co.uk/era> 2004
- *ERIC: Current Index to Journals in Education (CIJE)*
  <http://www.ericacve.org> 2003
- *Family & Society Studies Worldwide <http://www.nisc.com>* 2003
- *Family Index Database <http://www.familyscholar.com>* 2003
- *Family Violence & Sexual Assault Bulletin* 2003
- *GeroLit <http://www.dza.de/english/english.html>* 2003
- *Google <http://www.google.com>* 2004
- *Google Scholar <http://www.scholar.google.com* 2004
- *Index to Periodical Articles Related to Law*
  <http://www.law.utexas.edu> 2003
- *International Bibliography of the Social Sciences*
  <http://www.ibss.ac.uk> 2004
- *New Literature on Old Age <http://www.cpa.org.uk>* 2003
- *Sage Family Studies Abstracts (SFSA)* 2004
- *Sociological Abstracts (SA) <http://www.csa.com>* 2003

*Special Bibliographic Notes related to special journal issues
(separates) and indexing/abstracting:*

- indexing/abstracting services in this list will also cover material in any "separate" that is co-published simultaneously with Haworth's special thematic journal issue or DocuSerial. Indexing/abstracting usually covers material at the article/chapter level.
- monographic co-editions are intended for either non-subscribers or libraries which intend to purchase a second copy for their circulating collections.
- monographic co-editions are reported to all jobbers/wholesalers/approval plans. The source journal is listed as the "series" to assist the prevention of duplicate purchasing in the same manner utilized for books-in-series.
- to facilitate user/access services all indexing/abstracting services are encouraged to utilize the co-indexing entry note indicated at the bottom of the first page of each article/chapter/contribution.
- this is intended to assist a library user of any reference tool (whether print, electronic, online, or CD-ROM) to locate the monographic version if the library has purchased this version but not a subscription to the source journal.
- individual articles/chapters in any Haworth publication are also available through the Haworth Document Delivery Service (HDDS).

Intergenerational Relationships: Conversations on Practice and Research Across Cultures

CONTENTS

Preface   xi
  Dov Friedlander

Introduction   1
  Elizabeth Larkin

SECTION I: INTERGENERATIONAL RELATIONSHIPS
  IN FAMILIES

Family Studies and Intergenerational Studies:
  Intersections and Opportunities   5
    Roma Stovall Hanks
    James J. Ponzetti, Jr.

Intergenerational Cultural Transmission
  Among the Akan of Ghana   23
    Joseph K. Adjaye
    Osei-Mensah Aborampah

Intergenerational Impact of the AIDS Pandemic in Nigeria   39
  Bede Eke

The Elder in African Society: The View from Folklore
  and Literature   53
    Joseph Mbele

Understanding Intergenerational Relationships in India   63
  N. K. Chadha

Intergenerational Theory in Society: Building on the Past,
  Questions for the Future   75
    Karen VanderVen

SECTION II: INTERGENERATIONAL RELATIONSHIPS IN COMMUNITIES

Intergenerational Initiatives in Sweden 95
 Ann-Kristin Boström

A Faith-Based Intergenerational Health and Wellness Program 105
 Mary Duquin
 James McCrea
 David Fetterman
 Sabrina Nash

Futures Festivals: An Intergenerational Strategy
 for Promoting Community Participation 119
 Matthew Kaplan
 Frank Higdon
 Nancy Crago
 Lucinda Robbins

Terms for Intergenerational Relations Among the Tumbuka
 of Northern Malawi 147
 Lupenga Mphande

Transformations over Time in Generational Relationships
 in Africa 171
 Choja Oduaran
 Akpovire Oduaran

Where We Are Now with Intergenerational Developments:
 An English Perspective 187
 Norma Raynes

". . . the (unbearable) 'in-betweenness' of being . . .":
 A Postmodern Exploration of Intergenerational Practices
 in Africa: A Framework Towards Programming 197
 Jaco Hoffman

SECTION III: CONCLUDING DISCUSSION

Global Intergenerational Research, Programs and Policy:
 What Does the Future Hold? 215
 Paul A. Roodin

Index 221

ABOUT THE EDITORS

Elizabeth Larkin, EdD, is Associate Professor in the College of Education at the University of South Florida Sarasota-Manatee. She has received awards for her intergenerational research from the National Intergenerational Caucus of Early Childhood Professionals and Big Brothers Big Sisters of the Suncoast. Dr. Larkin's research interests include looking at the professional development of educators as well as studying intergenerational initiatives that bring older adults and younger populations together for their mutual benefit. She is on the editorial board of the *Journal of Intergenerational Relationships* and is a founding member of ICIP.

Dov Friedlander, PhD, served as both Lecturer and Program Coordinator at York University, Toronto, Canada, in the field of Clinical Psychology until 1970 when he returned to Israel to accept the joint positions of Senior Lecturer in Clinical Psychology and founder and Director of the Student Counseling Services at the Hebrew University of Jerusalem, Israel. Since his retirement in 2002, Dr. Friedlander has been elected to be the Chairman of the Israel Association for Adult Education. He is a member of the ICIP International Management Committee and serves on the Editorial Board for the *Journal of Intergenerational Relationships.* He has published numerous articles and co-edited a number of books on the subjects of clinical psychology, adult education, and intergenerational topics.

Sally Newman, PhD, is emerita faculty of the University of Pittsburgh, School of Education, Senior Researcher (retired) at the University of Pittsburgh Center for Social and Urban Research, and Founder and former Executive Director of Generations Together, an intergenerational studies program there. Dr. Newman is the Founding Chair of the International Consortium for Intergenerational Programs (ICIP) and Founding Editor of the *Journal of Intergenerational Relationships: Programs, Policy, and Research.* She edited and co-authored the first textbook on intergenerational issues, *Intergenerational Programs: Imperatives, Strategies, Impacts, and Trends,* and is senior author of the textbook *Intergenerational Programs: Past, Present, and Future.* A pioneer in intergenerational programs, she is known internationally as an author, lecturer, and researcher.

Richard Goff, ABD, is a PhD candidate in history at the University of Pittsburgh. He is adjunct faculty at Chatham College where he teaches American social history. He has served as Graduate Advisory Editor for Social Science History and is currently the editorial assistant for the *Journal of Intergenerational Relationships.*

Preface

*One way to cope with the complexity of today's world is to pro-
mote global intergenerational relationships.*

On October 19-20, 2003, a colloquium on global intergenerational
research, programs and policy entitled "Enhancing Global Social
Change Through Intergenerational Initiatives" was convened at the
University of Pittsburgh. The colloquium focused on "how international intergenerational initiatives could contribute to understanding
among different groups and cultures." During this two-day event, University of Pittsburgh faculty and students, international faculty colleagues, and faculty board members of the *Journal of Intergenerational
Relationships* described intergenerational collaboration from a global
perspective.

Participants from fourteen countries and four continents presented
papers that identified and explored intergenerational concepts, programs, and research and discussed future action for international intergenerational initiatives through information and exchange. One needs
to capture the tone of the colloquium. The atmosphere among the participants was one of quiet and careful listening to each other, and trying to
understand what others were attempting to convey, without immediately filtering it through one's own cultural and educational experiences.

The feeling in this friendly environment was that a real conversation
between people of very different backgrounds was occurring. It is my
impression, that this colloquium managed to go beyond the level of
shared knowledge, but in fact created rich and diversified understanding
between the different cultures and ideas represented. Furthermore, I believe these "Conversations" did much to lay the groundwork for contin-

[Haworth co-indexing entry note]: "Preface." Friedlander, Dov. Co-published simultaneously in *Journal
of Intergenerational Relationships* (The Haworth Press, Inc.) Vol. 2. No. 3/4, 2004, pp. xvii-xix; and:
Intergenerational Relationships: Conversations on Practice and Research Across Cultures (ed: Elizabeth
Larkin et al.) The Haworth Press, Inc., 2004, pp. xi-xiii. Single or multiple copies of this article are available
for a fee from The Haworth Document Delivery Service [1-800-HAWORTH, 9:00 a.m. - 5:00 p.m. (EST).
E-mail address: docdelivery@haworthpress.com].

xi

uing international dialogue and to enhance international communication in the intergenerational field. A significant aspect of this event was the diversity of the content and the geographic representation of the participants.

From the thirty-five papers that were delivered at the colloquium, fourteen appear in this volume entitled *Intergenerational Relationships: Conversations on Practice and Research Across Cultures.*

The contents of this volume reflect the diversity of approaches to intergenerational issues by its authors from many different corners of the globe and from a variety of academic disciplines. In organizing the material, it naturally fell into two general categories: Relationships in Families and Relationships in Communities. A concluding article on global intergenerational research synthesizes the papers and highlights the common ground in this diversified field.

What is striking in this collection of articles is the diversity of content and cross-cultural representation that find their expression in these papers that was also reflected in the "Conversations" among the participants.

I would venture to say that the colloquium has opened avenues that had hardly existed for international cooperation. We shared information on joint ventures and promulgated the development of a variety of international intergenerational initiatives.

Finally, as a co-editor of this volume, I wish to express my personal sincere thanks to the person who introduced me, as she has many others like me, to the field of intergenerational processes, to Professor Emerita Sally Newman, best known to her very many friends throughout the world as "Sally, the founding mother" of the discipline of intergenerational concepts and practice. I wish also to acknowledge her assistant Richard Goff for his commitment and tireless efforts to prepare this unique volume. Without the constant support, help, and focus of the editorial team, this volume would not have reached fruition.

Also, thanks to the co-sponsors including University of Pittsburgh, The Haworth Press, Inc., and the Pittsburgh Council for International Volunteers who assured the success of the colloquium.[1]

Finally, allow me to thank my guest co-editor, Professor Elizabeth Larkin of the University of South Florida. In the many years I have been involved in cooperative research and publishing endeavors, I have never experienced a more joyous and effortless process as I did in working and cooperating with Liz.

Dov Friedlander

NOTE

1. "Enhancing Global Social Change Through Intergenerational Initiatives" co-sponsors:

    Center for International Studies, William Brustein, Director
      Africana Studies, Joseph Adjaye, Director/Chair
      Asian Studies, Bell Yung, Director
      Latin American Studies, Kathleen DeWalt, Director
      Western European Studies, Alberta Sbragia, Director
    College of General Studies, Susan Kinsey, Dean
    Graduate School of Public Health, Bernard Goldstein, Dean
    School of Education, Alan Lesgold, Dean
    School of Law, David Herring, Dean
    University Center for Social and Urban Research Richard Schulz, Director
    The Haworth Press, Inc., Bill Cohen, President and Publisher
    Pittsburgh Council for International Visitors, Gail Shrott, Executive Director

Introduction

This collection of papers by experts in the field of intergenerational work furthers the dialogue about the importance of intergenerational practices around the world. Because this is still an emerging field, we continue to face the need to justify the critical importance of addressing social issues with an intergenerational lens, both here in the U.S. and abroad. The dialogue has moved from what was once narrowly defined as programming for skipped generations of people who are not related to a much broader view of intergenerational work that now embraces family relationships and multigenerational connections as well. These papers present the "state of our art" as it is today, and they provoke thought about how both families and communities are being transformed for the better by an intergenerational approach.

What was started by the International Consortium of Intergenerational Programmes (ICIP) in 1999, and carried forward in the conferences and journal articles that followed, is a truly international conversation about intergenerational approaches to solving social issues. Understanding how different cultural groups value connections among people of different ages, how they endeavor to promote interdependencies that benefit all generations, and what modern-day complexities shape their program goals are elements of the discussion that can increase global awareness and perhaps even make a small contribution toward peaceful coexistence worldwide.

At a time when national security is in crisis, we must do whatever we can to reach across international boundaries to make the world a safer place. As Dr. Narender Chadha from Delhi University taught us at the

[Haworth co-indexing entry note]: "Introduction." Larkin. Elizabeth. Co-published simultaneously in *Journal of Intergenerational Relationships* (The Haworth Press. Inc.) Vol. 2, No. 3/4, 2004, pp. 1-3; and: *Intergenerational Relationships: Conversations on Practice and Research Across Cultures* (ed: Elizabeth Larkin et al.) The Haworth Press, Inc., 2004, pp. 1-3. Single or multiple copies of this article are available for a fee from The Haworth Document Delivery Service [1-800-HAWORTH. 9:00 a.m. - 5:00 p.m. (EST). E-mail address: docdelivery@haworthpress.com].

Digital Object Identifier: 10.1300/J194v02n03_01

2003 Colloquium in Pittsburgh, we can learn to greet one another with the words, "I respect you" rather than simply wishing a good morning or afternoon. We can begin to appreciate what it means to have a whole generation of parents dying of AIDS, and help by sharing knowledge and resources. And we can learn to value the stories and traditions that have bound people together over centuries of struggle, so that we don't lose what matters most as the world rapidly changes.

Threads in the conversation that link articles from Africa, Europe, Asia, and the U.S. include the critical importance of building cultural capital and ensuring cultural transfer across ages. As modern technologies rapidly transform societies, the need to recognize the essential elements of who we are and maintain a cultural identity is clear. The challenge to adapt and accommodate change while also preserving our heritage is inherent in the intergenerational perspective of these authors.

The conversations cross disciplinary boundaries as well as geographic ones. Through different lenses, such as education, family studies, cultural anthropology, psychology and gerontology we look at the meaning of generational connections. Rites of passage, language, art and literature, community events, and academic research are all brought to bear on why we must not allow isolation or competition to divide our common interests. As no man is an island, so is no generation–we cannot survive without the collective gifts and strengths of all.

This volume is divided into two sections: the first on intergenerational relationships in the family, the second on intergenerational relationships in the community. In the former, Hanks and Ponzetti, and VanderVen contribute to the ongoing dialogue about defining the field of intergenerational studies, and they present a broader spectrum of theoretical frameworks to inform our understanding of interpersonal relationships among partners of different ages. The second section includes papers that address community-wide concerns. Some program initiatives are organized at the grassroots level, while others stem from formal social policies that address quality of life issues. Looking at social policies as they affect all age groups within a community expands our understanding of intergenerational relationships as being a matter of multigenerational ties where the middle groups have a key role in connecting younger and older generations to one another. The third section contains summarizing reflections on the intergenerational practices, policies, and research that this international group of authors has presented.

We have a relatively large cluster of papers that address intergenerational concerns in Africa. To have so many perspectives on family and social relationships from this part of the world is truly unique, and they lend a powerful voice to the conversation about the rationale for inter-generational programming in a part of the world that is undergoing rapid social change. One paper presents the disturbing picture of how AIDS has decimated the middle generation, leaving younger and older generations to suffer the consequences. Several of the papers on African cultures describe how central family is to the fabric of a society, and how important elders are in transferring language, values, and history to younger generations. In comparison, the intergenerational thrust in modernized western countries tends to be more on redeveloping community cohesiveness and creating a society for all ages.

Whether the focus of intergenerational practice is on families or communities, the critical nature of our interdependencies is apparent in either context.

This multicultural collection of papers presents strong reasons for taking an intergenerational approach to solving social problems, to understanding how culture changes practice, and to appreciating the importance of protecting human values in times of technological innovation, geographic mobility, and shifting economies. The important roles of grandparents and the beauty of their stories are made clear. These authors have communicated critical ideas in an effort to collaborate across the geographic and academic boundaries that divide us day-to-day in order to foster greater understanding of why we need intergenerational relationships.

Elizabeth Larkin

SECTION I:
INTERGENERATIONAL RELATIONSHIPS
IN FAMILIES

Family Studies
and Intergenerational Studies:
Intersections and Opportunities

Roma Stovall Hanks
James J. Ponzetti, Jr.

SUMMARY. This paper reviews key sources in the field of family studies in order to identify, in research and program development, intersections of theoretical, methodological, or programmatic interests. The
purpose of the paper is to begin a dialogue between researchers and practitioners in the fields of family studies and intergenerational studies to
foster collaborative projects in research and programming. The authors
have chosen to limit the literature reviewed to sources that contain landmark reviews of research on intergenerational relationships from the
perspective of the family studies field: Decade reviews that appeared in
the primary journal of the National Council on Family Relations, the

Roma Stovall Hanks is affiliated with the University of South Alabama, Alabama.
James J. Ponzetti, Jr. is affiliated with the University of British Columbia, Vancouver.

[Haworth co-indexing entry note]: "Family Studies and Intergenerational Studies: Intersections and
Opportunities." Hanks, Roma Stovall, and James J. Ponzetti, Jr. Co-published simultaneously in *Journal of
Intergenerational Relationships* (The Haworth Press, Inc.) Vol. 2, No. 3/4, 2004, pp. 5-22; and: *Intergenera-
tional Relationships: Conversations on Practice and Research Across Cultures* (ed: Elizabeth Larkin et al.)
The Haworth Press, Inc., 2004, pp. 5-22. Single or multiple copies of this article are available for a fee from
The Haworth Document Delivery Service [1-800- HAWORTH, 9:00 a.m. - 5:00 p.m. (EST). E-mail address:
docdelivery@haworthpress.com].

Journal of Marriage and the Family (Broderick, 1971a; Berardo, 1980; Booth, 1990; Milardo, 2000); the *Handbook of Marriage and the Family* (Sussman & Steinmetz, 1987; Sussman, Steinmetz, & Peterson, 1999); *Families: Intergenerational and Generational Connections* (Pfeifer & Sussman, 1991). *[Article copies available for a fee from The Haworth Document Delivery Service: 1-800-HAWORTH. E-mail address: <docdelivery@ haworthpress.com> Website: <http://www.HaworthPress.com> © 2004 by The Haworth Press, Inc. All rights reserved.]*

KEYWORDS. Family studies, intergenerational studies, collaborative projects, intergenerational relationships, marriage and the family

INTRODUCTION

Intergenerational relationships have a particularly salient role in contemporary family networks because families are constituted by a multitude of cross-generational linkages. Families, by definition, consist of two or more individuals of varying ages who are linked together over time through a matrix of intimate relationships. Thus, family life is typically multigenerational in nature. These generational arrangements promote unique interpersonal processes that are very influential for the individuals who exist within the familial context (Day, 2003).

Family structures and processes are typically intergenerational in nature. The structure of families is defined and maintained by generational boundaries; that is, the rules differentiating the rights and responsibilities between older and younger cohorts. A variety of arrangements can be tenable if generational boundaries are clear and not breached.

Generational processes influence family members across their entire life span. Cross-generational linkages are essential for both personal and family connectedness and continuity. The horizontal connections between family members representing several generations explicate the daily interactions at the same historical time. The vertical connections across generations in families are important for understanding family life over time.

The purpose of the paper is threefold. First, family studies and intergenerational studies are defined as distinct fields of study. Second, research on intergenerational relationships from the perspective of the family studies field is reviewed. Finally, how this information can develop and foster collaborative projects in research and programming between the two fields is discussed.

FAMILY STUDIES

The academic study of families is not new. It began as an interdisciplinary area of inquiry in the early 20th century. Scholars from a variety of established disciplines (e.g., home economics, sociology, anthropology, theology) focused their attention specifically on families. As a coherent body of family theory and research developed, scholarly journals emerged that focused on family issues. In addition, more colleges established family studies departments which led to the development of new knowledge and theoretical frameworks about family life (Christen- sen, 1964).

Interest in family studies continued to evolve from the 1950s until the early 1980s when the recognition of family studies as a unique discipline in its own right was broached at meetings of the National Council for Family Relations (Burr & Leigh, 1983). The fact that family studies is recognized as a discipline rather than a profession is a critical one for understanding the primary difference between family studies and intergenerational studies which is an area of professional practice.

Professions include fields such as nursing, social work, engineering, or education. Students graduating from professional education have been prepared for specific types of employment, and they have a job title or identity based on that profession. In contrast, students with a degree in a discipline (such as sociology, mathematics, or geology) are trained in bodies of knowledge, skills and critical thinking that can be applied to a wide variety of jobs. Students with degrees in family studies enter careers in a variety of sectors such as social services, business and industry, health professions, education, journalism and publishing, public administration, criminal justice and corrections, government, and international affairs.

The parallels between family studies and intergenerational studies are most obvious in the life span developmental perspective evident in each field. In later life, parents place a high value on caring and sharing ties with their children. They continue to be interested in the activities and welfare of their children and subsequent generations. Despite popular myths to the contrary, parents continue to provide help or attention to other family members, as well as to receive support. The reciprocal interaction that occurs across all the generations is a sign of family well-being. The elderly can continue to provide care for their children and their grandchildren until they are no longer able. Middle-aged children receive love and aid from their parents and can also help their parents as needed. Grandchildren and children both give to and receive from the older generations.

INTERGENERATIONAL STUDIES

The field of intergenerational studies began in the 1960s with the growing interest and development of programs that brought children and elders together (Newman, 1989). The field developed around program initiatives and policy concerns. Interest in intergenerational activities involving adults and children continues to grow as the size and composition of nuclear families continue to change. This increase is probably attributable to the fact that the idea makes such good sense. Anecdotal reports based on firsthand experiences have probably spread enthusiasm as well.

Intergenerational studies has always had a strong applied emphasis. Programming efforts have been more prominent than the articulation of theory or research (VanderVen, 1999). What, then, is intergenerational programming? Intergenerational programming has been defined as the ". . . purposeful bringing together of different generations in ongoing mutually beneficial planned activities designed to achieve specified program goals. Through intergenerational programs, young and old share their talents and resources, supporting each other in relationships that benefit both the individuals and the community . . ." (AARP, 1994). Intergenerational programs are most frequently found in schools, child and adult day care programs, community centers, and with civic organizations and youth groups. In some cases, older adults act as caregiving staff, tutors, mentors, or role models. In other instances, they participate in joint activities with younger people. Some research has documented the value of intergenerational programs; larger-scale studies are needed.

The establishment of academic sponsorship for intergenerational studies is still nascent despite calls for such advanced education (VanderVen, 1989). The advent of the *Journal of Intergenerational Relationships* is the first scholarly periodical devoted exclusively to the area.

Although both intergenerational studies and family studies consider cross-generation interaction, family scholars utilize a broader definition of intergenerational relationships than the one widely accepted in the field of intergenerational studies. Specifically, family studies includes parent-child relationships, and other kin relationships, among those relationships that are viewed as intergenerational, while intergenerational studies focuses on non-kin relationships and family relationships that skip a generation. Intergenerational simply means "between generations" and thus the inclusion of studies on parent-child interaction is considered important here.

REVIEW OF RELEVANT FAMILY STUDIES LITERATURE

The literature reviewed is limited to significant review articles that address intergenerational relationships from major perspectives within the discipline of family studies. To be specific, *Families: Intergenerational and Generational Connections* edited by Pfeifer and Sussman (1991), and pertinent chapters in both editions of the *Handbook of Marriage and the Family* (Sussman & Steinmetz, 1987; Sussman, Steinmetz, & Peterson, 1999), and, the *Journal of Marriage and the Family* decade review volumes (Broderick, 1971a; Berardo, 1980; Booth, 1990; Milardo, 2000) are considered.

Intergenerational Family Studies Research in the 1960s (Broderick, 1971a)

Early investigation of family relationships focused on the nuclear family. Sussman (1951) challenged the prevailing view that nuclear families are disconnected from the kin network. During the 1960s, the study of kinship began to consider intergenerational relationships (Sussman & Burchinal, 1962; Adams, 1968; Farber, 1968). The study of kinship provided both theoretical and methodological underpinnings for future intergenerational research. Work on kin networks dominated research, with less attention given to parent-child relationships as intergenerational connections. As he introduced his decade review volume, Editor Carlfred Broderick (1971b) pointed to significant development of research and theory in comparative intergenerational studies.

Intergenerational Family Studies Research in the 1970s (Berardo, 1980)

In the decade review of the 1970s (Berardo, 1980) (Figure 1), the tone was one of a discipline finding itself. Discussions around theory and methodology point to growth and emerging self-confidence among scholars in the family studies field. Troll reviewed literature on kin availability, residential propinquity between elders and other family members, economic interdependence between elders and their adult

FIGURE 1. Review of literature summarized in NCFR decade reviews.

Research on intergenerational relationships from family studies perspective: Decade review of the 1960s (Broderick, 1971)
- Kinship
  - Family structure
  - Parent-child; in-law; frequency of contact; generational conflicts; strength of ties
- Inheritance
  - Application of exchange theory
  - Transmission of wealth
  - Sharing of resources
- Caregiving
  - Availability/residential propinquity
  - Gendered work
  - Economic differences
- Grandparenting
  - Transmission of values
  - Meaning of role for grandparents
  - Impact of interaction on child development

Research on intergenerational relationships from family studies perspective: Decade review of the 1970s (Berardo, 1980)
- Parent-child relationships
  - Bi-directional influences in the relationship
- Advocacy
  - "Government intrusion into the parent-child relationship" (Walters & Walters, 1980)
- Kin networks in African American families
- Bureaucratic linkages
  - Organizations assume nurturing roles of family
- Non-traditional family forms
- Isolation of the nuclear family
  - Gary Lee (1980) observed that isolation became "a variable, not a condition"
- Kin availability and intergenerational economic interdependence

Research on intergenerational relationships from family studies perspective: Decade review of the 1980s (Booth, 1990)	Research on intergenerational relationships from family studies perspective: Decade review of 1990s (Milardo, 2000)

• Policy
  • Growing individualism
  • Lessening civil engagement
• African American families
  • Racial socialization
  • Black women in extended kin networks
  • "Early" grandparenting
  • Church as informal support network
• Later life families
  • Adult children and their parents
  • Grandparenting
  • Family caregiving
  • Gender differences
• Adolescence
  • Parent/peer influences
  • "Youth culture"
• Marital and family enrichment programs
  • Evaluation research encouraged
	• Family structure in multicultural perspective
	• Grandparent involvement
	  • Grandparents raising grandchildren
	• Neighborhood and peer influences
	  • Acculturation and intergenerational conflict in immigrant families
	• Comparison of friendship and kin networks
	• Application of theories to intergenerational relations
	  • Life course
	  • Feminist
	  • Socioemotional selectivity
	  • Family solidarity
	• Methodological issues explored
	  • Qualitative and quantitative

children, and qualitative differences in kin relationships. However, Troll (1971) lamented the lack of research on grandparents. Troll presented the concept of "filial maturity" as an essential component of family and individual development.

Walters and Walters (1980) reviewed parent-child relationships. They delineated 10 areas of research on parent-child relationships: physiological influences, parent-infant relationships, divorce, separating, child abuse and neglect, intervention strategies, the value of children, adolescent asexuality, legal influences, and methodological issues. Throughout this review, they embrace a concept that can be seen in much of the development of intergenerational programming, i.e., relationships between parents and children are bi-directional. Indeed, the intergenerational programming perspective pushes this concept beyond the family into relationships such as mentoring, learning, and social support. Walters and Walters also mention a relationship that has become a feature of research on intergenerational relationships: the father-child relationship.

Lee (1980) contributed the article on kinship in the 1970s. Lee discussed conditions that create need for multiple generations to share living space and drew some interesting conclusions about kin interaction. Perhaps most noteworthy, however, in Lee's article is his observation regarding intergenerational research in the 1960s. Lee (1980: p. 193) noted, "Perhaps the most significant accomplishment of the sixties was the recognition that nuclear isolation is a variable not a condition." This principle paved the way for programs to *do something about* the separation between generations.

Intergenerational Family Studies Research in the 1980s (Booth, 1990)

During the 1980s, research on intergenerational relationships continued to focus on parent-child relationships and the relationships between elders and their family members.

Taylor, Chatters, Tucker, and Lewis (1990) reviewed research on African American families. The majority of research on intergenerational relationships concerned the roles of adult children in supporting elderly family members and the role of grandmothers in providing assistance to their grandchildren. Intergenerational relationships are discussed as support net- works, including reviews of literature that relate extended family network support to child development and aging. One intergenerational issue covered was racial socialization as a strategy to prepare their children for adulthood in the broader society. Extended family networks, including intergenerational ties, were important considerations for research in the 1980s on black women, black men, and black elderly.

Brubaker (1990) noted substantial growth in research interest on families that had passed the child launching stage. Brubaker recognized Mancini and Blieszner's (1989) review of research on adult children and older parents, as well as reviews by Bengtson and colleagues (Bengtson, 1989; Bengtson, Cutler, Mangen, & Marshall, 1985) on intergenerational relationships. Brubaker provides an extensive review of literature on grandparenting and on family caregiving, including gender differences in both perception and enactment of roles related to each. Women were more involved as both grandparents and caregivers.

In his overview of marital and family enrichment programs, Berardo called for continued evaluation research in order to discover which programs work best for which populations and to use the accumulated knowledge for program improvement. Certainly, this programmatic arena offers a common ground for family and intergenerational studies to contribute to program development and evaluation.

1987 Handbook on Marriage and the Family
(Sussman & Steinmetz, 1987)

An important stream of family research has been the historical analysis of family relations. Hareven's (1987) chapter on family history dispels myths that the pre-industrial family was three-generational in a household, that these families were more harmonious and connected than post-industrial families, and that furthermore the Industrial Revolution destroyed the prevailing family structure and created the isolated nuclear family. Indeed, Hareven and the researchers she cites agree that the predominant family structure that has persisted over time is the nuclear household with members of the family closely connected with ties to extended kin, including both same generational and cross-generational connections (see Figure 2).

This discussion of family structure over family time and historical time is of great interest to researchers and practitioners in intergenerational programming and research. There is much room for debate and subsequent research as to the family's loss of intergenerational ties over historical time–especially as a result of historically significant events, such as the Industrial Revolution or the large-scale entrance of women into the workforce. Hareven says that it was actually the extended kin

FIGURE 2. Review of literature summarized from other landmark sources.

Intergenerational relationships reviewed in the *Handbook on Marriage and the Family*, First Edition (Sussman & Steinmetz, 1987)
- Historical research on family structure
  - Persistence of nuclear family
  - Aid in extended kin networks
  - Fluidity of household structure over the life span
- Life course perspective
  - Mid-life transitions
  - Gender differences
- Parent and child socialization
  - Bi-directional influence
- Family solidarity

Intergenerational relationships reviewed in the *Handbook on Marriage and the Family*, Second Edition (Sussman, Steinmetz, & Peterson, 1991)
- Parent-child relationship continues to interest family scholars
- Focus on adulthood—the middle generation

Intergenerational relationships reviewed in Pfeifer and Sussman (1991)
- Process of modernization and emergence of bureaucratic organization; viability of intergenerational connections in the face of residential distance between generations (Sussman)
- Intergenerational solidarity—refinements in operational definitions and methodologies (Roberts, Richards, & Bengtson)
- Application of life course perspective—focus on "the middle ground" (George & Gold)
- "Differential pull" of family and non-family intergenerational relationships as basis for obligation (Hanks)
- Convoys of social support (Antonucci & Akiyama)
- Policy and generational conflict (Hirshorn)
- Role timing and meaning (Kivett)

Questions for further discussion
- What are reasons to include parent-child relationships in intergenerational studies? What are reasons to limit intergenerational studies to skip-generation relationships?
- How can theories applied to intergenerational relationships in families inform analyses of non-family intergenerational relationships?
- What methodologies for intergenerational research and programming are transferable between family studies and intergenerational studies perspectives?

networks of families that facilitated industrialization because the extended family aided migration and socialization.

Although the Peterson and Rollins (1987) chapter is rich with discussion that offers potential bridges between family studies and intergenerational studies, we will select only one as an illustration–the shift in focus in research on parents and children from unidirectional influence to bi-directional influence. There seems to be vast opportunity for collaboration of family studies and intergenerational studies researchers in simply replicating findings for these approaches in non-familial cross-generational dyads or comparing family and non-family relationships and child outcomes.

Vern Bengtson and his colleagues have generated a substantial body of research on intergenerational relationships over the last thirty years. Much of this work has been presented at conferences on gerontology and published in research journals that focus on aging. Although Treas and Bengtson (1987) take the perspective of the late life family in their *Handbook* chapter, they recognize, "No account of the constraints on family relations would be complete without a consideration of the changing social roles of mid-life Americans" (page 633). They note that increasing demands for elder care are particularly challenging for women, since they provide most of the informal care in families. Increased participation of women in the paid workforce has decreased their time available for caregiving, but has not diminished their representation in caregiving roles. Treas and Bengtson note that women provide 75% of family caregiver assistance. As women become less available to provide informal care, the caregiver pool must be sustained from other sources. Non-family caregivers can help to fill gaps. Programs that encourage non-familial intergenerational relationships go directly to this problem and its solution.

Family solidarity has been a major theme in Bengtson's research on intergenerational relationships. Too little has been done to apply his research questions and methods to non-family groups in order to explain cross-generation friendships, mentoring relationships, voluntary assistance, and choice of careers in caring professions. The work of Bengtson and his colleagues is rich with questions about intergenerational relationships that need to be answered for non-family as well as family groups.

Contributions to Pfeifer and Sussman (1991)

Sussman's (1991) introduction to the volume traces the process of modernization as a major influence on intergenerational relationships in families. Interestingly, the perceived isolation of the nuclear family has its place in the founding of the field of intergenerational programming. As families of residence shrank in size from extended to nuclear, children had less day-to-day access to older family members. Founders of the field of intergenerational programming believed that negative stereotypes of elders were a direct result of lack of contact between the generations and they sought to correct the problem of generational isolation. Within family studies, researchers took a different tack. Numerous articles, books, and book chapters reported results of research that suggested the viability of intergenerational relationships in the face of residential distance between the older and younger generations.

The chapter on intergenerational solidarity by Roberts, Richards, and Bengtson (1991) is a "must read" for anyone interested in understanding the impact of modernization on intergenerational relationships. The authors go back to the Durkheimian roots of the argument that the Industrial Revolution interfered with family solidarity. They encourage more research on the topic, using refined methodologies and operational definitions of the various components of solidarity in family relationships. In her discussion of "wider definitions of intergenerational responsibility," Hanks (1991) argued that it is not necessary for individuals to be related in a family in order to feel the special obligations within their relationship, similar to the feelings that are the basis of family caregiving. Intergenerational programming has certainly demonstrated that non-family caregiving can be rewarding for members of both generations involved. Qualitative research and program evaluation are needed in order to understand how familial and non-familial caregiving are related.

George and Gold (1991) applied the life course perspective to intergenerational relationships in families. As in other life course articles, George and Gold focus on the middle generation as the most promising for understanding the family's links to the larger society and to history. Again, some resolution needs to be reached between family researchers and intergenerational researchers regarding the importance of the middle generation in understanding the life course. The family emphasis on the middle generation runs counter to the intergenerational perspective of skipping a generation.

George and Gold (1991) raise interesting questions about transitions and trajectories in the life course. Knowledge of the life course of partners in non-family intergenerational relationships could inform program design. Research on intergenerational relationships in life course perspective has focused on family. Hareven (1987) advocates for the life course perspective. It is in the life course perspective that intergenerational studies and family studies may find the origin of their intersection. The life course perspective has contributed to the under-standing of family and non-family intergenerational relationships by setting both in the context of historical time, thereby linking them to so-cial change.

The study of non-family relationships could extend knowledge of the life course, as well as knowledge of the relationships themselves. De-mographic changes that have been observed to coincide with observed changes in family intergenerational relationships may also create change in non-family intergenerational relationships (Hanks, 1991). Here is an opportunity for further discussion and collaboration between family and intergenerational specialists.

Gubrium and Rittman's (1991) chapter was perhaps the most promis-ing to serve as a basis for collaboration between family and intergenerational specialists because in that chapter, the authors focus on inter- organizational contexts–small worlds–that provide insights into intergenerational interaction. While their focus is beyond family, Gubrium and Rittman apply family intergenerational perspectives.

Hirshorn (1991) examines the various arguments regarding the dis-tribution of resources by generation, categorizing these arguments as: conflict-based, solidarity-based, and heterogeneity-based. These argu-ments have become all too familiar since 1991, but neither the family field nor the intergenerational field has reached full potential in apply-ing the various perspectives to research and programming.

Sprey (1991) contributes methodological insights on the study of family intergenerational relationships–specifically the study of family solidarity. He observes that researchers often draw conclusions about families merely by adding individual data. The complexity of family re-lationships cannot be captured by simple addition. Recent research on intergenerational service-learning suggests that individuals of both gen-erations may be changed by interaction. The reflection required by ser-vice-learning is a methodology to understand processes by which a relationship emerges from interaction of individuals from different gen-erations. In a sense, these methodologies answer Sprey's call to attend to the whole, rather than the sum of parts.

Kivett's (1991) review of grandparent research is a call for application of theory to the study of intergenerational relationships. Role interpreta-tions, age and role timing, and gender and ethnic differences contribute to theory building in the study of grandparenting. Similarly, they can explain non-family intergenerational interaction. For example, research that explores mentoring relationships might also explore the meaning of the mentoring role, the timing of volunteer activities across the life course of the mentor, and gender and ethnic differences associated with taking the role of mentor.

1999 Handbook on Marriage and the Family (Sussman, Steinmetz, & Peterson, 1999)

An interesting aspect of intergenerational relationships emerges from the discussion of direction of effect in parent-child interaction. Peterson and Hann (1999) challenge the notion that socialization of children is unidirectional. Here is an intersection of family studies and intergenerational programming in their perspectives on relationships between the generations. Evidence is abundant in intergenerational programming to support bi-directional impact of cross-generational interaction.

Treas and Lawton's 1999 contribution to the *Handbook on Marriage and the Family* is an example of one of the fundamental differences between the family studies field and the intergenerational field. Research and programming in intergenerational studies focus on relationships that skip a generation, i.e., they leave out the middle generation; family research and programming are increasingly interested in the middle generation and the dynamics of relationships of that generation with younger and older family members. Treas and Lawton (1999) focus on adulthood, emphasizing changes in the life course that result from demographic changes such as extended life expectancy.

Intergenerational Family Studies Research in the 1990s (Milardo, 2000)

Certainly, the 1990s decade review showed an increase in research on grandparent involvement, in particular the involvement of grandmothers, but the results are mixed on child outcomes. Of interest to scholars and program developers in intergenerational studies may be the authors' discussion of neighborhood and peer influences and immigration influences. These studies examine the process of acculturation as it influences parent-child interaction, while looking closely at values and conflict in families and communities. McLoyd, Cauce, Tekeuchi, and Wilson (2000) reviewed considerable evidence on ethnicity that addressed intergenerational issues under the topic of parenting behavior. A number of parent-child interaction topics are included in the review: parental involvement, discipline, parenting styles.

Allen, Blieszner, and Roberto (2000) make a substantial contribution to the understanding of intergenerational relationships in families with their article for the 1990s decade review. This article is essential for new or experienced researchers and practitioners who want to gain a better understanding of intergenerational relationships from the family studies perspective. Certainly, the fusion of family and intergenerational studies can find a starting point in the conceptual, theoretical, methodological, and substantive perspectives presented by Allen et al. The recognition that older individuals create effective helping networks by converting friends into kin, suggests intergenerational programming can appropriately aim to provide kin-like aid and anticipate kin-like relationships to develop.

CONCLUSIONS

These landmark publications in family studies suggest considerable grounds for collaboration between researchers and program specialists from family and intergenerational perspectives. We observe these opportunities for further dialogue:

1. What are reasons to include parent-child relationships in intergenerational studies? What are reasons to limit intergenerational studies to skip-generation relationships?
2. How can theories applied to intergenerational relationships in families inform analyses of non-family intergenerational relationships?
3. What methodologies for intergenerational research and programming are transferable between family studies and intergenerational studies perspectives?

The *Journal of Intergenerational Relationships* encourages discussion that will foster collaboration. The journal's Forum provides a setting to continue looking for common ground.

REFERENCES

AARP (1994). 1994 *Connecting the generations: A guide to intergenerational resources.* Washington, DC: Author

Adams, B. N. (1968). *Kinship in an urban setting.* Chicago: Markham Publishing Co.

Allen, K. R., Blieszner, R., & Roberto, K. (2000, November). Families in the middle and later years: A review and critique of research in the 1990s. In R. M. Milardo (Ed.), *Understanding families into the new millennium: A decade in review* (pp. 911-927). *Journal of Marriage & Family, 62.* Minnesota: National Council on Family Relations.

Antonucci, T. C., & Akiyama, H. (1991). Convoys of social support: Generational issues. In S. P. Pfeifer & M. B. Sussman (Eds.), *Families: Intergenerational and generational connections* (pp. 103-123). New York: The Haworth Press.

Bengtson, V. L. (1989). The problem of generations: Age group contrasts, continuities, and social change. In V. L. Bengtson (Ed.), *The course of later life: Research and reflections* (pp. 25-54). New York: Springer.

Bengtson, V. L., Cutler, N. E., Mangen, D. J., & Marshall, V. W. (1985). Generations, cohorts, and relations between age groups. In R. H. Binstock and E. Shanas (Eds.), *Handbook of aging and the social sciences* (pp. 304-338). New York: Van Nostrand Reinhold.

Berardo, F. M. (Ed.). (1980, November). *Decade review: Family research 1970-1979. Journal of Marriage and the Family, 42,* 1-264. Minnesota: National Council on Family Relations.

Booth, A. (Ed.). (1990, November). *Family research in the 1980s: The decade in review. Journal of Marriage & Family, 52.* Minnesota: National Council on Family Relations.

Broderick, C. B. (Ed.). (1971a, May). *A decade of family research and action.* Minnesota: National Council on Family Relations.

Broderick, C. B. (1971b, May). Beyond the five conceptual frameworks: A decade of development in family theory. In C. B. Broderick (Ed.), *A decade of family research and action* (pp. 3-23). Minnesota: National Council on Family Relations.

Brubaker, T. H. (1990, November). Families in later life: A burgeoning research area. In A. Booth (Ed.), *Family research in the 1980s: The decade in review* (pp. 959-982). *Journal of Marriage & Family, 52.* Minnesota: National Council on Family Relations.

Burr, W., & Leigh, G. (1983). Famology: A new discipline. *Journal of Marriage and the Family, 45,* 467-480.

Christensen, H. (1964). Development of the family field of study. In H. Christensen (Ed.), *Handbook of marriage and the family* (pp. 3-32). Chicago: Rand McNally & Co.

Day, R. (2003). *Introduction to family processes* (4th edition). Mahwah, NJ: Lawrence Erlbaum.

Farber, B. (1968). *Comparative kinship systems.* New York: John Wiley and Sons, Inc.

George, L. K., & Gold, D. T. (1991). Life course perspectives on intergenerational and generational connections. In S. P. Pfeifer & M. B. Sussman (Eds.), *Families: Intergenerational and generational connections* (pp. 67-88). New York: The Haworth Press.

Gubrium, J. F., & Rittman, M. R. (1991). Small worlds and intergenerational relationships. In S. P. Pfeifer & M. B. Sussman (Eds.), *Families: Intergenerational and generational connections* (pp. 89-102). New York: The Haworth Press.

Hanks, R. S. (1991). An intergenerational perspective on family ethical dilemmas. In S. P. Pfeifer & M. B. Sussman (Eds.), *Families: Intergenerational and generational connections* (pp. 161-173). New York: The Haworth Press.

Hareven, T. K. (1987). Historical analysis of the family. In M. B. Sussman & S. K. Steinmetz (Eds.), *Handbook of marriage and the family,* 1st Ed. (37-58). New York: Plenum Press.

Hirshorn, B. (1991). Sharing or competition: Multiple views of the intergenerational flow of society's resources. In S. P. Pfeifer & M. B. Sussman (Eds.), *Families: Intergenerational and generational connections* (pp. 175-193). New York: The Haworth Press.

Kivett, V. R. (1991). The grandparent-grandchild connection. In S. P. Pfeifer & M. B. Sussman (Eds.), *Families: Intergenerational and generational connections* (pp. 267-290). New York: The Haworth Press.

Lee, G. R. (1980, November). Kinship in the seventies: A decade review of research and theory. In E. M. Berardo (Ed.), *Decade review: Family research 1970-1979* (pp. 193-204). *Journal of Marriage and the Family, 42.* Minnesota: National Council on Family Relations.

Mancini, J. A., & Blieszner, R. (1989). Aging parents and adult children: Research themes in intergenerational relationships. *Journal of Marriage and the Family, 51,* 275-290.

McLoyd, V. C., Cauce, A. M., Takeuchi, D., & Wilson, L. (2000, November). Marital processes and parental socialization in families of color: A decade of review of research. In R. M. Milardo (Ed.), *Understanding families into the new millennium: A decade in review* (pp. 1070-1094). *Journal of Marriage & Family, 62.* Minnesota: National Council on Family Relations.

Milardo, R. M. (Ed.). (2000a, November). *Understanding families into the new millennium: A decade in review. Journal of Marriage & Family, 62.* Minnesota: National Council on Family Relations.

Milardo, R. M. (2000b, November). The decade in review. In R. M. Milardo (Ed.), *Understanding families into the new millennium: A decade in review* (pp. 873-876). *Journal of Marriage & Family, 62.* Minnesota: National Council on Family Relations.

Newman, S. (1989). A history of intergenerational programs. *Journal of Children in Contemporary Society, 20* (3/4), 1-16.

Peterson, G. W., & Hann, D. (1999). Socializing children and parents in families. In M. B. Sussman, S. K. Steinmetz, & G. W. Peterson (Eds.), *Handbook of marriage and the family,* 2nd Ed. (327-370). New York: Plenum Press.

Peterson, G. W. & Rollins, B. C. (1987). Parent-child socialization. In M. B. Sussman & S. K. Steinmetz (Eds.), *Handbook of marriage and the family,* 1st Ed. (471-508). New York: Plenum Press.

Pfeifer, S. P., & Sussman, M. B. (Eds.). (1991). *Families: Intergenerational and generational connections.* New York: The Haworth Press.

Roberts, R. E., Richards, L. N., & Bengston, V. L. (1991). Intergenerational solidarity in families: Untangling the ties that bind. In S. P. Pheifer & M. B. Sussman (Eds.), *Families: Intergenerational and generational connections* (pp. 11-46). New York: The Haworth Press.

Sprey, J. (1991). Studying adult children and their parents. In S. P. Pfeifer & M. B. Sussman (Eds.), *Families: Intergenerational and generational connections* (pp. 221-235). New York: The Haworth Press.

Sussman, M. B. (1951). Family continuity: A study of factors which affect relationships between families at generational levels. Doctoral dissertation. New Haven, CT: Yale University.

Sussman, M. B. (1991). Reflections on intergenerational and kin connections. In S. P. Pheifer & M. B. Sussman (Eds.), *Families: Intergenerational and generational connections* (pp. 3-9). New York: The Haworth Press.

Sussman, M. B., & Burchinal, L. (1962). Kin family network: Unheralded structure in current conceptualization of family functioning. *Journal of Marriage and the Family, 24,* 231-240.

Sussman, M. B. & Steinmetz, S. K. (1987). *Handbook of marriage and the family* (1st edition). New York: Plenum.

Sussman, M. B., Steinmetz, S. K., & Peterson, G. W. (1999). *Handbook of marriage and the family* (2nd edition). New York: Plenum.

Taylor, R. J., Chatters, L. M., Tucker, M. B., & Lewis, E. (1990, November). Developments in research on black families: A decade review. In A. Booth (Ed.), *Family research in the 1980s: The decade in review* (pp. 993-1015). *Journal of Marriage & Family, 52.* Minnesota: National Council on Family Relations.

Treas, J., & Bengtson, V. L. (1987). The family in later years. In M. B. Sussman & S. K. Steinmetz (Eds.), *Handbook of marriage and the family,* 1st Ed. (625-648). New York: Plenum Press.

Treas, J., & Lawton, L. (1999). Family relations in adulthood. In M. B. Sussman, S. K. Steinmetz, & G. W. Peterson (Eds.), *Handbook of marriage and the family,* 2nd Ed. (425-474). New York: Plenum Press.

Troll, L. (1971, May). The family of later life: A decade review. In C. B. Broderick (Ed.), *A decade of family research and action* (pp. 187-214). Minnesota: National Council on Family Relations.

VanderVen, K. (1989). Training and education for intergenerational activities: An agenda for the future. *Journal of Children in Contemporary Society, 20* (3/4), 135-145.

VanderVen, K. (1999). Intergenerational theory: The missing element in today's intergenerational programs. *Child & Youth Services, 20* (1/2), 33-47.

Walters, J., & Walters, L. H. (1980, November). Parent-child relationships: A review, 1970-1979. In F. M. Berardo (Ed.), *Decade review: Family research 1970-1979* (pp. 80-95). *Journal of Marriage and the Family, 42.* Minnesota: National Council on Family Relations.

Intergenerational Cultural Transmission Among the Akan of Ghana

Joseph K. Adjaye
Osei-Mensah Aborampah

SUMMARY. Sociocultural transmission is a necessary ingredient in societal stability, cohesion, and continuity everywhere. For the Akan of central and southern Ghana, an important aspect of societal cohesion occurred through intergenerational solidarity which existed principally in the extended family, with the elders acting as the primary instruments in cultural transmission. The extended family, especially as represented in the Akan traditional household, was regarded as one family. Elders were viewed as the embodiment of the past as well as members with the largest store of memories from the past. Reminiscences, remembrances, and oral narratives were passed down to children in whose lives these elders were intimately involved, and stories always contained some moral values that children were expected to learn from and apply. What appears to be occurring in contemporary Ghana are processes of change and persistence, and the task of this study is to assess changes in the Akan family, particularly the extended family, and their impact on the transmission of cultural values across generations. *[Article copies available for a fee from The Haworth Document Delivery Service: 1-800-HAWORTH. E-mail address: <docdelivery@haworthpress.com> Website: <http://www.HaworthPress.com> © 2004 by The Haworth Press, Inc. All rights reserved.]*

Joseph K. Adjaye is affiliated with the University of Pittsburgh, Pennsylvania.
Osei-Mensah Aborampah is affiliated with the University of Wisconsin-Milwaukee, Wisconsin.

[Haworth co-indexing entry note]: "Intergenerational Cultural Transmission Among the Akan of Ghana." Adjaye, Joseph K., and Osei-Mensah Aborampah. Co-published simultaneously in *Journal of Intergenerational Relationships* (The Haworth Press, Inc.) Vol. 2, No. 3/4, 2004, pp. 23-38; and: *Intergenerational Relationships: Conversations on Practices and Research Across Cultures* (ed: Elizabeth Larkin et al.) The Haworth Press, Inc., 2004, pp. 23-38. Single or multiple copies of this article are available for a fee from The Haworth Document Delivery Service [1-800-HAWORTH, 9:00 a.m. - 5:00 p.m. (EST). E-mail address: docdelivery@haworthpress.com].

http://www.haworthpress.com/web/JIR
© 2004 by The Haworth Press, Inc. All rights reserved.
Digital Object Identifier: 10.1300/J194v02n03_03

KEYWORDS. Sociocultural transmission, Ghana, extended family

... [P]henomena such as individualization; the erosion of the traditional structures of neighborhood, family and the church; the notion of deteriorating public morals and growing violence seem to
be arousing concern about solidarity and cohesion in our society.
Urbanization, increased geographic mobility, changes in the labor
market as a consequence of economic globalization, a higher level
of education, and changes in the way children are socialized are
said to be reflected in changes in values and intergenerational solidarity. (Komter & Vollebergh 2002: 171)

INTRODUCTION

Sociocultural transmission is a necessary ingredient in societal stability, cohesion, and continuity everywhere. For the Akan of central and
southern Ghana, an important aspect of societal cohesion occurred
through intergenerational solidarity which existed principally in the extended family, with the elders acting as the primary instruments in cultural transmission. Even though the extended family covered a wide
range of different residential and householding arrangements, it acted as
one productive unit under one or a pair of family heads who exercised
authority over and discharged ritual duties for the protection and well
being of the family members. Thus, the extended family, especially as
represented in the Akan traditional household, was regarded as one
family. It provided the practical basis for membership of a domestic unit
and the emerging social relations served to assign prestige, control, responsibility, and rights over property and services to certain categories
of persons within the unit.

Elders tended to hold more vital economic, political, status, and ritual
functions than younger adults. They held much of the traditional knowledge in terms of the secrets of the natural environment and Akan worldview. Growing children acquired this knowledge through training,
socialization and education that was provided by the elders. From infancy, children constantly learnt from elders who were considered to
have the same roles and responsibilities as parents, surrogate parents,
older siblings, or as significant others. Elders were viewed as the embodiment of the past as well as members with the largest store of memories from the past. Reminiscences, remembrances, and oral narratives

were passed down to children in whose lives these elders were intimately involved, and stories always contained some moral values that children were expected to learn from and apply.

In processes of skills acquisition, a system of patrifiliation existed whereby sons generally followed their parents' occupations, whether as farmers, fishermen, hunters, or craftsmen. This father-son dyad made possible the intergenerational cultural transmission of values. Indeed, it was common practice that the expertise and knowledge of each generation be passed on to the next, thus affording older persons an important role in society. In turn, the younger generation was expected to live up to the ideals that society held for young adults. However, it is apparent everywhere that the efficacy of the traditional modes of intergenerational transmission of cultural values is being eroded in modern Akan society, where expanded Western educational opportunities, rapid social and technological change, and transformations in familial organization have increasingly impinged upon the role of the older generation as cultural transmitters. Although Komter and Vollebergh's study (cited above) focused on Dutch families, their observations about transformations in intergenerational solidarity are equally applicable to the experience of the Akan of Ghana.

This essay, then, examines intergenerational cultural transmission among the Akan. How do elders view their role as transmitters of cultural values? Do they see their role as central to cultural continuity? What values are transmitted, and how do these values, especially collectivist ones, promote group and culture maintenance? What transmission belts, i.e., conditions and contexts that are favorable for cultural transmission, are most effective, and are they Akan-specific? Is mutual assistance gendered? Above all, what modern-day constraints or moderators are impeding the process of intergenerational cultural transmission? And what are the implications of these transformations in intergenerational cultural transmission for processes of cultural continuity?

Modernization theorists have long been interested in the effects of social changes on traditional structures of African societies. Some (e.g., Southall 1961; Goode 1970; Caldwell et al. 1975; Gugler & Flanagan 1978) contend that technological advancement and modernization lead to a breakdown of extended family networks. Caldwell (1982) further asserts that changes in socioeconomic circumstances as well are causing transformations in reproductive behavioral patterns. The argument is predicated on the assumption that developing countries, like Ghana, expose their populations to western nuclear family ideals through their educational systems. However, it is possible that transformation in family structure may not occur at the same rate as changes in socioeconomic circumstances. Indeed, it has been suggested that an institution as powerful as the extended family may strengthen, rather than weaken, over time, reinforced, as it were, not merely by religion and custom, but also by ordinary day-to-day living (Deyrup 1962: 183). After all, modern technology also provides mechanisms for maintaining kinship ties and modern means of communication–the telephone, the Internet, the automobile, the airplane, etc.–have made it increasingly easy for families and individuals to communicate with each other.

What appears to be occurring in contemporary Ghana are processes of change and persistence, and the task of this study is to assess changes in the Akan family, particularly the extended family, and their impact on the transmission of cultural values across generations. We argue that the extended family, with its system of mutual obligations, more adequately provides for the group's security, in the absence of any meaningful and effective national social security system. Thus, the net balance of the direction of exchanges (from the old to the young and vice versa) would be an important determinant of intergenerational cultural transmission.

METHODOLOGY

In pursuance of these issues, the authors developed a battery of questions to elicit respondents' opinions on an array of cultural themes, including the Akan concept of the elder, the extended family, and the elder's role in everyday life as well as in specific roles such as in life cycle transitional events. Given the exploratory nature of the study, survey questionnaires were administered to a non-random sample of 28 adult Ghanaians, half of whom live in an urban area and the other half in a rural environment. The two communities were selected on the basis of the lead author's familiarity with those areas. The ages of the respondents ranged from 19 to 65 and included individuals with such diverse occupational backgrounds as farmers, bakers, students, nurses, and military personnel. Where applicable, Likert-type instruments were developed for respondents to indicate whether they (1) strongly agreed, (2) agreed, (3) disagreed, or (4) strongly disagreed with certain opinions/statements, or (5) had no opinion about them. All the respondents spoke the Akan language, even though a few were born in non-Akan communities. In our study, we also examined critical issues in intergenerational transmission such as collectivist versus individual values, cultural transmission belts, whether cultural transmission is gendered, and emergent social changes and their impact on intergenerational relations. We conclude with an assessment of our findings and their implications for policymakers and stakeholders concerned with the education of today's youth.

THE AKAN OF GHANA

To assist readers place this study within the appropriate context, we provide here a brief description of Akan society and its social organization. The Akan occupy central and southern Ghana and consist of culture clusters including the Asante, Fante, Bono, Akyem, Akuapem, Kwawu, Akwamu, Asen, Denkyira, Twifo, and Wasa. Kinship structure among the Akan is matrilineal. This means that an individual, from birth to death, remains a component of her/his matrilineage, which consists of a woman, her brothers and sisters, as well as her sisters' sons and daughters. The line of descent for any given matrilineage is traced through the female members of the group and living adults of the group form the core of blood or consanguineal relatives around whom lineage decision-making occurs.

Family for the Akan means the extended family, which is formed by linking one lineage to another in networks of alliance and cooperation through marriage. While the matrilineage is based solely on descent, the extended family is based on descent and marriage. Thus, both units could be viewed as the organizing principles for family stability and solidarity. Both concepts will be used interchangeably in this report. Another point worth noting is that Akan matrilineages involve not only the living but also the dead and those yet to be born. In the past, the deceased were remembered through periodic rituals. Ancestors were regarded as the main means of social order and social control.

Ancestors served to give assurances about lineage desires, including peace, good health, long life, fertility, and lineage solidarity. Thus, ancestral wisdom served to promote group cohesion and group belonging. Older living members, being closest to the ancestors, were the repositories of ancestral wisdom. Elders, then, served as critical links between the dead and younger members for the transmission of cultural values. Bearing this brief description in mind, we proceed to report our findings.

The Akan Concept of the Elder

Among the Akan, the concept of the elder embodies competence, which is traditionally endowed in age and seniority; the older generation is viewed as the custodian of tradition. Hence, responsibility for the transmission of values necessary to sustain Akan societies devolves on them. For these reasons, the younger generation is expected to show veneration and deference toward the elder. However, the elder is not a homogenous group. There exists a great deal of variation. Indeed seventeen of the 28 respondents (61%) in our study saw age cohorts as arbitrarily defined criteria for distinguishing one generation from another and felt that any person who is 50 or more years old could be considered an elder. About a quarter defined persons in their mothers' and fathers' generation as elders. Interestingly, 39% of the respondents agreed that eldership may be conferred by virtue of being a role-occupant, such as a chief, queen, or priest(ess). In contrast, only 11% would confer the status of eldership on someone by virtue of personal accomplishments. On the issue of whether ageing enhances a person's status and enriches his/her life satisfaction, 67% either strongly agreed or agreed with the proposition.

Among the Akan, as elsewhere in Africa, the family is considered one of the most important and cherished cornerstones of society. It was regarded as a strong social community that was grounded on shared norms and interdependency. Indeed, the family was traditionally a social *and* economic unit, based on mutuality of support, help and care. Thus, economic cooperation was critical to the family. In the absence of social security from the state, the family carried responsibility for providing welfare and insurance, ensuring that the aged, infirm and disabled were taken care of. Within the context of such an informal social security system, an elder could look forward to old age and eventual death, knowing that members of the extended family would care for him/her and provide a fitting burial. When asked whether children must bear responsibility for caring for the elder, 68% of our respondents either strongly agreed or agreed, with only 32% disagreeing. It is interesting to note that 82% either strongly agreed or agreed with the proposition that a learning community should be created for the youth to inform the elderly about latest events.

The Akan Extended Family

Concerning the Akan matrilineal system and transitional rituals (e.g., child naming, puberty, marriage, and death) performed by elders of the kin group, no less than 60% either strongly agreed or agreed with the following propositions:

a. The matrilineal principle of descent should continue to operate as the basis for unity and solidarity (64%);
b. Social capital (education, training, etc.) should continue to be invested in all members of the matrilineage (76%);
c. Puberty rites (*bragoro*) should continue to be practiced (60%);
d. Customary marriage should continue to be practiced (93%);
e. Bridewealth should continue to be given upon marriage (86%);
f. Marriage ceremonies should continue to be practiced (100%);
g. Members of the matrilineage should stick together in times of stress (93%); and
h. Childbirth should continue to receive top priority from all members of the matrilineage (71%).

We also attempted to ascertain respondents' opinions about changes perceived to be occurring within the Akan matrilineage. For example, while 93% agreed that marriage should be viewed as an economic duty to the matrilineage, 91% agreed that it should be based on individual love. While all agreed that individuals should marry persons of their own choice, at the same time, 78% agreed that inter-ethnic marital relations should be encouraged among members of the matrilineage. There was a clear preference for small family sizes (78%) as the mechanism for building the political base of the matrilineage.

Given that the traditional compound housing structure of the Akan tends to promote face-to-face interaction and caring, and serves as the physical space for the major cultural activities of the matrilineage, we wanted our respondents to react to changes perceived to be occurring in that area as well. As expected, 82% agreed that members of the matrilineage should continue to maintain family compounds for lineage ceremonies. However, 57% disagreed with the proposition that members of the matrilineage should be obligated to build their homes in their matrilineal homelands, and 71% agreed that single family homes should be preferred to traditional family compound units. Moreover, 57% disagreed with the suggestion that the single-family home as a housing structure tends to undermine lineage solidarity. This finding may be interpreted to reflect an apparent absence of a systemic conflict between residence in a single family unit and participation in one's extended family network. Although the structure of the residential building largely determines the number of people that can reside in a unit, family residential patterns, per se, may have little or nothing to do with existing extended family networks of mutual obligations. Regardless of where they reside, many Akans (both literate and preliterate) travel to their hometowns to participate in funeral and other family ceremonies.

Mutual Assistance

Is the changing structure of the family, both in rural and urban environments, leading to a weakening of the sense of interdependence? Do the older and younger generations continue to believe that they owe an obligation toward each other? Do the elders continue to perform their critical roles relative to transitional rituals that provided avenues for the intergenerational transmission of cultural values? Toward these ends, some of our questions were developed to ascertain respondents' perceptions about the elder's role concerning puberty rituals for the induction of the youth into adulthood, the institution of marriage, and mortuary rituals to guide the deceased to the afterlife. Additionally, respondents were asked to determine the types of mutual/reciprocal assistance provided and/or received within the past year, the level of importance attached to selected family values, the strength or otherwise of selected dyadic relationships within the family, as well as the effectiveness of selected family/cultural value transmission belts.

When asked whether, over the past year, respondents had provided and/or received assistance from other members of the family, 75% responded in the affirmative. The types of assistance provided/received included the following: money (71%); medicines (32%); advice (71%); clothing (39%); food (57%); house care (36%); and free transportation (18%). This would seem to suggest that members of the matrilineage continue to provide for the economic well-being and psychological health of other members. The majority of the respondents continue to perceive each of the eight pair bonds (dyadic relationships) within the family as strong, which supports prevailing perceptions of mutual/reciprocal assistance. However, all agreed that the co-wife to co-wife relationships in multiple-spouse marriages are weak, which is to be expected given their earlier indication of a strong preference for marriage based on individual love as well as individual choice.

Cultural Values

On the issue of what cultural values should be considered most important in terms of intergenerational transmission, our interviewees responded as follows: communal labor/civic engagement: 100%; respect for elders: 97%; social connectedness: 90%; Christian spirituality: 89%;

personal success: 86%; inclusion: 86%; reciprocity: 78%; lineage success: 78%; interdependence: 75%; and lineage decision-making: 64%. Sixty-four percent of the respondents felt that individualism was not important as a family value. In the same vein, only 35% viewed secularism as an important value. To be urbane was not considered important by 54% of the respondents, and so was traditional spirituality (57%). The latter should come as no surprise as 64% agreed that traditional religious beliefs have waned and that Christian and Islamic family values have supplanted traditional family values (92%). Additionally, 61% disagreed with the proposition that ancestors can visit family members with misfortune if family values are betrayed by the youth. Nonetheless, 53% agreed that belief in ancestors as the guardians of the highest moral values should continue to be promoted.

Cultural Transmission

In any given society, as among the Akan, there exists an array of what may be called cultural transmission belts, that is, certain processes, conditions and contexts that enhance transmission of values. Adults teach the younger generation through direct instruction, and indirectly through advice, proverbs, and maxims, and by example. The younger generation learns from the former through imitation, observation, socialization and enculturation; transmission occurs largely through social orientation. Though cultural transmission is mostly vertical, that is, from parent generation to offspring, intergenerational transmission is not necessarily symmetrical or bi-directional, for it is more oriented from the older to the younger generation than vice versa. Bearing these observations in mind, we asked our respondents to identify various modes of cultural transmission that they perceive to be effective. Participation in group activities on the part of the young, direct training, and socialization were offered by the majority of our respondents as the most effective cultural transmission belts (71%, 54%, and 54%, respectively). These modes were followed by formal education (39%), observation (36%), and imitation (18%). However, it must be emphasized that different transmission modes were viewed as effective under certain circumstances.

Gender

The question of gender in intergenerational cultural transmission is very complex. Akan society is largely male-dominated and yet women play very crucial roles in many arenas, not the least of which is their role in the transitional rituals and in the domestic field. In the survey, we attempted to assess the position of women vis-à-vis men and the perceived changes occurring therein. When asked whether older women have less power within their matrilineages than older men, 67% of the respondents agreed, while 36% disagreed with the suggestion that older women are more dependent than older men. Perhaps, the relatively high proportion disagreeing with the latter suggestion could be explained by the fact that a large majority (86%) felt that children give more support to their mothers than to their fathers. Nonetheless, perceptions about role specificity in gender relations remain among our respondents, as they have been in the past. Thus, ninety-three percent agreed that women do most of the domestic chores and 91% believed that men do very little domestic work. Fifty-four percent disapproved of the idea of a joint bank account for husband and wife, although 68% favored separate bank accounts. In addition, 68% preferred separate sleeping and eating arrangements for boys and girls rather than mixing them up. Thus, there was a clear preference for gendered spaces for the sexes. The implication is that socialization may be gendered in the sense that mothers transmit to their daughters what girls/women are supposed to do and correspondingly, fathers transmit male values to sons. However, we noticed some signs of perceptual changes among our respondents. Past practices concerning property transfers in the course of Akan funeral ceremonies tended to perpetuate gender difference. Consequently, we asked our respondents whether wives should inherit husbands' and whether husbands should inherit wives' personally acquired properties. The proportions agreeing with the two propositions were 78% and 75%, respectively.

Discussion

According to Bhat and Dhruvarajan (2001: 621),

> urbanisation, modernisation and globalisation have led to changes in economic structure, erosion of societal values and the weakening of social institutions such as the joint family. In this changing economic and social milieu, the younger generation is searching for new identities encompassing economic independence and redefined social roles within, as well as outside, the family. The changing economic structure has reduced the dependence of rural families on land, which had provided strength to bonds between generations. The traditional sense of duty and obligation of the younger generation towards their older generation is being eroded.

The older generation is caught between the decline in traditional values on the one hand, and the absence of an adequate social security system, on the other.

Bhat and Dhruvarajan made these observations about Indian societies, which, like other traditional societies around the world, are undergoing rapid social changes. To what extent are these changes being experienced by the Akan? It can be discerned from our study that social changes are indeed occurring in Ghana, as in other developing societies of the world, and that intergenerational cultural transmission has not remained immune to these changes. While some critical roles in the transmission of cultural values continue to be assigned to the elders within the Akan extended family/matrilineage, at the same time there is a strong preference for single-family homes, for example. As explained earlier, this preference is viewed as being compatible with the discharge of one's extended family obligations. On the other hand, Christian spirituality has definitely supplanted traditional spirituality. Nonetheless, continued adherence to the dictates and demands of tradition in many areas of social life is an ever-present testimony to the authority of the elders. Christianization and Western formal education were perceived to have exerted the strongest impact on the changing dynamics of the Akan extended family/matrilineage. On this issue, Assimeng (1981: 41) observes that "In terms of change in education, economy, aspirations . . . religious diversity, and the ultimate stratification of Ghanaian societies as we see it now, the efforts of Christian missionaries have been quite outstanding." Other factors said to be impacting processes of intergenerational transmission of cultural values include Western popular culture, industrialization, urbanization, growing autonomy or individualization, modernization, and demographic changes.

Similarly, income, residence, age, class, family size, and educational level are also impinging on cultural transmission. At the same time, pull factors such as greater economic opportunity and the attraction of the city are causing the younger to increasingly migrate to the urban centers, leading to an erosion in family togetherness and elderly authority, and the promotion of individualism and independence (Assimeng 1981: 24). In practical terms, while these changes are taking place in contemporary Ghana, it is worth noting that our findings did not support individualism, secularism, and urbanity as important family values. To us, the apparent contradictions go to confirm our view that persistence and change in traditional social organization are part and parcel of the contemporary Ghanaian scene. Nonetheless, care of the elderly by children cannot be taken for granted any more. Demographic constraints such as a decrease in family sizes and educated women postponing childbearing are all eroding trans-generational cultural transmission.

Concerning extended family networks, our findings also point to specific patterns of intergenerational mutual assistance that prevail among the Akan, as indicated earlier. For the majority of our respondents, the role of mutual assistance in maintaining continuity across generations and perpetuating the family in the face of the erosion of modernity and social change continues to be viewed as crucial. Obviously, through socialization and the other modes of transmission, the act of giving has become part of the broader cultural ethos of Akan family relationships. In addition, cultural transmission serves as a means by which the elders maintain power over the younger generation. Dowd (1975; 1983) postulated that older people must have some "negotiable commodity to exchange in order to maintain their status in society." For the Akan, that commodity may be interpreted to mean the elders' large store of traditional knowledge and experience that are abundantly displayed on celebratory occasions such as those involving the transitional rituals. This form of cultural transmission not only enables the older to maintain power but also serves as an antidote to social disruption, and thus promotes social cohesion. In other words, the net balance of exchanges, as mentioned earlier, favors the older generation.

Thus, there is a strong belief that intergenerational support still increases well-being and therefore is a positive thing, even though some younger people feel that offering support to older relations is sometimes a burden. The nature, types, and frequency of assistance given obviously varies. Respondents drew a distinction between what may be regarded as obligatory support such as monetary and emotional support on the one hand, and occasional or incidental support such as ceremonial gift-giving (e.g., at Christmas) on the other. The evidence conclusively points to the extended family as a valued source of economic sustenance and emotional support, and to social exchange as vital to social continuity. Mutual assistance is a critical element in intergenerational cultural transmission and is deeply embedded in the cultural context of family life.

Our study also validated the contention that intergenerational transmission of values is a culturally meaningful responsibility and that intergenerational assistance is shaped by cultural traditions, norms and expectations. Our respondents evinced an attachment to a variety of traditional values including respect for elders, lineage success, reciprocity, social connectedness, and communal labor. Hence, culturally specific expression of mutual assistance is an important means of maintaining family and social continuity. Indeed, the very concept of continuity is culture-specific. The ways in which family members envision continuity is directly related to their particular cultural ethos, a view confirmed by Becker (1997), as well as Becker et al. (2003). Families provide the primary setting through which culture is defined, transmitted, and interpreted (see, e.g., Luborsky & Rubinstein 1987). Thus, the Akan family is the principal conduit in the transmission of knowledge concerning belief systems, social organization, and transitional rituals that represent and ensure cultural continuity. As Schonpflug (2001) and others have observed with respect to other societies,

> The transmission of value orientations may be seen as a core issue of culture maintenance and culture change. Values provide standards for actions and thus regulate day-to-day behavior as well as important critical life decisions. (Schonpflug 2001: 175)

Yet, it must be remembered that the family is shaped not only by continuities but also by discontinuities caused by migration, economic deprivation, civil unrest, and so forth. Therefore critical disruptions that intervene in personal history could threaten intergenerational continuity.

It is also clear that responsibility within the family, especially on the part of elders, provide them with ongoing status and roles. Their social roles are a source of self-esteem. Deference for the elder on the part of the younger generation represents continuity of cultural traditions, and for this reason, cultural values reciprocated through deferential behavior on the part of children are taught and encouraged. When the traditional roles of the older generation are removed from them, they stand the risk of being isolated from their families. What is not clear is whether they have the flexibility to adjust to these changing times and contexts. The connection between cultural transmission and cultural continuity is predicated on the assumption/premise that the familial values that are transmitted have continuity that overrides individual discontinuities.

Our study also confirmed that intergenerational cultural transmission is important not only within parent-child dyads, but also with grandchildren, nephews, nieces and other extended family relations. It leads to feelings of being emotionally connected to relatives.

Implications

It must be emphasized again that the sample studied in this project was rather small and non-random. Thus, the results should be treated as preliminary. The findings point to areas that could be further explored through a more rigorous research. For example, what is the impact of the proliferation of single family housing structures on family solidarity and hence, on intergenerational cultural transmission? Further, to what extent are our respondents representative of the general population?

Additionally, we emphasize the necessity for studies on intergenerational cultural transmission to provide an assessment of the development level of the society or a given subgroup in the society if at all possible. In the course of socioeconomic development, some traditional institutions like the Akan matrilineage and the extended family may prove themselves resilient by adapting to changing situations. Both institutions continue to be relevant in terms of Akan marriages and funeral celebrations, in spite of the introduction of Christian and Islamic weddings and the creeping impact of modern mortuary rituals.

Finally, our study suggests a few preliminary policy implications. In the context of minimal state support, we suggest that the *abusua mpaninfoo* (family heads) may do well to educate the older generation about their familial obligations toward the younger and vice versa. Also, we suggest that increased support should be given to non-governmental organizations (NGOs) and citizen groups to create friendly environments for a more sustained and effective interaction between the old and the young.

REFERENCES

Assimeng, M. *Social Structure of Ghana: A Study in Persistence and Change*. Accra: Ghana Publishing Corporation, 1981.

Becker, G. *Disrupted Lives: How People Create Meaning in a Chaotic World*. Berkeley, UCP, 1997.

Becker, Gay et al. "Creating Continuity Through Mutual Assistance: Intergenerational Reciprocity in Four Ethnic Groups." *Jr. of Gerontology: Social Sciences*, 58B, 3 (2003): S151-59.

Bhat, A. K. & Dhruvarajan, R. "Ageing in India: Drifting Intergenerational Relations, Challenges and Options." *Ageing and Society* 21 (2001): 621-40.

Caldwell, J. C. *Theory of Fertility Decline*. New York, AP, 1982.

Caldwell, J. C. et al. *Population Growth and Social Change in West Africa*. New York, CUP, 1975.

Cavalli-Sforza, L. L. & Feldman M. *Cultural Transmission and Evolution: A Quantitative Approach*. Princeton, PUP, 1981.

Clay, D. C. and Vander, J. E. "Patterns of Intergenerational Support and Childbearing in the Third World." *Population Studies*, 47, 1 (1993): 67-84.

Deyrup, F. J. "Family Dominance as a Factor in Population Growth of Developing Countries." *Social Research* 29 (1962): 177-189.

Dowd, J. J. "Aging as Exchange: A Preface to Theory." *Jr. of Gerontology*, 30 (1975): 584-94.

_____. "Social Exchange, Class, and Old People." In J. Sokolovsky (ed.), *Growing Old in Different Societies: Cross-Culture Perspectives*. Belmont (CA), 1983, pp. 29-42.

Fry, D. P. "The Intergenerational Transmission of Disciplinary Practices and Approaches to Conflict." *Human Organization*, 52, 2(1993): 176-85.

Goode, W. J. *World Revolution and Family Patterns*. New York, Free Press, 1970.

Gugler, J. & Flanagan, W. G., *Urbanization and Social Change in West Africa*. Cambridge, CUP, 1978.

Hammerstrom, G. "Solidarity and Values in Three Generations." In H. A. Becker and P. L. Hermkens (ed.), *Solidarity of Generations: Demographic, Economic, and Social Change and Its Consequences*, v. 1-3, 1993.

Hoddinott, J. "Rotten Kids or Manipulative Parents: Are Children Old Age Security in Western Kenya?" *Economic Development & Cultural Change*, 40, 3 (1992): 545-75.

Johnson, M. L. "Interdependency and the Generational Compact." *Ageing and Society*, 15, 2 (1995): 243-65.

Komter, A. E. & Vollebergh, W. "Gift Giving and the Emotional Significance of Family and Friends." *Jr. of Marriage and Family*, 59 (1997): 747-57.

_____. "Solidarity in Dutch Families: Family Ties Under Strain?" *Jr. of Family Issues*, 22, 2 (2002): 171-88.

Luborsky, M. & Rubinstein, R. L. "Ethnicity and Lifetimes: Self-Concepts and Situational Contexts of Ethnic Identity in Late Life." In Gelfand, D. and C. Barresi (eds.), *Ethnic Dimensions of Aging*. New York, Springer, pp. 35-50.

Martin, L. G. "Changing Intergenerational Family Relations in East Asia." *The Annals of the American Academy of Political and Social Science*, 510 (1990): 102-14.

Moller, V. "Intergenerational Relations in a Society in Transition: A South African Case Study." *Ageing and Society*, 14, 2 (1994): 155-89.

Peil, M. "Family Support for the Nigerian Elderly." *Journal of Comparative Family Studies*, 22, 1 (1991): 85-100.

Radcliffe-Brown, A. R. & Forde, D. (eds.) *African Systems of Kinship and Marriage*. London: KPI in association with the International African Institute; and New York: Columbia University Press, 1987.

Schonpflug, U. "Intergenerational Transmission of Values: The Role of Transmission Belts." *Jr. of Cross-Cultural Psychology*, 32, 2 (2001): 174-85.

Simons, R. L. et al. "Gender Differences in the Intergenerational Transmission of Parenting Beliefs." *Journal of Marriage and the Family*, 54, 4 (1992): 823-36.

Sokolovsky, J. (ed.). *The Cultural Context of Aging: Worldwide Perspectives*, 2nd ed., Westport (CT), Bergin & Garvey, 1997.

Southall, A. *Social Change in Modern Africa*. Oxford, OUP, 1961.

Taylor, R. J. et al. "A Profile of Familial Relations Among Three-Generation Black Families." *Family Relations*, 42, 3 (1993): 332-41.

Thompson, J. "Inherited Obligations and Generational Continuity." *Canadian Journal of Philosophy*, 29, 4 (1999): 493-515.

Unanka, G. O. "Family Support and Health Status of the Elderly in Imo State of Nigeria," *Jr. of Social Issues,* 58, 4 (2002): 681-95.

Van der Geest, S. "Opanin: The Ideal of Elder in the Akan Culture of Ghana." *Canadian Journal of African Studies,* 32, 3 (1998): 449-93.

Vercruijsse, E. "The Dynamics of Fanti Domestic Organization: A Comparison with Fortes' Ashanti Survey," Cape Coast (Ghana): University of Cape Coast Social Studies Project: Research Report Series, Paper no. 12, 1972.

Whitbeck, L., Hoyt, D. R., and Huck, S. M. "Early Family Relationships, Intergenerational Solidarity, and Support Provided to Parents by their Adult Children." *Journal of Gerontology,* 49, 2 (1994): S85-94.

Intergenerational Impact
of the AIDS Pandemic in Nigeria

Bede Eke, MGS, PhD (cand.)

SUMMARY. This paper articulates and assesses the intergenerational impact of the AIDS pandemic in Nigeria based on literature reviews and mailed surveys. The findings reveal that, with the advent of colonialism in the 19th century, the wave of modernization, and the new idea of nuclear family system, intergenerational bonds and relationships were weakened to an extent. But the arrival of the AIDS epidemic in the 1980s and its steady increase worsened the situation. Intergenerational relationships have been affected to the extent that bonds between generations are collapsing. The AIDS pandemic creates social isolation and stigmatization of the infected and affected population. Since the middle generation is mostly infected, the older and younger generations who depend on them suffer most of the consequences. Some efforts have been made by the government and non-governmental organizations to address the increasing rate of infection. But little has been done to mitigate the impact of the pandemic especially on intergenerational relationships. As a possible solution, this paper suggests some intergenerational programming and policy approaches to address the problem, and achieve better intergenerational relationships in Nigeria at this time of crisis. *[Article copies available for a fee from The Haworth Document Delivery Service: 1-800-HAWORTH. E-mail address: <docdelivery@haworthpress.com> Website: <http://www.HaworthPress.com> © 2004 by The Haworth Press, Inc. All rights reserved.]*

Bede Eke is affiliated with Miami University, Ohio.

[Haworth co-indexing entry note]: "Intergenerational Impact of the AIDS Pandemic in Nigeria." Eke, Bede. Co-published simultaneously in *Journal of Intergenerational Relationships* (The Haworth Press, Inc.) Vol. 2, No. 3/4, 2004, pp. 39-52; and: *Intergenerational Relationships: Conversations on Practice and Research Across Cultures* (ed: Elizabeth Larkin et al.) The Haworth Press, Inc., 2004, pp. 39-52. Single or multiple copies of this article are available for a fee from The Haworth Document Delivery Service [1-800-HAWORTH, 9:00 a.m. - 5:00 p.m. (EST). E-mail address: docdelivery@haworthpress.com].

KEYWORDS. Intergenerational relationships, HIV/AIDS, Nigeria

One of the greatest challenges of this century is the AIDS epidemic (Eke, 2003a). Globally, AIDS has claimed over 20 million lives, and over 40 million are estimated to be living with HIV/AIDS (Kaiser Family Report, 2002). Nigeria has 3.5 million of the 28.5 million individuals living with AIDS in Sub-Saharan Africa (UNAIDS/WHO, 2001). In Nigeria, AIDS and its consequences for both the young and the old cannot be overstated.

Traditionally, the aged in Nigeria rely more on family and kin for social and economic support than on formal services (Griffin, 1995). Most of this support comes from adult children. With the AIDS epidemic ravaging the middle cohort, the aged face two major challenges–less or no support from adult children and becoming a caregiver for both the dying child and for the child's offspring. Children in Nigeria also face severe consequences as their parents suffer or die from AIDS.

It is against this backdrop that the following questions are addressed in this paper:

1. What is the nature of intergenerational impact of AIDS in Nigeria?
2. How does the AIDS epidemic affect the social, economic, and emotional health of the younger and older population in Nigeria?
3. What policy recommendations can be made for supporting the older and younger population affected by the pandemic?

AIDS is a complex phenomenon. In order to answer the above questions, information was accessed from historical documents, public health publications, epidemiological case studies, demographic documents, ethnographic record, pilot studies, medical research, and Internet sources. A review of historical records provided an assessment of traditional relationships and role expectations for children, young adults, and elders. Through health and epidemiological documents, information on the spread of the disease in Nigeria was gathered. Some case study documents provided additional knowledge about the extent of the impact of AIDS on intergenerational relationships in various Nigerian communities. Additionally, a brief mailed survey was sent to eight Nigerian Health Officials and AIDS relief workers.

TRADITIONAL NIGERIAN PATTERNS
OF INTERGENERATIONAL RELATIONSHIPS

Intergenerational relationships exist when younger and older generations live in sustained mutual cooperation and coordination that benefit members of each generation (Newman, Ward, Smith, Wilson, & McCrea, 1997). These relationships occur at both the familial and community levels. Largely governed by exchange and norms of reciprocity (Goulder, 1960), traditional intergenerational relationships in Nigeria are greatly challenged as a result of the AIDS epidemic.

In Nigeria, especially the southeastern part, a hierarchical age grading system accords great respect to elders. In some part of Igboland (southeastern Nigeria), elders are not addressed by their first name by younger ones without also including a prefix expressing respect such as "elder," "mommy," or "daddy." "Family relationships are guided by a strict system of seniority. The freedom to use first names is given only to seniors and superiors. It is an insult to call an elder sibling by his or her first name" (George, 1999, 1). As in most parts of Africa (especially West Africa), in Nigeria elders are respected, adored and revered (Appiah-Kubi, 1982). They are regarded as sacred and thus deserving of honor (Brown, 1992 as cited in Unanka, 1999).

Children are also highly valued in Nigerian families. They are considered to belong to their parents, to the community, and to society at large. The importance of children underscores the reason for giving birth to as many children as possible, and for the elaborate naming ceremonies that follow a child's birth. Parents believe that their children are a source of glory to them and will provide support in their old age (Cattel, 1990). Traditionally, it is perceived as unacceptable for couples to live without producing children.

Children assist their parents in economic activities, household chores, farming activities. In turn, parents provide for their children and train them to become useful adults. In other words, tasks are shared between men, women, and children, but every person's duty is supportive of the entire family's well-being.

Elders also function as agents of socialization for the children who shall follow in their footsteps. Children are taught community values and cultural norms, and are expected to uphold moral decorum. Children commonly serve apprenticeships with elders in order to learn trades.

Family living arrangements in Nigeria promote a sense of caring that characterizes the traditional life of the people. Extended families, in which children, their spouses, grandchildren and other relatives live under one roof, are common in rural areas (George, 1999; Peil, Bamisaiye, & Ekpenyong, 1989). Caring among generations is viewed as part of daily obligation. Parents care for their children and see it as their responsibility to raise them. In turn as they mature, children see it as an obligation and a reciprocal norm to serve as caregivers to their parents and other elders around them. Caregiving is seen as a family responsibility based on family ties and bonds (Brown, 1984; Cattel, 1990; Bai- yewu & Bella, 1997; Unanka, 1999; George, 1999). One can view the system of caring among generations in Nigeria from Caldwell's (1982) "Life-Time Intergenerational Exchange/Wealth Flow" model, and Cain's (1985) "old age security" motive for fertility. Caldwell's model explains that in the exchanges of wealth between generations, wealth or economic benefits flow upward from adult children to parents as an exchange for the care they received from parents (Unanka, 1999). According to Cain, people tend to have children because of the expectation of being cared for in old age. Cattel (1990) notes that "children in developing countries are the best security assets in an environment where there are no extra-familial welfare institutions such as exist in Europe and America" (pg. 377). Individualism and detachment are uncommon elements in interpersonal relationships. Rather, responsibilities are shared and collectively shouldered for individual and community benefits (Brown, 1984; Olaniyan, 1985; Cattel, 1990; Unanka, 1999; & Falola, 2001).

In most Nigerian communities the younger and older populations cooperate for sustainable economic and social benefits. Caregiving to sick individuals and older people is usually the responsibility of the family members (Brown, 1984; Cattel, 1990), but other community or clan members provide caregiving to the sick when there is no family member available or when the family members are incapacitated.

The idealized cultural patterns of intergenerational relationships in Nigeria, as described above, have been altered by the process of modernization, including migration of younger generations to the cities. But clearly the greatest threat to traditional intergenerational support and solidarity in Nigeria is from the AIDS pandemic.

CHANGING PATTERN
OF INTERGENERATIONAL RELATIONSHIPS

Traditional patterns of intergenerational relationships in Nigeria are changing as family structure evolves. As noted by Unanka (1999), "The caregiving system in Africa began to change with the advent of colonialism by the late 19th century, the spread of Christianity, formal education, and subsequent rural-urban migration" (pg. 6). With the wave of modernization that created new conditions (job opportunities in cities, migration, and so on) caregiving to elders in Africa in general and Nigeria in particular started changing its reciprocal nature (Togonu-Bickersteth, 1989). Today, a role reversal quite unlike that described in modern western literature is often seen in cases where elders are forced by circumstances to care for their adult children and/or their grandchildren. The astronomical spread of AIDS, which began in the mid-1980s, is envisaged to worsen the already altered pattern of intergenerational relationships, and mutual support at both the family and community levels.

BRIEF HISTORY OF THE AIDS PANDEMIC
AND ITS EPIDEMIOLOGICAL STATISTICS IN NIGERIA

It has been almost two decades since the first AIDS case was reported in Nigeria (Igbanugo, 2001). Subsequently, there has been a steady increase in the number of cases. With a population of about 120 million (representing 1/5 of the total population of Africa), Nigeria to date has lost 1.7 million people to AIDS (Akukwe, 2001). According to the results of the Sentinel Survey, 5.4% of the adult population (2.6 million) is already infected with HIV (Akinsete, 2000). Of these, 1.4 million are women between the ages of 15 and 49, while the number of children infected is 120,000 (UNAIDS/WHO, June 2000). In Nigeria's hardest hit zones, mainly in the urban centers, the prevalence rates range from 15 percent among the adult population to 20 percent of pregnant women. With a 17% infection rate among adults (20-39) (Akukwe, 2001), AIDS is claiming the "engine house" of Nigeria's workforce.

Initially, AIDS was considered a trivial matter and received little government attention. Perhaps, this early lack of concern explains why Nigeria's programs against AIDS started later than in most other African nations. However, with a steady increase in the rate of infection, the Nigerian government launched a war against HIV/AIDS in 1992 (Igbanugo, 2001). Although some successes have been recorded, AIDS infections are still increasing. At the current rate, it is projected that 75 million Nigerians will likely be HIV positive or dying of AIDS by the year 2020.

THE NATURE OF INTERGENERATIONAL IMPACT
OF THE AIDS PANDEMIC IN NIGERIA

The impact of AIDS goes well beyond the number of individuals it sickens and lives it claims. Its secondary impacts are varied and substantial. For example, the number of AIDS orphans in Nigeria is estimated to be 971,472 and is increasing at an alarming rate. As noted above, there is a social tradition in Nigeria whereby children are viewed as belonging to the community and society at large. This view, contrary to the individualism of the west, may make it easier, or more natural, for community to step in to assist individuals, especially children and older people, who are less privileged.

Because of the crucial role of the infected population cohorts, the most pronounced impact of AIDS upon intergenerational relationships in Nigeria comes as a result of the prevalence of its infection of the middle generation. The loss of caregiving support to the older population by adult children, and the new role reversal of caregiving to the infected and affected children and grandchildren respectively by the aged population, is now occurring as a result of AIDS.

"One of the most vital elements in successful aging is the ability to achieve a sense of personal integration and continuity as part of a meaningful historical process that not only links the experience of a single lifetime, but also places the individual in a sequence of intergenerational ties" (Simic, 1993, 10). For families and communities where the AIDS pandemic has taken its toll, mutual interdependence among generations is now collapsing. Exchange does not thrive where there is lack of resources. The infected adult children are no longer resourceful and have little or nothing to offer in the exchange relation. The older population in Nigeria is at high risk of losing both financial and social supports they had hitherto derived from their adult children. In addition, they now assume a new caregiving role. Ironically, they have become caregivers to their children and grandchildren who are infected or affected by HIV/AIDS; on the other hand the level of social support for the younger generation is dropping due to much pressure and fewer resources at the disposal of the elders.

Among children and youth, the story is also painful. The AIDS epidemic has affected many children and denies them some of the services that orphans traditionally have. As noted by one of the questionnaire respondents, "It is a hopeless position as the children are at risk. Survival here (in Nigeria) is hard, it is extra burden for them" (CEO, Sabaoth Mission–an AIDS rescue mission, aged 42). According to Jonathan Silvers (Online NewsHour, May 9, 2002), ". . . millions of children are discovering that AIDS and economic turmoil are destroying social traditions, leading relatives and neighbors to reject them when they're at their most vulnerable."

There is a wave of change in intergenerational relationships occasioned by the effects of AIDS. The younger generation is becoming more of a burden to the older generation without adequate reciprocal services and support. Additionally, there is a changing role of the elders–either as parents or grandparents. Grandparents are raising their grandchildren in increasing numbers. This relationship, while founded on familial ties and commitment, still experiences tension and strain. Often, older persons who are caregivers to their orphaned grandchildren find it very difficult to cope with this challenge. The level of understanding and communication between a grandparent and a grandchild is weak because of the generation gap. The grandparents would like to raise these children just the way they raised their own children without realizing the generational differences. This may lead to misunderstandings. Often, grandparent caregivers complain that their grandchildren are stubborn and rebellious while the grandchildren accuse their grandparents as not understanding their needs. Consequently, the intergenerational relationship becomes weak and less cordial.

Compared with the traditional roles, grandparents are now assuming a caregiver role instead of a care recipient role. The following quotation summarizes the survey respondents' assessment of the impact of AIDS on the older generation:

> The older population who have lost their children to AIDS and are caring for their grandchildren are overwhelmed by grief and unexpected economic responsibilities, compounding their dwindling or non-existent finances, and failing health. (Medical Officer/Industrial Physician, aged 42)

SOCIAL, ECONOMIC, AND EMOTIONAL HEALTH IMPACT OF AIDS ON OLDER AND YOUNGER POPULATIONS IN NIGERIA

AIDS is creating social isolation and ostracism of the infected and affected people in Nigeria and other African nations (Obi, 2001; WHO, 2002; Ankrah, 1994; Bor & Elford, 1994). Due to its stigma, individuals in some communities fear any association with families or individuals suffering from the disease (Obi, 2001; Online NewsHour, 2002; Online NewsHour, 2001). For example, a report on AIDS in South Africa quoted Moetlo, a nurse practitioner, as saying, "women risk being thrown out in the street if they reveal their HIV status" (Online NewsHour: December 2, 1998). The work of Obi (2001) made vivid the fact of abandonment rejection and isolation of people suspected to have HIV/AIDS. One survey respondent described AIDS as "an abnorma, an aberration, an omen, and an evil wind that must be stopped" (AIDS Relief Mission worker, age 42).

Not only are AIDS victims isolated by their communities, findings also reveal that they tend to withdraw and isolate themselves in order to maintain their dignity (McGrath, Rwabukwali, Schumann, Pearson- Marks, Nakayiwa et al., 1994). They also fear disclosing their AIDS status because of the negative consequences associated with this information. For instance, a study reported the testimonies of two HIV/AIDS victims:

> Nobody knows, but I do not know what will happen if they come to know. Please do not let my sister know of it. Because she will let everybody around here know. She is a person who cannot keep a secret. And it may affect my staying here. (Ganda female, aged 28)

> I am afraid that if they learn that I have AIDS they may decide to send me home to die. They may fear to keep me in their house any longer let alone paying out money for a patient without any hope of permanent recovery. (Ankole male, aged 35) (McGrath et al., 1994)

With AIDS claiming thousands of lives of schoolteachers, the educational process is also being disrupted. Some schools are forced to close due to the loss of teachers (World Bank, 2002; Eke, 2003b).

Economically, every nation or community where the epidemic has taken its toll suffers from a decrease in productivity. As the productive cohorts of young able-bodied men and women are being claimed, leaving older people and children, there is economic devastation. Cost of medications further drains the meager income of the infected and affected people. Some uninfected adults may adopt a distant posture in their relationships with the young and old as a way to shield themselves from severe financial depletion.

According to one respondent, "The older population suffer the impact of changes in house/family structure, loss of income, impoverishment, grief, psychosocial distress, increased malnutrition, and reduced ability to care for children" (Consultant Physician, aged 40). Onyenechere (1999) found a large financial impact on people living with AIDS and their families in Nigeria. This situation is aggravated by the fact that most people living with AIDS who are productive have an average income of less than N2,000 (US$22) per month (Onyenechere, 1999). Four survey respondents believe that the older population 'especially' bears the brunt economically of AIDS. They see it as a responsibility to preserve the family name and to step forward in times of need. Given their meager financial resources which decline in most cases as they age, caring for an AIDS victim in the family increases this burden.

Caregivers experience significant levels of emotional stress. Such stress may assume a unique dimension for an elder who must confront a double dilemma of observing one's own children deteriorate in health and knowing that their sick and dying children will not be there to provide care when needed. It is emotionally stressful to observe one's offspring die and now assume a new role of parenting their children who also may be very sick and emotionally unstable. Griffin (1995) notes that "elders may be experiencing extreme emotional stress from witnessing the death of successive children while at the same time, caring for the orphans who are undergoing the serious psychological effects of watching parents die" (pg. 17).

A great sense of uncertainty and insecurity about the future provide another significant source of stress for elders. It has always been the prayer of older people in Africa for their children to outlive them and give them a befitting burial. For elders, to be involved in burying their own children is heartbreaking. Now they have the added worry that they will not receive an adequate funeral because they have lost their children to AIDS.

Children whose parents are infected with the disease often face the challenge of caring for them. At the time they need their parental support, they turn (very early in life) to being supporters and caregivers to their young dying parents. In addition, they face the trauma of stigmatization. This situation clearly does not promote happy intergenerational relationships which are supposed to be mutually supportive and benefiting.

When their parent or parents die, they face all the problems associated with "orphanhood" (Preble, 1994; Akukwe, 2001). Some of them are left sick (sometimes of AIDS), and may not have anybody to take care of them. Even when they receive care, the quality may be at its barest minimum. These orphans are expected to run errands and engage in economic activities in order to assist their caregivers (grandparents/relations) to be able to provide their basic needs. Where this is not possible, some end up as "street children," and often without any formal education or trade.

NEED FOR INTERVENTION

Steps Taken by Nigeria to Respond to the Problem

Several efforts have been made by Nigeria to assist infected individuals and their families, and to prevent the spread of the disease. Such efforts include subsidized antiretroviral drugs; functional social support groups that provide information, counseling and care to victims; and radio/TV adverts asking people not to discriminate against those who have AIDS (Eke, 2003b). Some policy efforts by the Nigerian government have been criticized for being ineffective because they mainly target the infected individuals while overlooking those who are affected. As noted by a respondent to the mailed survey, "So far we have not seen a blue print of such impact alleviation policies . . ." (COE, Sabaoth Rescue Mission, NGO that fights against HIV/AIDS).

The fact remains that even if AIDS were eradicated today, its impact, especially with regard to intergenerational relationships, will last for decades. Consequently, there is a serious need to address the impact of the disease on intergenerational relationships. So far, not much effort has been made in this direction.

Suggested New Strategies

Several new strategies, programs, and initiatives are needed to better deal with the realities of HIV/AIDS in Nigeria. These strategies must carefully consider the impact of AIDS on traditional intergenerational relationships in Nigeria, but also must consider the benefits of intergenerational solutions.

To slow the spread of AIDS and to improve intergenerational relationship in the face of AIDS, measures must be taken to remove the stigma of AIDS through grassroots information and education campaigns. Many citizens simply do not understand the nature of the disease and its spread; many, including most of the older population who become caregivers to their infected and affected children, are illiterate. Using local languages and dialects to explain issues of AIDS will reduce many of the misconceptions that lead to stigma.

The fear of financial burden, which also results in some people avoiding responsibility for the affected populations, must be addressed by government policies and programs aimed at subsidizing housing, funding for transportation, and feeding allowances for children and older adult victims of AIDS. These funds could be disbursed through the local government health and social services agencies so that the service can be provided nationwide.

"Policies on orphan care and support for the aged with food, clothing, school fees, medicare, etc., are necessary" (CEO Sabaoth Rescue Mission, age 42 years). Because the economic burden is becoming too heavy for individual families and even communities to bear, government should provide funding to compensate caregivers and intergenerational volunteers for services they provide. Centers should be established for AIDS orphans. If such orphanages are established, older caregivers can periodically visit their orphaned grandchildren and give them a sense of support. Support centers and programs should be developed to assist grandparents providing foster care to their grandchildren. "All parents of HIV/AIDS victims can belong for discussions of their common problems and find solutions to them. Such association can apply for and receive targeted donations and assistance from international donors, and other charitable organizations" (Survey respondent).

Policy must look beyond the nuclear and extended family and develop community-wide intergenerational support systems (Eke, 2003b). For example, programs should be developed to provide assistance to older AIDS caregivers by the community's youth. Elders who are able can also be encouraged to assist others' children who are victims of AIDS. Healthy and well-to-do youth should be encouraged to form or participate in volunteer groups to assist both the older and younger victims. "Formation of family forum for the creation of HIV/AIDS awareness/prevention is needed. UNAIDS should urgently work to safeguard the intergenerational relationship which is breaking apart because of AIDS" (CEO, Sabaoth Rescue Mission, NGO that fights against HIV/AIDS).

National and international religious organizations have been providing extensive volunteer services in Nigeria for many years, but it is now time for them to more specifically target HIV/AIDS victims and families for emotional, social and economic supports. Other traditional organizations/institutions, such as the Age Grades, the youth organization, married women organization, Elders' meeting and organized children services, should be encouraged to provide supports and services to individuals and families struggling with AIDS. As suggested by one of the respondents, "Advocacy programs utilizing the traditional, religious and educational authorities are necessary" (Consultant Physician, age 40 years).

Most Nigerian communities are "age graded." In other words, members are hierarchically organized according to their age or cohorts. Although many organizations focus on specific age groups and on their members' welfare (Eke, 2003b), they can and should be encouraged to respond to calls for assistance made by non-members if such calls fall within what they consider as their mission. Governmental policies should aim at joint efforts of the different generations. Program development should involve the participation of different generational cohorts both for preventive measures and for caring for victims. When community efforts are unified, these organizations can prove very strong because they have personal funds and other resources that can assist in times of crisis.

This notion of building intergenerational relationships as a collective effort in problem solving by different organizations of cohorts is yet to be harnessed. In fact, this is perhaps the most significant aspect that has not been fully explored in the campaign efforts against the spread and effects of AIDS. Other international agencies that fight AIDS should be more sensitive in their support for programs that will help build and strengthen intergenerational relationships in the face of AIDS.

CONCLUSION

The intergenerational impact of AIDS in Nigeria is troubling. Those infected or affected by the pandemic suffer isolation; deprivation of traditional patterns of care, support and nurturance; and emotional devastation. Parents and children of AIDS victims bear much of the economic and psychological impact of the epidemic. While there is some hope that adopting new preventive strategies will slow HIV/AIDS infection, it is clear that slowing the trend of the infection is only one step to redress the impact of the pandemic upon intergenerational relationships. Protecting and building upon traditional intergenerational relationships at both the family and community level should become a national priority. More community-based intergenerational programs could serve as a viable tool for assisting affected individuals who may not have family members to help them. In addition, new dimensions of intergenerational relationships among existing traditional organizations which encourage unity, coordination, and cooperation would be helpful.

The time has come for government to create policies aimed at financially supporting affected persons and caregivers. Reactivating the well-known intergenerational bonds at both the family and community levels will help Nigerians, especially the aged, and children to live more happy and productive lives even in the face of the HIV/AIDS challenges. Future research on this aspect of the impact of AIDS is encouraged.

REFERENCES

Akinsete, I. (2000). Situation Analysis Report on STD/HIV/AIDS in Nigeria. Federal Ministry of Health, National Action Committee on AIDS.

Akukwe, C. (2000, September 25). HIV/AIDS in Nigeria: Averting an impending catastrophe. *Nigeriaworld*. Available online: http://www.nigeriaworld.com/feature/article/aidshiv_in_Nigeria.html

Appiah-Kubi, K. (1982). Knowledge is power, but age is wisdom: The challenge of active aging from African perspective. In F.V. Tiso (Ed), *Aging: Spiritual Perspective*. Lake Worth, FL: Sunday Publications, Inc.

Baiyewu, O. & Bella, A.F. (1997). Attitude to aging among different groups in Nigeria. *International Journal of Aging and Human Development, 44(4)*, 283-292.

Bor, R. & Elford, J. (1994). *The Family and HIV*. Great Britain: Redwood Books.

Brown, C.K. (1984). *Improving the Social Protection of the Aging Population in Ghana*. Legon: Institute of Statistical, Social & Economic Research, University of Ghana.

Cain, M. (1985). Fertility as an adjustment to risk. In A.S. Rossi (Ed), *Gender and the Life Course*, pp. 145-149. New York: Aldrine.

Caldwell, J.C. (1982). *Theory of Fertility Decline*. New York: Academic Press.

Cattel, M.G. (1990). Models of old age among the Samia of Kenya: Family support of the Elderly. *Journal of Cross-cultural Gerontology*, 5, 375-394.

Dowd, J.J. (1975). Aging as exchange: A preface to theory. *Journal of Gerontology*, 30, 584-594.

Eke, B. (2003a). The impact of AIDS on intergenerational relationships in Africa. *Journal of Intergenerational Relationships, 1(3)*, 9-24.

Eke, B. (2003b). The Impact of AIDS on Intergenerational Relationships in Nigeria. A research thesis submitted to the faculty of Miami University, Oxford, Ohio.

Falola, T. (2001). *Culture and Customs of Nigeria*. London: Greenwood Press.

George, U. (1999). Nigeria-Family Life. Available online: http://cwr.utoronto.ca/cultural/english/nigeria/family.html

Gouldner, A.W. (1960). The norms of reciprocity: Preliminary statement. *American Sociological Review*, 25, 161-178.

Griffin, C.L. (1995). The effects of AIDS mortality on the elders of Sub-Saharan Africa. A master's degree thesis presented to the department of sociology & gerontology, Miami University, Oxford, Ohio.

Grant-Miller, J. (2003). An intergenerational journey. Available at: http://www.eden midwest.com

Igbanugo, V. (2001). Evaluation of the efforts to contain HIV/AIDS in Oyo State (Nigeria): Successes, constraints, and the way forward. Lagos, Nigeria: (JAAIDS). Available at: http://www.nigeria-aids.org/reports.cfm?read=24

Iwuagwu, S. (2001). Attitude of Nigerians towards the human rights of people living with HIV/AIDS. Nigeria: JAAIDS.

Kaiser Family Report (2002). The Global HIV/AIDS Epidemic. Fact Sheet #3030-03. Available at: http://www.kff.org/hivaids/

Kaslow, R.A. & Francis D.P. (1989). *The Epidemiology of AIDS*. New York: Oxford University Press.

Laszlo, E. (2001). *Microshift: Navigating the Transformation to a Sustainable World*. San Francisco: Berrett-Koehler Publishers, Inc.

Mann, J.M., Tarantola, D.J.M., & Netter, T.W. (1992). *AIDS in the World: A Global Report*. Cambridge, Massachusetts: Harvard University Press.

McGrath, W.J., Rwabukwali, C.B., Schumann, D.A., Pearson-Marks, J., Nakayiwa, S. et al. (1994). Anthropology and AIDS: The cultural context of sexual risk behavior among urban Baganda women in Kampala, Uganda. In R. Bor & J. Elford (Eds), *The Family and HIV*. London: Cassell.

Newman, S., Ward, C.R., Smith, T.B., Wilson, J.O., & McCrea, J.M. (1997). *Intergenerational Programs: Past, Present, & Future*. Washington, DC: Taylor & Francis.

Obi, G.L.O. (2001). The care of HIV/AIDS patients: A taboo among the slum communities. Nigeria: JAAIDS.

Olaniyan, R. (1985). *Nigerian History and Culture*. Hong Kong: Longman Group Ltd.

Online NewsHour (2001, May 15). *AIDS in Africa: The Botswana Battle*. Available at: http://www.pbs.org/newshour/bb/health/jan-june01/aids_5-15.html

Online NewsHour (2002, May 9). *Orphaned by AIDS*. Available at: http://www.pbs.org/newhour/bb/health/jan-june02/aids_zambia_5-9.html

Onwujekwe, D.I. (2001). *The Epidemiology of HIV in Nigeria: Changing Trends and New Challenges*. Nigeria: JAAID.

Onyenechere, E. (1999). *A geo-economic analysis of community home based care for PLWAs and their families in Africa (case study Nigeria): Implications for the future*. Paper presented at the 11th International Conference on AIDS/STDS in Africa (ICASA 99).

Peil, M., Bamisaiye, A., & Ekpenyong, S. (1989). Health and physical support for the elderly in Nigeria. *Journal of Cross-cultural Gerontology, 3,* 3-20.

Preble, E.A. (1994). Impact of HIV/AIDS on African children. In R. Bor & J. Elford (Eds), *The Family and HIV*. London: Cassell.

Simic, A. (1993). Aging and ethnic identity: A refutation of double-jeopardy theory. *Journal of Case Management, 2 (1),* 9-13.

Togonu-Bickersteth, F. (1989). Conflicts over caregiving: A discussion of filial obligations among adult Nigerian Children. *Journal of Cross-Cultural Gerontology, 4 (1),* 35-48.

UNAIDS (2000, June). *AIDS in Africa*. Available at: http://www.aidsandafrica.com/2001_aids_country_data.htm

UNAIDS (2002, July). *Global estimates of HIV/AIDS epidemic as of end 2001*. Available at: http://www.unaids.org/EN/other/functionalities/advancedSearch.asp

UNAIDS/WHO (2001). *Epidemiology Fact Sheet*. Available at: *http://www.who.int/emc-hiv/fact_sheets/pdfs/Nigeria_EN.pdf*

Unanka, G.O. (1999). *Caregiving and the impact of health and functional status: A study of aging problems and prospects in the African nation–Nigeria*. A master's degree thesis presented to the Department of Sociology, Gerontology, & Anthropology, Miami University, Oxford, Ohio.

Will, G.F. (2000, Jan. 10). AIDS crushes a continent. *Newsweek*, New York; p. 174.

World Bank, (2002). *Education and HIV/AIDS: A Window of Hope*. Available online: http://www1.worldbank.org/education/pdf/Ed%20&%20HIV_AIDS%20cover%20print.pdf

World Health Organization (2002). Report on the Global HIV/AIDS EPIDEMIC 2002. XIV International Conference on AIDS, Barcelona, 7-12 July.

The Elder in African Society:
The View from Folklore and Literature

Joseph Mbele

SUMMARY. Conventional wisdom presents the elder in African society as a wise, dignified and powerful figure, who keeps the culture alive and guides the young. This paper tries to demonstrate that this image of the elders in Africa is simplistic, using evidence from folklore and literature. Folklore, though a rarely used source for studies of this nature, is the most authentic expression of a people's reality and experience. Since it springs from the remote past, folklore bears the evidence of where the Africans have come from. Together with folklore, there are some literary works which are also used, since they spring from and appropriate key aspects of the folklore heritage. *[Article copies available for a fee from The Haworth Document Delivery Service: 1-800-HAWORTH. E-mail address: <docdelivery@haworthpress.com> Website: <http://www.HaworthPress.com> © 2004 by The Haworth Press, Inc. All rights reserved.]*

KEYWORDS. Elders, African society, folklore

The very notion of the elder in African society conjures up an image of dignified, solemn, and serious old men or women who wield unchallenged authority in the community and are wise counselors of the young.

Joseph Mbele is affiliated with St. Olaf College, Minnesota.

[Haworth co-indexing entry note]: "The Elder in African Society: The View from Folklore and Literature." Mbele, Joseph. Co-published simultaneously in *Journal of Intergenerational Relationships* (The Haworth Press, Inc.) Vol. 2, No. 3/4, 2004, pp. 53-61; and: *Intergenerational Relationships: Conversations on Practice and Research Across Cultures* (ed: Elizabeth Larkin et al.) The Haworth Press, Inc., 2004, pp. 53-61. Single or multiple copies of this article are available for a fee from The Haworth Document Delivery Service [1-800-HAWORTH, 9:00 a.m. - 5:00 p.m. (EST). E-mail address: docdelivery@haworthpress.com].

http://www.haworthpress.com/web/JIR
Digital Object Identifier: 10.1300/J194v02n03_05

We associate the notion of the elder with respect, wisdom, power, and authority. How truthful is this perception of the image and role of elder in Africa? It appears to me that this view of the elder both reveals and conceals the truth about the elder in African society. I will develop my argument not with conventional social science data, but the evidence of folklore and literature. In the course of my discussion, I will state the reasons for my choice.

There is no doubt that, at least in the olden days, African elders held much power and authority, the greatest power and authority that can be invested in human beings. The elders made decisions for the society, either on their own or as councils of elders. This has been the case since time immemorial. About precolonial Igbo society, Ohadike writes:

> Each town, lineage, and town was headed by a headman, *onyisi*, who acquired the position by virtue of his age. Town meetings were usually held in the town square, but the most important lineage and house meetings were held in the *obi* (meeting shed) of the most senior elders. (Ohadike, 2000, p. xxiii)

Even where monarchs ruled, they were assisted by and responsive to such a councils of elders. The elders played central roles in rituals as well; for example, they controlled the "Poro" secret society of the Mende of Sierra Leone.

It is common, however, to romanticize the image of the African elder, imagining the elder as the repository of a society's values and wisdom, which apparently have remained unchanged over the ages. Such beliefs drive researchers in folklore, for example, to go in search of the elders, hoping to rescue their great knowledge before they die. I wonder whether this simplistic view of elders has evolved only in recent times, promoted through simple observation of social life and the tradition of writing. A cursory observation of social life might have yielded the conventional view of the elders, in the sense that it did not dwell too deeply on the reality being observed. The belief that elders embody wisdom may have clouded or prevented a more careful look at the issue. The tradition of writing may also have contributed to the consolidation and perpetuation of the same view of elders. What writers have said about elders has tended to assume canonical significance, and the durability of the written word reinforced the view. Amadou Hampaté Bâ wrote, for example: "In Africa, when an old person dies, it's a library burning down" (quoted by Irele, ix). This statement has been picked up and taken for granted as canonical wisdom. I feel that such observations and writings do not present the complex reality of the elder in African society. It appears that in the past, as evidenced by folklore, African societies had a complex and therefore more sophisticated view of the elders.

For this reason, I have decided to discuss the image and role of the elder using folklore, a source that is rarely considered in such discussions. The concept of folklore that I am using here involves primarily traditional narratives, proverbs, sayings, and songs. I will also invoke the artistic expressions that flow from folklore, including contemporary written literature. Using these sources, together with descriptions and analysis of actual behaviour, is likely to yield the most authentic understanding of the question of the elder in African society. Folklore is a reliable index of people's consciousness, perhaps more so than standard responses people might provide to questions posed by researchers or officials. Folklore is the people's collective expression, authentic embodiment of values, aspirations, critiques of social life and individual experience, its tensions, contradictions, problems and promise. Folklore is more reliable than most social science approaches of arriving at such knowledge, because folklore is the voice of the people themselves, not mediated through any other perspective. As unmediated discourse, folklore is the most authentic expression of the people's experience, values, sentiments, aspirations, thoughts and understanding. At the same time, folklore springs from the distant past and represents the distillation of the collective memory of a people.

African folklore expresses the complexity of the subject of the elder in African society. While affirming the conventional view of the elders as the custodians and source of the collective wisdom of a society, folklore brings up many other perspectives. Let us examine some examples. The conventional view is stated, for example, in the Swahili proverb: "Kuishi kwingi ni kuona mengi," living a long life is witnessing many things. Another proverb states, "Penye wazee haliharibiki neno," where there are elders, nothing can go wrong. Another proverb restates this truth with a warning: "Asiyesikia la mkuu huona makuu," a person who does heed the elder will meet face serious consequences. Another version of the proverb goes "Asiyesikia la mkuu huvunjika guu." The one who does not listen to an elder will end up breaking his leg.

These proverbs accurately express and reinforce the reverence Africans hold for elders. Only the most reckless African will dare defy the will of the elders. The elders are considered wise precisely because they have lived longer and have seen more than anyone else. The Swahili refer to someone old with the saying, "amekula chumvi nyingi," which means he or she has eaten much salt. Having lived long is described in terms of how much salt the person has eaten, and one supposes that in the Swahili mind, the eating of much salt over the years signifies the accumulation of wisdom and experience.

African folklore proves adequately that Africans take these beliefs seriously. In the folktales, for example, we see that whenever people have a difficult problem, they bring it in front of the elders. What the elders decide is final. In fact, the Ashanti tale, "How Spider Obtained the Sky-god's Stories," takes us beyond the realm of human existence and shows Nyankonpon, the sky-god, consulting his elders and other dignitaries when an important matter arises (Radin, 1953, p. 27). The folktales thereby reinforce the idea of the wisdom of the elders.

While affirming the view that with age comes experience, and that the elders are the storehouse and founts of wisdom, Africans were also aware that this was not always the case. Again, folklore affords ample evidence of this awareness. There are, for example, folktales which challenge the conventional wisdom. The Matengo folktale "Hare, Civet and Antelope" presents elders who are neither wise nor responsible (Mbele, 2001, pp. 12-19). Given the task of watching the village to find out who is stealing the livestock and fowl while everyone is in the fields, the elders succumb to bribery and abandon their duty. The image of elders presented in this tale is quite disturbing. At the same time, it offers proof of the society's capacity and willingness to investigate unpleasant realities and possibilities in life. It alerts us to the fact that the elders are not a monolithic group of like- minded people; there are differences among them, and some may not live up to the image we entertain about elders. Folklore thus presents a more realistic, more truthful view of the elders.

We see a similar dialectical perspective in Chinua Achebe's famous novel *Things Fall Apart* (2000) which makes skillful use of Igbo folklore. While stressing the role of elders as the memory of the community, the voice of reason, and the arbiters of what is right and wrong, this novel does not present the elders as a monolithic group. Just as in folklore, it presents different kinds of elders, from Uchendu, who is a sober and grave old man, to Unoka, who is universally despised and considered good for nothing. Regarding Unoka, the novel states that "[i]n his day he was lazy and improvident and was quite incapable of thinking about tomorrow" (3). In a society that emphasized hard work, Unoka was interested only in having a good time, playing music, entertaining people with music, drink, and good cheer. Between the polarities represented by Unoka and Uchendu there is Obierika, who is such a thoughtful elder that he questions some of the values and customs of his culture.

Obierika represents the elder who is not just a custodian of the African culture, but a critic and thus potentially a catalyst for change. In some strange way, Unoka can also be seen as person who offers an alternative to the conventional ways of living and is, therefore, also a potential catalyst for change.

Unoka represents a pattern we see in African folklore, which problematizes the phenomenon of elders in African society. Folklore, as I have noted, comes down from ancient times, and it is clear that the ancients knew that not all elders fit one pattern. They had a much more sophisticated view of the elders than the views we hold today. In folktales, for example, African societies present elders of different kinds: the wise and responsible, and also those who are not wise and responsible. For some reason, however, today this awareness is largely missing in conventional discourses about African elders, even among scholars. People generally fail to see that the mere passage of years might not necessarily transform an ignorant, lazy or mischievous young person into a wise elder.

Again and again, *Things Fall Apart* invokes the authority of the elders in various situations. The elders keep the collective memory of the society. We see this right in the first paragraph of the novel, where the big wrestling match between Okonkwo and Amalinze the cat is described. Achebe writes, "It was this man that Okonkwo threw in a fight which the old men agreed was one of the fiercest since the founder of their town engaged a spirit of the wild for seven days and seven nights" (3). The sayings of the elders have the same power in the society Achebe is describing as legal documents have in other societies. In discussing the way Okonkwo, the main character, moved from a lowly start to great success, Achebe says: "As the elders said, if a child washed his hands he could eat with kings. Okonkwo clearly had washed his hands and so he ate with kings and elders" (6).

As a researcher in folklore, I have encountered some unexpected situations with elders. While people everywhere I go tend to introduce me to old people as the best informants, some of the old people say that they are too old to remember much or anything. We all seem to be enraptured by the idea that the oldest people are the most knowledgeable. Rather than sticking to the stereotype of the wise elder, the elder who is the ultimate source of wisdom, we should remember that old age comes with its problems, such as forgetfulness.

The situation of elders in Africa is changing rather steadily. Though, as I have indicated, it is correct to say that traditionally, elders in Africa were highly esteemed, there are increasing tendencies which undermine their position and authority. While such tendencies were there to some degree throughout the ages, expressed, for example, as a generation gap or intergenerational tensions, the intervention of European colonialism accelerated and accentuated the disruptive tendencies: the statues of elders has been eroded by school education, urbanization and the general spread of western values. The elders themselves complain about the erosion of the respect that age used to command in the past. In the course of folklore research in Tanzania in recent years, I have encountered such complaints by the elders.

The irony is that it appears that throughout history, elders have complained about the young generation. This idea struck me in 1989 while reading issues of the old Swahili newspaper *Mambo Leo*, which dealt with life in East Africa. I noted that in the twenties, the elders were complaining about the behaviour of the young people, and when those young people had become elders, they complained about the young people, who are, of course, elders today. They, in turn, are complaining about today's young people. Despite appearances to the contrary, it is not easy being an elder in Africa. On the surface there is tremendous respect attached to being an elder, but on the other hand the elders face real hardships in their daily lives and experience life in ways we may not be fully aware of. In Sukumaland, Tanzania, witch killings target the old, especially old women. The irony is that when contemplating the plight of elders in the western world, such as the U.S.A. where the elders are consigned to nursing homes, Africans tend to wax eloquent about how properly they treat their own elders.

As a folklorist, I sense that there must be a wealth of folklore and other discourses through which the elders express their experiences, predicament, and perspectives in today's Africa. If no one recorded these discourses in the past, we might do well to do so in our own time. Maybe there are proverbs, sayings, jokes, rumours, and other forms of folklore through which the elders express themselves, as humans have done from time immemorial. There is a need to record and study all this, in order to get a better sense of the existential reality of the elders today. Otherwise our understanding of this reality is likely to be based on conjecture and illusions.

We get a glimpse of the problematic situation of African elders today through reading certain works of African literature. In Sembene Ousmane's novel, *God's Bits of Wood* (1995), which describes a strike by railway workers in Senegal during the time of French rule, we hear an elder trying to dissuade the young generation from going on strike, on the grounds that they did have the experiences he had in his life, which includes witnessing the bad effects of such a strike. He complains that their inexperience aside, the young people made such a momentous decision, whose consequences could be grave. There is also an old woman, Niakoro, who cautions the young from staging a strike, even though they have legitimate grievances. She is in the compound with younger women, who pay little attention to her. As the novelist writes: "But what did old Niakoro mean to these women, occupied only with the passing hour? She was just a leftover from a vanished time, slowly being forgotten" (3). There is a sense among the younger generation in *God's Bits of Wood* that the elders are old-fashioned, and one senses that these young people are under the influence of the encroaching European ways, including, of course, urbanization and the social and economic realities brought about by the railway, which is called the machine, and various other means of communication. As the old man Fa Keita says:

> I think it is the machine which has ground everything together this way. And brought everything to a single level. . . . How all this has come about I do not know, but we can see it happening already, before our eyes. Now, for instance, Tiemoko has had this idea, which he took from a book written in the white man's language. I have seen more suns rise than any of you, but this is the first time in my life that I have seen a [tribunal]. (94-95)

In discussing the elders, we are, obviously, implying a relationship between the elders and the young people. The question of how youths relate to the elders can be explored further. The conventional view that elders embody wisdom seems to imply that young people are not as wise as the elders. However, a study of African folklore shows that Africans recognized alternatives to this paradigm. There are, for example, many folktales in which the young people are shown to be wiser than the older people. Such tales convey the message that the young could be as good as the older people. Hence the need for respecting the young and the old alike, though each in their own way. *Things Fall Apart* states this fact through the Igbo proverb I have cited, that a child who washed his hands could eat with the elders.

Though the young in Africa are expected to respect the elders, this respect is often tempered with joking between the young and the elders. In other words, intergenerational relationships are not defined merely by respect of the young for the elders, but also mutual joking between the young and the elders. Among the Mande of West Africa the young are expected not only to seek to emulate the elders but also to outdo them.

The Mande have a saying that your father is your first rival (Traoré, p. 171). The idea of competing with the elders, in order to do better than them, is part of the Mande concept of fadenya, which describes the spirit of adventure, and the inclination towards breaking social boundaries in order to attain success and fame.

African traditions considered the elders and the young generation as part of an unbroken cycle of life, which involved also the ancestors and the unborn. As Mildred Hill-Lubin notes:

> In [Africa] grandparents were honored because it was believed that they were the closest to the ancestors, and the ancestors were important because they could assume revered status. It was from the grandparents that children learned their family history, family wisdom, community lore, and traditional values. Among certain groups, the grandparents named their newborn grandchildren. (259)

Mildred Hill-Lubin's reference to naming deserves some more comment. Africans often gave their children the names of elders or ancestors. The children thus became personifications or reincarnations, so to speak, of the elder or ancestors whose named they assumed. The names themselves signified a wish or a prayer that the child should be like the ancestor or elder. The Africans believed that if the elder or ancestor was a distinguished person, the child named after him or her would inherit and embody the qualities of that elder of ancestor. In a word, the name blessed the child and directed his or her destiny.

Problematic and complex as the situation of the elders is in contemporary Africa, overall, the elders continue to wield much power and authority. Though other forms of authority exist in Africa, such as central governments, the power of the elders persists. With this in mind, some people have suggested that Africa should create a council of elders to guide and regulate affairs among African countries. The idea is that the respect the elders command would make them effective counselors and mediators. When he was president of Tanzania, Ali Hassan Mwinyi used to hold meetings with the elders of Dar es Salaam, seeking their counsel. In keeping with African traditions, he was seeking legitimacy for his decisions from the elders. Indeed, western style government, including western style democracy, might not be the most suitable system for Africa. Councils of elders might be the ideal, since they resonate with the culture and spirit of Africans.

REFERENCES

Achebe, C. (2000). *Things Fall Apart*. Oxford: Heinemann.

Bâ, A.H. (1999). Quoted in "Introduction" by Abiola Irele. In Amadou Hampaté Bâ. *The Fortunes of Wangrin*. Trans. Aina Pavolini Taylor. Bloomington: Indiana University Press.

Hill Lubin, M. (1986). "The Grandmother in African and African American Literature." In *Ngambika: Studies of Women in African Literature*. Ed. Carole Boyce Davies and Ann Adams Graves. Trenton: Africa World Press, Inc.

Mbele, J. L. (2001). *Matengo Folktales*. Haverford: Infinity Publishing Company, Inc.

Ohadike, D.C. (2000). "Igbo Culture and History." In Chinua Achebe, *Things Fall Apart*. Oxford: Heinemann.

Ousmane. S. (1995). *God's Bits of Wood*. Trans. Francis Price. Oxford: Heinemann.

Radin, P. (1953). *African Folktales & Sculpture*. New York: Bollingen Foundation, Inc.

Traoré, K. (1999). "Jeli and *Sere*: The Dialectic of the Word in the Manden." In *In Search of Sunjata: The Mande Oral Epic as History Literature, and Performance*, ed. Ralph A. Austen. Bloomington: Indiana University Press.

Understanding Intergenerational Relationships in India

N. K. Chadha

SUMMARY. This paper makes an attempt to describe the status and role of elderly within the family and community institutions as a source of wisdom and knowledge, particularly to have an understanding of the intergenerational relationships in the Indian context. As the countries and areas of Asia develop economically and become more heavily urban, the familial support of the elderly has eroded. There are a number of reasons to think that traditional systems of familial care for the elderly in Asia have started to reflect this changing scenario in terms of increasing problems for the elderly. The Indian subcontinent too has experienced these transitional changes. But despite the changes in the structures and functions of Indian societies, families do preserve the norms of social hierarchy (of which the elderly are an important part), cultural styles and mode of living. At the same time elderly who are regarded as the sources of wisdom and knowledge are given due respect and place in the society within the ambit of the family and community contexts. *[Article copies available for a fee from The Haworth Document Delivery Service: 1-800-HAWORTH. E-mail address: <docdelivery@haworthpress.com> Website: <http://www.HaworthPress.com> © 2004 by The Haworth Press, Inc. All rights reserved.]*

N. K. Chadha is affiliated with the Department of Psychology, University of Delhi, Delhi, India.

[Haworth co-indexing entry note]: "Understanding Intergenerational Relationships in India." Chadha, N. K. Co-published simultaneously in *Journal of Intergenerational Relationships* (The Haworth Press, Inc.) Vol. 2, No. 3/4, 2004, pp. 63-73; and: *Intergenerational Relationships: Conversations on Practice and Research Across Cultures* (ed: Elizabeth Larkin et al.) The Haworth Press, Inc., 2004, pp. 63-73. Single or multiple copies of this article are available for a fee from The Haworth Document Delivery Service [1-800-HAWORTH, 9:00 a.m. - 5:00 p.m. (EST). E-mail address: docdelivery@haworthpress.com].

KEYWORDS. Elderly, family, community, India

As the countries and areas of Asia develop economically and become more heavily urban, the familial support of the elderly has eroded. There are a number of reasons to think that traditional systems of familial care for the elderly in Asia have started to reflect this changing scenario in terms of increasing problems for the elderly. The Indian subcontinent too has experienced these transitional changes. But despite the changes in the structures and functions of Indian societies, families do preserve the norms of social hierarchy (of which the elderly are an important part), cultural styles and mode of living (Singh, 2001). At the same time elderly who are regarded as the sources of wisdom and knowledge are given due respect and place in the society within the ambit of the family and community contexts.

This paper makes an attempt to describe the status and role of elderly within the family and community institutions as a source of wisdom and knowledge, particularly to have an understanding of the intergenerational relationships in the Indian context.

ELDERLY AND INSTITUTION OF FAMILY IN INDIA

The Indian family, which is predominantly joint or extended, has remained remarkably stable despite some marked and drastic social, political, economic and religious changes over the last thirty years. Family has retained its primarily joint or extended characteristics. In general, the Indian family has the following structural features: In the cyclical family pattern, that is, joint family-nuclear family-joint family, the agrarian nature of the society in the majority of rural population areas have been able to sustain this multi-couple lifestyle for a longer time while non-cultivating landowners retain this family pattern for a shorter period; landless laborers tend to adhere to the extended family system.

The socialization process is composed of a series of ceremonies beginning with the bathing and naming of the infant till the death of an individual; the process of celebrating rituals, religious ceremonies, and other events as a mark of reverence, remembrance and peace for the departed souls continue even after the death.

In many family rituals, key roles are customarily assigned to the oldest male. Older women also have important roles, although they usually have less centrality than men. These practices create an important place for older people in ritual settings relating to the household. The relative age and generation serve as important organizing principles in these rituals. Folklore and tales form an important tool of transcending knowledge and wisdom down to younger generations as an important mode of communication. The importance of the role played by elderly in these rituals and ceremonies can best be seen in the following story about a grandfather and a wedding party.

> One boy longed to marry a particular girl. After thinking very carefully about his prospect, he arranged a meeting with her and made a proposal to marry. The girl's father accepted the proposal but with a condition. This was that no old person would come along with the marriage party. The young man was hesitant to accept the condition because he loved his grandfather and knew it meant that he could not be part of the wedding. He thought about it and hesitatingly accepted the condition because he was just deeply interested in the girl. He came back home and told his grandfather that the proposal was accepted under the condition, established by the girl's father, that no old person could be part of the procession from the groom's home to that of the bride. The father said, "How is it possible without taking your grandfather? He is the eldest man of the household." The grandfather was very keen to accompany the marriage party and seeing his grandson walk around the sacred fire and repeat the vows. At last, a decision was made. They would take the grandfather along with the marriage party but would lock him in a wooden box. They would cut a hole in the side of the box so that the grandfather could see and breathe. In this way they left with the procession consisting of 100 younger and old aged people. When they arrived at the girl's family home, her father greeted them. He said, "There is another condition. I will allow my daughter to marry you provided the groom's party will eat the meat of a hundred goats. If you don't succeed, then I will not allow my daughter to marry you and you will have to return." The boy's heart sank. He thought it impossible to meet this condition. "How can 100 goats be eaten by 1000 people?" he thought. Sad and dejected, he returned to the guesthouse where the marriage party was staying. Through the hole in the box, the old man saw his grandson, sad and dejected. He could not remain silent. He asked from the box, "What is the matter?" The grandson told the whole incident. The old man spoke, "it is very simple; I will give you the answer: you tell the girl's father that I accept your proposal on one

condition. That is, that you will cook one goat and serve us. At the moment we finish the goat, you will cook another and serve us." Eating a hundred goats would be a pleasure one at a time. The boy went to the girl's house and told her father of his condition. Immediately, the girl's father smiled and said, "it seems you must have an old wise person in your wedding party who gave you this solution. Only an old person can think so intelligently. I want to meet that old person and then I will allow my daughter to marry you." The boy confessed, "I brought my grandfather with me locked in a box because of your condition not to bring any elderly along with the marriage party." (van Willigen and Chadha, 1999: 76-77)

This story presents a glimpse of the importance given to the experienced knowledge of the elderly in the Indian cultural setting. Even though India is an abode to people of diverse origins, religious beliefs, practices and modes of living, the commonality of deep respect for the elderly and taking them as traditional authority figures is evidenced across cultures and regional zones. Older people are very much involved in every ritual and ceremony and actually they are the ones who initiate the process of organizing these rituals and ceremonies in day-to-day life affairs. The process of marriage, marking the social recognition and permission for members of two opposite sexes to cohabit and fulfill the social obligations in the framework of the family system is a very significant event in the family life of Indian societies for a number of reasons. This process not only helps in bringing two opposite sexes together for the rest of their lives, but also acts as a bridge in extending the relationships between two families and, above all, two communities together and binds them. In the Indian context particularly, with majority of the population from rural traditional background, the trend of westernization and urbanization due to industrialization has not been able to replace the traditional family values of loyalty towards parents, reverence for elderly, values in regard to rites and rituals, marriage and other ceremonies. So this marriage arrangement process also signifies the role of elderly members of the family in introducing the younger generation to social obligations. How the elderly play a significant role and are referred to with high respect can best be elucidated by the example of a typical Hindu family marriage arrangement custom of northern India. In case of the marriage process within this sect of traditional northern India Hindu family, the initial contact is made by younger adults, such as the bride and groom's parents. Later as negotiations proceed, older members of the family are consulted and participate in the final decision. An older person may have substantial control over the outcome. Often the eldest male serves as a "point person" for the interaction between the two families. This means that the boy's grandfather plays a very important role in transactions.

When an agreement is reached, a brief ceremony called *Roka* is held and is sometimes referred to as the "initial fixing." The name comes from the word "to stop": with the *Roka* ceremony, the two families will stop looking for a suitable boy or girl. The *Roka* is usually conducted at an outside location like a temple or restaurant and seldom at the boy's house. There is a minor presentation of sweets by the girl's grandfather or father and is expressed with folding hands by the girl's grandparents and parents as a request to the boy's parents or grandparents to accept their daughter in their house. From a few weeks to months, the families meet again for presentations of gifts *(Sagan)* to the groom's family. Prior to the visit, the girl's family discuss with the elder males who should get gifts of cash and the appropriate amounts. *Sagan* will be given to relatives such as the grandfather, grandmother, father, mother, father's brothers and their wives, father's sisters and their husbands, mother's parents, mother's sister and brother. The *Sagan* may be presented to the older male and distributed by him within the circle of *Sagan* recipients.

A day after *Sagan,* the ring is presented. A group, including the boy, from the boy's side visits the girl's house. They make a presentation of the gift of a gold ring and a scarf. The boy's family makes a cash *sagan* to the girl but not to any other member of her family. This is made by the elder member of the boy's family, such as his grandfather. Food appropriate to the time of the day is served to the visiting guests. *Shaadi,* the proper marriage marking the social recognition of the union of two opposite sexes, is usually held on the third day in a grand ceremony. Older people are intensively involved in the marriage. The eldest man in the boy's family, preferably the grandfather, plays an important ritual role in this ceremony. As a mark of reverence, the name of the eldest member of the family, always the elderly men and women, are even listed on the wedding invitation itself as the one extending invitation to the guest for the occasion (including the relatives, neighbors and friends).

An important part of the wedding is the seven circumbulations of the sacred hearth altar under the directions of the priest, who serves as the chief to conduct rituals. These are referred to as *Pharas.* At each circumbulation a *mantra* is spoken along with a vow. The completion of each vow is marked by the removal of a line of *Atta* (i.e., wheat flour) that had been placed on the floor earlier as part of ritual. Among the vows for the girl are two that are directed at her relationships with older members of the household. She is asked to promise to care for all the elders of the household and not annoy them with bad behaviour. She is also asked to promise to treat her mother-in-law as a she would treat her own parents. The boy doesn't take a vow to care for her parents. This can be due to patrilineal descent pattern and domination of the male role in the family life. The girl is also asked to vow to keep the secrets of her new family. After these vows, the grandfather or the father stands in back of the bride and groom holding their heads, joining them together as a kind of blessing. After that, the bride and the groom get up and touch the feet of the grandparents. The bride also touches the feet of her father-in-law and other older close relatives on the boy's side. After the marriage ceremony is over, the girl goes to the boy's house where she will be living for the rest of her life. Her mother-in-law greets her at the gate of the home and does worship with special oil lamps at the gate itself, pouring mustard oil on the two sides of the gate. After the first night in her home, the girl, when she gets up in the morning, goes to the older persons' rooms and touches their feet to get their blessings.

After a few days, the girl cooks first food in the house, always a sweet dish, which she offers to her elders. Elders may be involved in the naming of children. The husband's elder sister might suggest names but only with the grandparents' and parents' approval. During the hair cutting ceremony for the boys, the grandfather has a special role. The father typically holds boy as the barber cuts his hair and priest does a *puja*. After about a week before *Diwalii,* some families will do the *Ahoi mata puja.* During this day, women fast to help assure the long lives of their sons. This is done from dawn till the women can see the stars. After the sun sets and the evening stars rise, there will be a *puja* at home. This is concerned with the happiness of the family and the growth of the sons. Importantly, the *puja* is performed by the oldest male member and acts as a priest giving sacred *tikka* on the forehead, tying sacred threads (*Moli*), giving consecrated food *(Prasad)* and reciting *mantras.*

This account shows how the elderly occupy an important position in a typical North Indian Hindu family. But in fact the vitality of the elderly involvement in the solemnizing of the marriage ceremony is central across other communities and religious belief groups as well.

CHANGING SCENARIO

No doubt family patterns in India are undergoing a change. The main factors of change are modern education, development programmes and urbanization. The direction of change is from the hold of collectivity (tribe, clan and family) to increasing individuality.

M. N. Srinivas (1996), after conducting a study in Indian village (i.e., Mysore in Karnataka State), writes: "the westernization of the Brahmins of Mysore brought about a number of changes in their life. There was change in their appearance and dress. The tuft gave way to cropped hair and the traditional dress gave place, at least partially, to western type dress and shoes." So this implies that reflections of westernization are visible even in the far of peripheral areas of Indian villages as well. But importantly the value system still by and large remains unaffected. At the same time the culture of the western lifestyle even in the metropolis is governed by the historicity of the regional cultural traditions (Singh, 2000). The impact of globalization and westernization has a role in this decline of the joint family (Cohen, 1995: 315) to whichever extent this has occurred in the Indian context. That traditional family collectivity in the form of joint system still prevails and the aged continue to command respect and power (Sharma and Dak, 1987: viii).

But this viewpoint also holds significance that in a society as large and culturally diverse and complex as India, changes take place at different speeds and at different levels of population not affecting the larger overall situation.

BINDING FACTORS

Of the total population of India, about one-third lives in cities, and the population actually is undergoing distortion in their family lives due to the urbanization, industrialization and inclination towards a materialist life driven by the globally competitive life. Obviously India is still a rural society and the nature of its urban spread is regionalized. The intensity of urban cultural influences is largely concentrated in the major metropolitan cities like Delhi, Kolkatta, Chennai, Mumbai, and Bangalore. So the strong linkages which exist in the traditional Indian cultural setting need to be strengthened to fill the gaps arising out of the changing scenario. In fact the traditional value system, order structure and functioning of family has a huge potential of absorbing these jerks and shocks of intergenerational problems, especially the deteriorating plight of elderly brought about by the so-called globalization. The traditional value system embodying the reverence for elderly in households with high cohesiveness, largely seen in the form of grandparents to grandchildren living together, under the same roof, and even the workplaces also bear testimony to the prevalence of such attitude where the elderly or most seniors enjoy the central power authority in every matter.

The shared commonalties in the diverse local cultures of India in the from of cultural traits, rituals beliefs and customs evidenced from states like Utter Pradesh and Rajasthan, etc., have shown remarkable similarity in the ritual styles, songs, and the centrality of the themes (Singh, 1973; Unnithan et al., 1965; Erosov and Singh, 1991). These commonalties do reflect that the strong traditional community ethos of village life is based on ties of caste, family, religion and rituals. These are the spheres where the intergenerational interactions also take place and the elderly have a vital and driving role. This vitality is derived from the status of elderly as central figures in matters concerning the transmission of the values and morality aspects which govern the daily life activities. Moreover, the eldest male of the family being vested with power and authority within the joint family (Lall 1976: 87) too plays a significant aspect. The elderly do have a strong emotional appeal within the family as well as outside family context. But within family as well as community contexts, the elderly do command respect and authority in varied roles not on the basis of emotionality only but because they are considered as the storehouses of knowledge and wisdom gained during their lifetimes. Within the family context the elderly as storytellers for their grandchildren and even actively involved in raising grandchildren serves as an important link in intergenerational bonds in the Indian context. This character of elderly representing duality of emotionality and authority in the family and community contexts proves very affective in conflict resolution within the family and also at the community levels.

This collective family type of the Indian society at large in fact revolves around the elderly who act as the building blocks and sustain its cohesiveness in the long run. So this collective family type actually serves as a joining point of two-three generations with the elderly being central to all of them. The concepts of reciprocity, sharing and care for children and elderly always get the priority. Hagestad (1998) posits that the communities which are safe, supportive and manageable for the old are also good for the children. And the value system of traditional Indian society by emphasizing the centrality of elders evidently leads to the development of society as a whole. The recent *Panchayati Raj* system also shows how especially in the majority of rural settings the elderly enjoy the status of decision making in the matters of village or block development just because of them being perceived as assets of wisdom.

Promoting family ties at the priority level and community ties at the secondary level will help overcome the barriers between generations while the institutionalization of the elderly through professional care only adds to the barriers and also drives away the storehouses of knowledge and wisdom from the younger generations. This also leads to deprivation of the love, affection and care between the older and younger generations. The traditional Indian family system can be presented as a model of absorbing the jerks and shocks of westernization and globalization impact. Man being a social animal has bio-psychic needs and the component of psychosocial needs can be met only by strengthening the familial ties of love, affection and authority within the ambit of family and community contexts and not in the institutionalized framework of professional care of the elderly. The model of the elderly being the central meeting point of generations holds prime significance. It is here where the elderly and the younger generation who deserve special tender care can actually also prove mutually reciprocal to each other as well. The sharing of knowledge by the elderly with the children in the form, even storytelling, acting as sources of fun, entertainment, in a way also leads to easing the young working parents from the extra burden of care towards children. So the elderly indirectly prove to be very essential in lessening the workload of the families and minimizing the efforts which should otherwise be spent on taking care of them as well. The involvement of the elderly with children and adolescents in the family situation is always friendly which lubricates the atmosphere of family as a whole. The familial context where the elderly and the younger generation share a closer tie implies healthy trend for the overall development of the society as a whole. And the Indian society has got all those ingredients which can sustain this reciprocal relationship of fostering care, love and affection in the intergenerational context.

The regional cultural stock of India, even though it comprises diverse beliefs and practices, shares commonalties including the respect for elderly, giving significance to their greater participation and role in the social hierarchy. So the strengthening of the family system at first instance is significant not only for the purpose of just caring for the elderly, but it also entails the overall prosperity and progress of the society and community as a whole thereby leading to national progress.

CONCLUSION

The inherent strengths of the Indian collective family and the traditional value system which emphasizes centrality of the elderly within family as well as community contexts can serve as models of strong intergenerational bonding which is based on reciprocity and care. Thus, supporting the familial ties, support and care in the context where the intergenerational ties have been eroded by the so called westernization/ globalization only can prove helpful in elderly care and not the institutionalization of the elderly care. It also brings to fore that the elderly enjoy high respect and command by being regarded as the storehouses of knowledge and wisdom within the family and community contexts. And that the involvement of elderly in these rituals, ceremonies, and religious functions is central in the Indian family life. Thus, supporting familial ties and programs and policies which are aimed at strengthening this basic unit of human collectivity can help in overall prosperity of the society at large and the safety and care of the elderly and children in better way. The strengthening of community ties at the secondary level also holds significance.

NOTES

- *Roka:* It is the first step in the process of two families looking for a match for their children.
- *Sagan:* It is the gift given by the parents of the bride to the family members of the bridegroom in the form of cash or kind.
- *Shaddi*: It is the marriage.
- *Pharas:* Rituals under the direction of a priest.
- *Mantra:* It is the way of seeking blessings of GOD.
- *Diwali:* It is the festival of light.
- *Ahoi mata puja:* It is the name of the Goddess.
- *Tikka:* It is the red power put on the forehead of the person to get a blessing from the spiritual leader.
- *Moli:* It is the red colour spiritual thread.
- *Prasad:* It is food given to the person as a blessing of GOD.

REFERENCES

Bamabala, U. (1993). *Growing old in young India: A sociological study of women and aging.* Pune: Snehavardhan Publishing House.
Cohen, L. (1992). No aging in India: The uses of gerontology. *Culture Medicine and Psychiatry, 16(2),* 123-161.

Erosov, B. and Singh, Y. (1991). *The sociology of culture*. Moscow: Progress Publishers.

Gangrede, K.D. (1988a). Crisis of values: A sociological study of the old and the young. In *The aging in India, problems and potentialities* edited by A.B. Bose and K.D. Gangrede. Delhi: Abhinav.

Guha, S. (1992). Loneliness and isolation in old age. In *Developed and developing world: Policies problems and perspectives*. Delhi: B.R. Publishing Corporation.

Hagestad, G. (1998). Towards a society for all ages: New thinking, language, new conversations (keynote address at a ceremony launching the 1999 international year of older persons). New York: United Nations.

Lall, A.K. (1976). Locus of power in the family. *The Indian Journal of Social Work*, 37(2), 187-193.

Sharma, M.L. and Dak, D. M. (1987). *Aging in India: Challenge for the society*. Delhi: Ajanta Publications.

Singh, Y. (1973). *Modernization of Indian tradition*. New Delhi: Thompson Press.

Singh,Y. (2000). *Culture change in India: Identity and globalization*. New Delhi: Rawat Publications.

Unnithan, T.K. Deva and Singh, Y. (1965) eds. *Towards a sociology of culture for India*. New Delhi: Prentice Hall of India.

Van Willigen, J. and Chadha, N.K. (1999). *Social aging in a Delhi neighborhood*. Westport, Connecticut: Bergin & Garvey (pp. 76-77).

Intergenerational Theory in Society:
Building on the Past,
Questions for the Future

Karen VanderVen

SUMMARY. Now that the 21st century is underway, society is changing more rapidly than ever. People of all ages are facing new kinds of psychological and interpersonal issues. They are living longer and pioneering new kinds of family patterns and relationships. Given this, then, how can intergenerational programs and relationships both adapt to these new contexts and serve to help people better meet these new societal demands and changes? This article extends, deepens and elaborates upon earlier efforts by describing new societal trends that affect people in the life span, selecting some relevant concepts, exploring them, and suggesting how they might enhance our understanding. Given that this is the postmodern age in which there are questions rather than answers, the discussion of each concept ends with questions for future theory construction. *[Article copies available for a fee from The Haworth Document Delivery Service: 1-800-HAWORTH. E-mail address: <docdelivery@haworthpress.com> Website: <http://www.HaworthPress.com> © 2004 by The Haworth Press, Inc. All rights reserved.]*

Karen VanderVen is affiliated with the University of Pittsburgh, Pennsylvania.

While the author takes complete responsibility for the content of this article, she wishes to acknowledge the significant insights and suggestions offered by Dr. Sally Newman which have greatly enhanced it.

This paper is based on a presentation given by the author, "Advancing Intergenerational Understanding: The Role of Relationship Theory," at the conference held at the University of Pittsburgh in October 2003.

[Haworth co-indexing entry note]: "Intergenerational Theory in Society: Building on the Past, Questions for the Future." VanderVen, Karen. Co-published simultaneously in *Journal of Intergenerational Relationships* (The Haworth Press, Inc.) Vol. 2, No. 3/4, 2004, pp. 75-94; and: *Intergenerational Relationships: Conversations on Practice and Research Across Cultures* (ed: Elizabeth Larkin et al.) The Haworth Press, Inc., 2004, pp. 75-94. Single or multiple copies of this article are available for a fee from The Haworth Document Delivery Service [1-800-HAWORTH, 9:00 a.m. - 5:00 p.m. (EST). E-mail address: docdelivery@haworthpress.com].

75

KEYWORDS. Intergenerational theory, intergenerational programs, family patterns

We continue to mount new intergenerational programs, but without an adequate conceptual framework to guide the design and implementation of these efforts. According to Newman and Smith in their seminal chapter on intergenerational theory, "As this new field matures, it becomes increasingly important to examine its fundamental premises" (1997, p. 4). They continue to say that "programs intended to help people grow" (i.e., intergenerational programs) "must apply theoretical concepts in ways that assist positive development . . ." (p. 5).

Lerner (2004) in describing "contemporary developmental science" indicates that it is "framed by theoretical modes that stress mutually influential and systemic *relations* between individuals and the multiple levels of their social, cultural and historical contexts . . . there is "the importance of understanding relations between people and contexts . . ." (p. 5). To illuminate these processes in the participants in intergenerational activities, in their relationships, in their mutual activities and in the settings that situate these, is the task of intergenerational theory as well. An intergenerational *theory* is essential to give the growing intergenerational field validity, credibility and a coherent, dynamic frame of reference for program development.

In 1999, building on the precedent and mandate set by Newman and Smith, I stressed the importance of a theory of intergenerational relationships and described some concepts that I thought could enhance the theory's applicability (VanderVen, 1999). However, theory construction and theory utilization in themselves are transactional processes, rather then one emphatic and permanent statement. Thus they must continually be reviewed and updated, taking into consideration the rapidly shifting context to which any developmental theory must adjust itself so that it "fits" in both explaining the trajectories of development, the meaning and nature of relationships within them, and in generating interventions that are successful.

There is no doubting that these trends affect the nature of requirements for positive development, their relationships, and the programs that are designed to help people attain them.

Society could not be undergoing more rapid change than it seems to be now that the 21st century is underway. People of all ages are facing new kinds of psychological and interpersonal issues. They are living longer, much longer, and pioneering new kinds of family patterns and relationships. Given this, then, how can intergenerational programs and relationships both adapt to these new contexts and serve to help people better meet these new societal demands?

Given the earlier comments of Lerner (2004), Newman and Smith (1997) and VanderVen (1999) stressing the need for an intergenerational theory that respects both societal changes and concomitant change in the course and dynamics of human development, this paper will use societal change as a springboard for examining a number of concepts relevant for continuing to shape intergenerational theory. Specifically the concepts are combinatory aspects, relationship and activity theory, cultural transmission, life span theory and generativity, relating to the relationship, reciprocal transformation, matching through needs and assets, and multigenerational relationships.

Some of the concepts have been considered previously and the intent is to suggest that we may re-examine them, sharpen our conception of them or take new contexts into account as we consider their applicability. Other concepts are introduced for the first time. This paper is also conceived in a postmodern vein, reflecting the premises that knowledge is co-constructed by many people, that the nature of knowledge is reflected by the contexts of those who construct it, and that it is legitimate in scholarship to raise questions rather than provide definitive answers. Thus the discussion of each concept ends with questions for future consideration by all of us involved in intergenerational work.

SOCIETAL TRENDS

A societal trend is an emerging pattern of characteristics in a particular domain, e.g., health, education, welfare, family relationships, and reflects "the social, political, cultural and economic contexts" (Naisbitt and Aburdene, 1990, p. xix) that determine it. Ward (1997) has pointed out the necessity for studying societal trends, particularly among the aging but among children as well, as we consider designing intergenerational programs. Because society as has been stated is changing so rapidly in areas related to family and relational patterns and to physical health, including the fact that people are living much longer lives (e.g., Ward, 1997), it is essential to continue to update our recognition of such societal trends.

Among children and youth there are such new trends. Because of the large growth of single parent and two working parent families, more and more children are in alternative care arrangements. With this have emerged new concerns. Many young children have behavior problems such as increased aggression, lack of self-regulation, and poorly developed social skills. Social and emotional preparation for school entrance is a profound concern (e.g., Hyson, 2002; Love, 2004). At a younger and younger age, children bully or exclude other children, setting both off into unhealthy developmental trajectories. For young adults, rather than marry and establish a household by the time they are in their mid-twenties, many remain or return to their parental homes. The average age at marriage, if young people get married at all, is rising.

Then we are an "aging society" (Manheimer, 2004). Not only that, "the characteristics of people in the later years have also been changing" (p. 119). Greengross (2003) points out that in our "changed world" . . . "traditional community ties are being eroded" and that to deal with this we "need new thinking from everybody." She proposes that intergenerational activities can help build and sustain true caring community among the generations who are in danger of being harmfully separated. Indeed.

It is important to note that there are some people for whom aging is not a happy experience. They may grieve for the loss of earlier connections through work and other activities, have been unable to find renewal in post-retirement interests, and suffer from ill health (e.g., Snowdon, 2001; Vaillant, 2002). An intergenerational theory needs to take these aspects into account and by doing so, perhaps can generate actual interventions that can provide the ingredients that will address those factors that contribute to healthy development, not only in old age but in earlier years as well. That is the potential power of intergenerational theory.

CONCEPTS FOR AN INTERGENERATIONAL THEORY

Combinatory Aspects

Intergenerational relationships are combinatory by definition (VanderVen, 1999). "Combinatory" simply means putting two things together or combining them. If two entities are put together, or in the case of an intergenerational pairing, two people, they are being combined and the question arises then, "What is the nature of this combination and what are its outcomes?" We often consider the characteristics identified as associated with an age range as fixed and invariant. However, an intergenerational pairing is a combination of two age ranges with internal variation, i.e., the developmental characteristics of those within each are different from those of the other, as well as each person negotiating the associated developmental tasks in an individual way. We need to consider then what is the *nature* of these pairings. Let us consider those that are well-established for childhood (e.g., Berk, 2002): Infancy (1-2), preschool (2-6), school age (6-11), and adolescence (11-18). Following more generally are young adulthood (18-30), mid-adulthood (30-40), midlife (40-50), post-midlife (50-55), pre-retirement (55-65), "young" old (65-75), "old" (75-85), and "old-old" (85-upwards). Each of these represents a general age span in which certain developmental tasks or attainments might be expected to occur, and which has identifiable features associated with the stage. For example, there is a great deal of recognition of the significance of the preschool years (ages 2-6) for setting the trajectory for subsequent development. Similarly, "midlife" is a frequently discussed stage of adult development.

The 13 named stages all seem to reflect the reality of differentiated age functions, although the number of years characteristic of each range vary. For example, the midlife range is considerably longer than the toddler range. This has implications for defining exactly what comprises an *intergenerational* relationship. Originally the idea of intergenerational relationships given was that there was something special about people at each end of the life span, i.e., the young (children) and the old (elderly, generally post-retirement adults). The question then arises, Is this notion still viable, especially given the fact that people live longer? Should an intergenerational relationship be *any* relationship in which participants are either two stages apart, or a generation apart? Furthermore, one can ask, If intergenerational relationships are as powerful a positive force as is generally believed (and supported by empirical research), then would it not be socially valuable to extend the notion of what kind of pairing constitutes an intergenerational relationship?

Let us further assume that an intergenerational relationship is one in which the participants are at least two stages or more, or twenty years (a standard generation) apart, e.g., a relationship between an adolescent and a person in young adulthood would not be intergenerational but one between an adolescent and a person in midlife would be. Mathematically, then, one can consider how many stage pairings might be possible given the above criteria. Without making a formal calculation there would be several dozen of these combinations. Given this larger number of combinatory possibilities, then are there common attributes that characterize any relationship two stages apart? Do the individual differences within stages along with their characteristic major themes make the relationships so complex that is difficult to understand the dynamics of any particular relationship?

RELATIONSHIP AND ACTIVITY THEORY

The ongoing development of intergenerational theory will be based on the selection and integration of relevant "source" theories. Two of these might be what are now known as "relationship" and "activity" theory. Because of the relationship between these two theory streams, they are presented in the same section.

The Centrality of Relationships

In the last decade or so, there as been a growing trend towards emphasizing the role of relationships as the wellspring of human development and certainly of child development (e.g., Fewster, 1990; Krueger, 1998). A primary relationship in the earliest years that leads to secure attachment, a blueprint for constructing subsequent relationships, one's ability to form positive relationships in the future (e.g., Berk, 2002). Furthermore, a growing body of research on development of resiliency–the ability to thrive under adverse circumstances–indicates that a close relationship with a caring adult is fundamental to being resilient (e.g., Werner and Smith, 1992). The need for human connection is forged through harmonious, gratifying relationships (e.g., Miller and Stiver, 1997; Gilligan, 2002). Relationships shape and give meaning to human development, and serve as "connective tissue" between individuals, others, and their ecology of home, neighborhood, community further highlighting their cruciality in development. Where relationships have not been successful and development disrupted, interventions such as mentoring (e.g., Freedman, 1993) have been designed to compensate for a relationship lack and promote resilience in the mentee. Intergenerational programs, like mentoring, have been designed to enhance and extend the relationships of people of different ages in a way that is developmentally enhancing.

The centrality of relationships is unquestionable. Many feel that relationships are the primary, even only major force in psychological development. Yet there is a body of theory that considers the "activity" engaged in by people as the central force in learning: "Conscious learning emerges from activity" (http://www.personal.psu.edu/users/). Activity theory is concerned with people "acting"; what they are *doing*, with the contexts in which they are acting and with the objects and tools that mediate the activity. Activity does embrace relationship: the relationship of people with their environment or context (e.g., Chaiklin and Lave, 1996).

An extensive explanation of both relationship theory and activity theory are beyond the scope of this paper, except to suggest that there is a dialectical relationship between how people interact, what they do, the tools and objects that mediate these interactions and activities, and the contexts that situate both. I suggest that one is not more significant than the other; rather each influences the other. It is like the proverbial "which came first, the chicken or the egg" question. For example, if a parent plays "peek-a-boo" with an infant and uses a large book to hide her head behind, that is a culturally constructed "activity" that is mediated by a tool (the book). The pre-existing relationship between the parent and infant may have situated the introduction of the activity. Doing the activity affects the relationship. Conversely, there can be no real relationship between two people–for example, a school age child and a senior volunteer in an art program–until the art activity is introduced and conducted.

Thus it could be time for the intergenerational field to consider more formally what "activity theory," taken along with "relationship theory" might contribute to it. There has certainly been attention to the types of activities engaged in by older adults, and to the kinds of activities that might be suitable for older and younger people to do together. However, there has been little if any consideration of how activities and relationships intersect, their contexts and what kinds of meanings are thus created. Activities situate and modify and shape interpersonal relationships, while interpersonal relationships in turn shape the selection of and nature of activities engaged in. While relationships have assumed a major place in thinking and practice in intergenerational work, the nature of the activities and their meanings, that are engaged in have received less attention, although there seems to be an integral relationship between them.

Another reason for bringing consideration of activity and activities into the mainstream of intergenerational theory is the fact that some theories of aging consider the amount of and nature of activity in the lives of older people. Cumming and Henry's "Disengagement Theory" has suggested that older adults tend to reduce their active involvement in society and the amount of activity in which they engage. Atchley, however, has contended that the inevitable loss of role and activities of aging can be coped with by replacing them with others that are more appropriate (e.g., Newman and Smith, 1997). Given this recognition of the significance of activity then, activity theory, in combination with relationship theory, would seem to have the potential to make a strong contribution to intergenerational theory and practice.

Thus the question at this point is, "How can activity theory inform intergenerational theory?" and "What contribution can a conjoint consideration of relationship theory and activity theory make?" Does the transactional relationship between relationships and activity (bringing it more into the forefront as an influence) offer us greater understanding of what might be going on in an intergenerational combination of people and suggest more ways of encouraging these pairings to be effective by supporting the replacement of lost roles, activities, and, for that matter, relationships?

CULTURAL TRANSMISSION

There is a well known "culture of childhood" that is considered to be the medium of transmission or sharing of traditional play activities among children. such as rituals, games, sayings, art and craft forms. This particular "culture" operates as younger children watch and are involved in various activities of older children. As children move around, this "lore" is transported across geographical boundaries and serves to help children on the move connect to a new group. This shared knowledge among children serves as "social coin," increasing a sense of belonging. If, for example, a new child knows how to play jacks or how to choose up sides, then that helps him or her gain entry into a new group that also has this knowledge (VanderVen, 1996). What has been unique about the "culture of childhood" has been that children themselves are the vehicle of transmission.

Interestingly today we see two changes in the "culture of childhood." While it still exists and can be observed, its content is vastly different than it was generations ago when today's older people were children. Now we have advanced technology featuring television, computers, and most particularly video games that in themselves comprise a compelling culture that consumes a great deal of children's time–and may not be healthy if engaged in excess. Certainly there is considerable evidence that violent themes in video games have negative effects It could be useful to replace them with more benign activities. If so many of today's children are hungry for individual attention and respond to older adults, could not they be strong agents in helping to at least modify the amount of time spent in video games and the like and their deleterious effects by passing along the "lore" of more active and wholesome occupations such as they experienced in their own childhood?

The other change is that some, perhaps an increasing number, of children, cannot acquire the lore of the "culture of childhood" due to some limitation in their own development, such as a physical or mental disability or lack of social skills, or life circumstances such as isolation or family dysfunction. Where this is the case, the *adults* must be the "transmitter" of the "culture of childhood" sharing activities and "lore" from *their* own childhood. While this is paradoxical, since the culture of childhood by definition is transmitted by children, nonetheless adults can assume this role. The proposal here is that an intergenerational relationship can be an ideal means for doing this. Older adults have memories of "traditional" childhood lore including more active games and construction type activities (for example) and can use the intergenerational forum for sharing them. In a sense, they use reminiscence to convey helpful, even healthy, knowledge and skills to younger people. Conversely children can share their interest in contemporary technology with older adults, and as the relationship evolves, perhaps reduce usage and replace it with other activities. A question is "How can intergenerational relationships serve to transmit the 'traditional' culture of older people's childhoods and how can such a consideration be integrated into intergenerational theory?"

LIFE SPAN THEORY AND GENERATIVITY

Erik Erikson's life span theory (e.g., Erikson, 1950) continues to be a predominant theory referred to in intergenerational activities (e.g., Newman and Smith, 1997; VanderVen, 1999). One reason for the continued acceptance of Eriksonian theory is the fact that it covers the complete life span. Eight stages are proposed, with each having the potential of having a positive or negative outcome as the crisis or major task of the stage is accomplished. For example, the task of infancy is to establish trust in the world, but with the potential to experience mistrust if caring experiences aren't supportive. The developmental task of most of adulthood is "generativity." The concept of Eriksonian generativity, especially is alive and well. Erikson originally defined generativity as "primarily the interest in establishing and guiding the next generation or whatever in a given case may become the absorbing object of a parental kind of responsibility. Where this enrichment fails, ..." there is "a per-

vading sense . . . of individual stagnation and interpersonal impoverishment" (1950, p. 231).

Erikson's son Kai suggests that generativity is more "complex" than
we might think (Erikson, K., 2004) and indeed there are now issues with
the concept. There is hardly thought of eliminating generativity as a developmental construct. As St. Aubin, McAdams and Kim (2004) point
out, generativity is now joining Erikson's concept of "identity" as having particular developmental significance. But we can ask, What does
generativity mean now given the numerous changes in society and
shifts in the customary ages at which certain events characteristically
occur. Thus of elaborating on it and describing it in finer detail in a way
that is relevant to the complexities of today's world and to the realities
of adults with increasing areas in which generativity can be further scru-
tinized and modified:

1. *Reconceptualizing its overall meaning.* In line with the premise of
   this paper that societal changes require ongoing re-examination
   and modification of developmental theories, the overall definition
   of generativity is being reconsidered. Generativity now needs to
   be viewed not only from the perspective of the individual, but also
   with regard to its role in society in general. Generativity is situated
   in and shaped by society and culture, society may (or may not) be
   generative itself, and generativity is expressed through social institutions (St. Aubin, McAdams and Kim, 2004).
2. *To retain the generativity concept with its breadth of coverage in
   years and meaning, but continue to consider the possibility of differentiated substages within it.* As a developmental theme for
   adults, generativity thus "covered" many, many years. If people
   are living longer, with even more adult years, and if the adult developmental process involves change, then it is possible that the
   concept of generativity needs to be broken down into differentiated substages within its overall purpose. In line with my propos-
   ing this earlier, I had suggested that around age 50, there would be
   efficacy vs. *passivity*, to reflect the fact that raising children, with
   all its challenges, and perhaps especially for women, develops a
   new sense of being able to cope with things and being instrumental. Following that would be *investment* vs. *detachment.* Investment means a special energy towards and valuing of both one's
   possessions and one's relationships–a kind of appreciation of
   what one has in life (VanderVen, 1999). However, it could now be

time to look again at these suggested substages with an eye to increasing attention to the social context in which they emerge.

3. *To redefine the major tasks of older people and ascribe new concepts and new terminology to them.* An example of this is offered by George Vaillant, who in his groundbreaking book *Aging Well* (2002) looks at different perspectives of Eriksonian generativity. These include generativity as 'caring for the next generation' in a giving and altruistic sense, and generativity as 'investing oneself in forms of life and work that outlive the self,' quoting Kotre's definition (p. 115). While not deviating widely from the overall concept of generativity, it is interesting to note that these definitions embrace the two major areas that are being suggested for a central place in intergenerational theory: Both relationship (implied by 'caring for the next generation') and activity (leaving something for perpetuity from one's work or accomplishments).

Vaillant (2002) introduces an important concept within his embracing of generativity: The older adult as "keeper of the meaning." If generativity is "caregiving," being a "keeper of the meaning" is "care taking": preserving heritage and history, Being a "keeper of the meaning" is a productive role once physical energy declines. One preserves what is meaningful from one's past life.

With evidence once again that people are living even longer, we need to look at the stages Integrity vs. Despair. Integrity was actually referred to as "ego integrity" by Erikson (1950). Summarizing, this means that one has a sense of acceptance of the lifestyle and accomplishments of the preceding years as being inevitable, and a sense of an order and meaning of life. Despair, the counterpart to integrity, refers to a fear of death because one's preceding life is felt not to be acceptable, yet there is little time to undertake a new life course. Should there be another life stage beyond Integrity vs. Despair? Or is there one or more before it? Nobody yet seems to have added new stages to Eriksonian life span theory, but while it is being re considered and reconceptualized, suggesting age-related extensions might be another challenge for the future.

The questions here are many: How can we continue to define, modify and apply Eriksonian theory, particularly the concept of generativity, so that it best relates to the reality of today's society and psychological and physical aging–the "new longevity" (Manheimer, 2004, p. 120)–along with all of the other changes in society and ways of living mentioned earlier?

RELATING TO THE RELATIONSHIP

As child and youth workers began to extend the scope of their practice from children and youth to their families, an interesting issue surfaced: How could a practitioner relate to the relationship between a young person and his or her parent(s)? The goal of developmental and therapeutic work is to try to support the parent-child relationship. If a worker overidentifies with the child, forming a strong relationship with him, that excludes the parent and increases the parental guilt and sense of failure, further damaging the parent-child relationship. On the other hand, if a worker overidentifies with a parent, perhaps feeling more comfortable with an adult, the child will feel alien- ated from both adults and seek positive gratification and positive relationships elsewhere. Anglin (1983) in a seminal paper describes these dynamics well. He then describes how an effective worker must stren- gthen the communication and interaction between parent and child and clarify the growing bond between them. The worker can teach each party effective communication skills as well as model them.

Ultimately, it would seem as if an effective intergenerational theory would consider the kinds of dynamics articulated by Anglin (1983). No matter how carefully matches are made they are subject to problems in communication and understanding. Thus any intergenerational worker must understand the dynamics of relationships and be able, so to speak, to "relate to the relationship" between participants in a supportive, non-dysfunctional way.

The question is, How can intergenerational theory highlight the interactive dynamics of intergenerational pairings so that a third or external party can adapt and support both parties in the relationship?

RECIPROCAL TRANSFORMATION

One of the key features of intergenerational theory from its inception has been the recognition that relationships are reciprocal–that each participant in the relationship is affected by the interaction with the other participant. However, it could be useful as intergenerational theory evolves to have a term that sharply defines the notion of reciprocity, and helps to further elaborate on the nature of a reciprocal relationships over time.

Increasingly in recent years, hermeneutic philosophy, which is concerned with how we interpret and make meaning of our experiences, has been applied to the social sciences, with special attention to how people enter into relationships and construct those relationships together over time. This is referred to as "reciprocal transformation" (Nakkula, 1998). In a "dialectic of mutual influence" (Ravitch, 1998, p. 113) each partner in a relationship brings to it his or her own particular background and value system, and in a process of mutual discovery and uncovering in the context of the relationship, not only learns more about the other person but also more about oneself. This ongoing reciprocity, a process of discovery and adjustment, leads to mutual change and transformation as each party discovers and learns more from the other. What could be a better framework for viewing the emergent processes of intergenerational relationships than that of "reciprocal transformation"? There is a great need for exploration of this concept in the context of intergenerational relationships, since by definition they are bi-directional and transactional. This is in great contrast to traditional adult-child relationships in particular, such as mentor-mentee, teacher-student, therapist-patient, and the like; traditionally these have been seen as unidirectional, flowing from the adult to the child as the receptacle or recipient. Naturally adult participants in such unidirectional relationships are implicitly changed but there has been little formal recognition of the fact that in a relationship with children, adults are affected as well.

A question is, Can the hermeneutic notion of reciprocal transformation and other aspects of hermeneutic philosophy focusing on how people make meaning and interpret their experience be given a more central role in intergenerational theory as it is developed in the future?

MATCHING THROUGH NEEDS AND ASSETS

A focus of intergenerational theory from the outset has been on the needs, tasks and assets of participants from both ends of the life span (e.g., Newman, undated; Newman and Smith, 1997). Because there is overlap and shared meaning between the terms *developmental task* and *need*, for clarity the word *need* alone will be used. *Needs* are just that: Developmental requirements that must be met for development to proceed. For example, food and water are needs. At least one primary attachment figure is a need. When these are identified, then better "matches" can be made of the participants in an intergenerational relationship. "Matching" is a concept used in mentoring programs such as Big Brothers and Sisters (e.g., deJong, 2004), and in that there are many commonalities between mentoring and intergenerational activities (VanderVen, in press), "matching" can be seen as relevant to intergenerational theory. While the meaning is quite obvious, specifically "matching" refers to the criteria for selecting participants in a relationship so that the relationship has the greatest probability of longevity and success for both parties. Recent advances can continue to enhance the concept of using needs and assets as the basis for such matches and ensure that the named tasks and assets resonate with the most contemporary knowledge there is, and with the rapid societal shifts that are affecting human development in general, as described earlier.

Needs

Considering needs of people at different stages of development can contribute to the conceptualization of how relationships transform and influence the participants. For example, Brazelton and Greenspan (2002) offer the following: Young children need nurturing relationships, physical protection and safety, experiences tailored to individual differences, developmentally appropriate activities, structure and limits, stable and supportive communities, and protection of their future. Youth need a sense of significance (knowing that they are important to somebody), competence (knowing they are good at something), power (a sense they can influence their world) and virtue (a sense of being a good person) (Brokenleg and van Brockern, 2003). For older people in post-retirement years, Vaillant (2002) poses four indicators of health. The first is the recreation of a social network to replace the one that might have been lost through leaving formal work. The second is the ability to play–to joyfully engage in various activities in a generally non-goal oriented way for their own sake. Then there is creativity. Creativity is more goal oriented than play and involves putting "into the world what was not there before" (p. 230). Engagement in creativity continues a more serious side to life and garners external recognition. Finally there is life-long learning which is simply that: the older adult continues to learn and holds a "gusto for education" (p. 246).

If one looks at these particular needs of children, youth and post-retirees particularly associated with their particular age range, these have implications for making intergenerational pairings that might be particularly meaningful. For example, an intergenerational relationship between a playful adult and a preschool or school age child who does not know how to play would have reciprocal benefits, as would that between a playful preschooler and an older adult who needs encouragement to reconnect with old play memories and be playful. A relationship between a younger person who has experienced disruption in the opportunity to make a primary attachment (increasingly the case) and an older adult who was experienced in creating a social network could be invaluable. A constricted and unexpressive child might thrive in the presence of a playful adult. Or, a creative older adult with a specific skill or talent could be connected with a youth who needs to develop something s/he is "good" in. Or, a youth who feels excluded and powerless can be connected with older people who need the strength and energy of younger people to maintain their life status. The possibilities are endless. The suggestion is that if we continue to use developmental needs and tasks relevant to the characteristics of different stages *and to the contemporary definitions of such needs*, to help make a match, these matches could be especially effective.

Developmental Assets

In her formulations of intergenerational attributes, Newman (undated) defined Assets as "Abilities, skills, functions, talents, and resources each generation can bring to intergenerational programs." Given this precedent of including Assets in intergenerational concerns, the concept can continue to be considered as a major component of intergenerational theory.

The notion of Developmental Assets has now been compiled into an empirically based framework that can be very useful in the future for intergenerational practice. This framework is the Developmental Asset Framework of Search Institute. Originally developed for youth, this empirically supported compendium of 40 attributes or characteristics that if present either in the environment (external assets) or internally–as attributes and abilities–contribute towards growth into useful, productive and happy citizens (e.g., Search Institute, 2002). Now there is a Developmental Asset Framework for young children (VanderVen and Mannes, 2004), the ECDAF, that adapts the Framework for youth to the specific developmental needs and characteristics of young children. This along with an Asset Framework for school age children offers a theory and empirically based practice model that for the first time brings coherence and connection into approaches to practice that heretofore have been targeted towards one age range only (e.g., Developmentally Appropriate Practice and young children to age 8). Internal Assets in four domains (social competencies, engagement in learning, positive values, positive identity) name developmental attributes encouraged by external actions, which are attributes and actions "outside" of children that contribute to positive development: support, constructive use of time, boundaries and expectations, and empowerment. The Developmental Asset Frameworks are being used in communities nationwide to encourage a holistic, consistent, and inclusive approach to promoting positive development.

One day hopefully there will be a Developmental Asset Framework for older people that ensures that they receive the ingredients they need for healthy aging, and that there are indicators for the degree to which such a process is occurring. Included in the discussion of the Assets for young children is a consideration of how intergenerational relationships specifically can serve to promote the particular Asset of "Other Adult Relationships" and "Caring Neighbors." A DAF for older people would perhaps include the Asset of "Relationships with Younger People" and a discussion of how young people could specifically contribute to helping older people attain this Asset.

A question here is, How can current concepts of developmental needs and developmental assets be incorporated into intergenerational theory as a means of helping to make effective matches leading to successful relationships?

MULTIGENERATIONAL RELATIONSHIPS

Scholars have already considered that there can be relationships between two generations: "intergenerational," and between three generations: what is now called a "multigenerational relationship." This introduces another ongoing issue to challenge intergenerational theorists: the potential for complexity among the scope of relationships. "Concept Complexity" might be the name for the phenomenon that once a new concept is established, inevitably as awareness grows of its relevance and applicability, it becomes more complex. New aspects are added to it. Thus, with the notion of intergenerational relationships, in the context of many societal shifts since the notion of intergenerational relationships was first proposed, one can ask how the movement into greater complexity will occur.

One way in which this might happen is embraced by the notion of multigenerational relationships. A multigenerational relationship now consists of a third person in a different stage relating to a pairing of others in an intergenerational relationship. Thus three different stages are represented in the relationship, increasing the complexity of the dynamics of the relationship. The most typical of these now is a middle-aged person relating to both an older and a younger person, sometimes within one's own family, i.e., the 'sandwich' generation. However, there could consists of other stages in a three-stage multigenerational relationship. These could involve, for example, a very old person or very young person relating to a grandparent and child; a midlife person relating to an infant and a teenage mother. Adding a third element certainly makes the relationship dynamics even more complex, a fact well known in family therapy with the concept of triangular relationships. A triangular relationship tends to be unstable with there being a stronger bond between two people and the third person being somewhat external to it. The pairings within a triangular relationship can shift, given changes in circumstances.

If people live longer and longer, the concept of multigenerational relationships may have to be extended to consider 4 different pairings of developmental stages. For example, a middle-aged person may be involved in a relationship with a young person, a "young old" person, and an "old-old" person. One can only imagine the complexities that will emerge from these multigenerational relationships involving more than two, or even three, people.

The question: How will we adapt our theories and practices to handle what may be now 3 age group multigenerational relationships to what soon might be 4 generational *multigenerational* relationships?

CONCLUSION

This article contends that a developmental theory, particularly an intergenerational one, needs continually to be revised in the light of rapid change in those factors, both societal and developmental, including longevity increases, that affect the course of the human life span. Examples of areas of society that have occurred in recent years with particular pertinence to intergenerational theory were given, such as increased physical health and length of life, changes in family and relationship patterns, and special needs of children and youth today.

Areas are covered that have been central to the development of intergenerational theory from the beginning as well as some new ones, all of which hold promise in the continued evolution of intergenerational theory, and has raised some questions about them. They converge around such areas as the nature of relationships and the activities that situate relationships, how older and younger are "matched" so that the needs of and assets of each party can be addressed, how the complexities inherent in a relationship can be recognized and worked with, and how some current well known concepts of adult development, such as Erikson's generativity, might be re-examined and even reformulated in light of the current social context.

However, at this point it was not the intent of the article in a short space to actually construct the new intergenerational theory. Rather it pointed out some issues and concerns relevant to theory construction and application that might serve to focus the ongoing development of intergenerational theory, and following an explanation of the concern and its significance, proposed questions that could guide the theory construction effort. It might be emphasized again that this article was written in a postmodern orientation, in which the intent is to offer questions, rather than answers, areas to be explored rather than to report a specific empirical justification. So that these questions are clear, they are summarized here:

- Combinatory aspects: How are people at different stages of life combined and what are the characteristics of these combinations?
- Relationship and activity theories: How can a consideration of the interactions between activity and relationship enhance intergenerational understanding?
- Cultural transmission: How can intergenerational theory consider the role of older adults as transmitters of important experiences from their own childhoods?
- Life span theory: How can we continue to modify and adapt Eriksonian theory to the societal changes affecting people's life span developmental trajectory?
- Relating to a relationship: How can intergenerational theory highlight the dynamics inherent in a third person relating to a relationship between two other persons?
- Reciprocal transformation: Can the hermeneutic concept of "reciprocal transformation" further adumbrate the reciprocity inherent in the definition of intergenerational relationships?
- Matching through developmental tasks and assets: How can current concepts of developmental tasks and developmental assets be incorporated into intergenerational theory as a means of helping to make effective matches?
- Multigenerational relationships: Can we adapt intergenerational theory to the possibility of multigenerational relationships involving three, or even four, people belonging to different generations?

Hopefully, these may serve as points for ongoing inquiry and proposals, and that there may be a continued quest for responses that will lead to an increasingly comprehensive, dynamic, and timely intergenerational theory.

REFERENCES

Activity Theory. http:www.personal.psu/edu/users.

Anglin, J. (1983). Counseling a single parent and child: Functional and dysfunctional patterns of communication. *Journal of Child Care*, 2(2), 33-45.

Berk, L. (2002). Infants, children and adolescents. Boston: Allyn and Bacon.

Brokenleg, M. and van Brockern, S. (2003). The science of raising courageous kids. *Reclaiming Child and Youth*, 12(1), 22-27.

Chaiklin, S. and Lave, J. (Eds.). *Understanding practice: Perspectives on activity and context.* Cambridge, UK: Cambridge University Press.

deJong, M. (2004). Metaphors and the mentoring process. *Child and Youth Care Forum*, 33(1), 3-17.

Erikson, E. (1977). *Toys and reasons: Stages in the ritualization of experience.* New York: WW Norton.

Erikson, K. (2004). Reflection on generativity and society: A sociologist's perspective. In St. Aubin, E., McAdams, D. and Kim, T-C. (2004). *The generative society: Caring for future generations.* Washington, DC: American Psychological Association

Fewster, G. (1990). *Being in child care: A journey into self.* New York: The Haworth Press.

Freedman, M. (1993). *The kindness of strangers.* San Francisco: Jossey-Bass.

Gilligan, C. (2002). *The birth of pleasure.* New York: Alfred P. Knopf.

Greengrass, S. Intergenerational programmes as a global approach to social issues. *Journal of Intergenerational Relationships*, 1(1), 2003, 11-13.

Hyson, M. (2002). Emotional development and school readiness. *Young Children* 57(6), 76-77.

Krueger, M. (1998). *Interactive youth work practice.* Washington, DC: Child Welfare League of America.

Kuehne, V. (Ed.). (1999). *Intergenerational programs: Understanding what we have created.* New York: The Haworth Press.

Lerner, R. (2004). Innovative method for studying lives in context: A view of the issues. *Research in Human Development*, 1, 1 and 2, 5-7.

Love, D. (2004). Supporting children's social and emotional growth. *The Provider.* Erie, PA: Pennsylvania Pathways.

Manheimer, R. (2004). Rope of ashes: Global aging, generativity, and education. In St. Aubin, E., McAdams, D. and Kim, T-C. (2004). *The generative society: Caring for future generations.* Washington, DC: American Psychological Association, 115-130.

Miller, J. and Stiver, I.P. (1997). *The healing connection: How women form relationships in therapy and in life.* Boston: Beacon Press.

Naisbitt, J. and Aburdene, P. (1990). *Megatrends 2000: Ten new directions for the 1990s.* New York: Avon Books.

Newman, S. Assets. Pittsburgh, PA: Undated ms.

Newman, S. and Smith, T. (1997). Developmental theories as the basis for intergenerational programs. In Newman, S., Ward, C., Smith, T., Wilson, J. and McCrea, J. (with Calhoun, G. and Kingson, E.) *Intergenerational programs: Past, present and future.* Washington, DC: Taylor and Francis. 3-19.

Ravitch, S. (1998). Becoming uncomfortable. In M. Nakkula and S. Ravitch. *Matters of interpretation: Reciprocal transformation in developmental and therapeutic relationships with youth.* San Francisco: Jossey Bass. 105-121.

Roazan, P. (1977,1997). *Erik H. Erikson: The power and limits of a vision.* Northvale, NJ: Jason Aronson.

St. Aubin, E., McAdams, D. and Kim, T-C. (2004). *The generative society: Caring for future generations.* Washington, DC: American Psychological Association

Snowdon, D. (2001). *Aging with grace. What the nun study teaches us about leading longer, healthier and more meaningful lives.* New York: Basic Books.

Vaillant, G. (2002). *Aging well.* Boston: Little Brown.

VanderVen, K. Adults are still needed: The role of intergenerational and mentoring activities with at risk children and youth. *Reclaiming Children and Youth.* In press.

VanderVen, K. (2003). Advancing intergenerational understanding–The role of relationship theory. Presentation given at "Advancing Intergenerational Understanding" conference. Pittsburgh, PA: University of Pittsburgh.

VanderVen, K. (1999). Intergenerational theory: The missing element in intergenerational programs. In Kuehne, V. (Ed.) *Intergenerational programs: Understanding what we have created.* New York: The Haworth Press.

VanderVen, K. (1996). Towards socialization and harmonious cross-cultural relationships. Integrating cultural universals and cultural specifics through the activities of "the culture of childhood." Cambridge, MA: Paper presented at the Many Cultures of Childhood conference, Harvard Graduate School of Education.

VanderVen, K. and Mannes, M. The Early Childhood Developmental Asset Framework (ECDAF). http://www.search-institute.org.

Ward. C. (199. The context of intergenerational programs. In Newman, S., Ward, C., Smith, T., Wilson, J. and McCrea, J. (with Calhoun, G. and Kingson, E.) *Intergenerational programs: Past, present and future.* Washington, DC: Taylor and Francis. 21-35.

Werner, E. and Smith, R. (1992). *Overcoming the odds: High risk children from birth to adulthood.* New York: Cornell University Press.

SECTION II:
INTERGENERATIONAL RELATIONSHIPS IN COMMUNITIES

Intergenerational Initiatives in Sweden

Ann-Kristin Boström, PhD

SUMMARY. It is pointed out in this report that the intergenerational perspective is conspicuous by its absence in Sweden, compared to several other countries where specific programmes exist for activities across generational boundaries. Activities across generational boundaries have also been a specific area where financial incentives for local projects have been provided in recent years through the government's project, Freedom of Choice/Older People and Public Health. But despite these efforts, comprehensive and systematic measures to develop and strengthen contacts across generational boundaries have been few and far between in Sweden. Instead, official measures within various areas have

Ann-Kristin Boström is affiliated with the Institute of International Education, Stockholm University, 106 91 Stockholm, Sweden.

[Haworth co-indexing entry note]: "Intergenerational Initiatives in Sweden." Boström, Ann-Kristin. Co-published simultaneously in *Journal of Intergenerational Relationships* (The Haworth Press, Inc.) Vol. 2, No. 3/4, 2004, pp. 95-103; and: *Intergenerational Relationships: Conversations on Practice and Research Across Cultures* (ed: Elizabeth Larkin et al.) The Haworth Press, Inc., 2004, pp. 95-103. Single or multiple copies of this article are available for a fee from The Haworth Document Delivery Service [1-800-HAWORTH, 9:00 a.m. - 5:00 p.m. (EST). E-mail address: docdelivery@haworthpress.com].

targeted different groups, often defined in terms of their age and stage of life course. *[Article copies available for a fee from The Haworth Document Delivery Service: 1-800-HAWORTH. E-mail address: <docdelivery@haworthpress. com> Website: <http://www.HaworthPress.com> © 2004 by The Haworth Press, Inc. All rights reserved.]*

KEYWORDS. Intergenerational initiatives, Sweden, government programs

INTRODUCTION

Recent demographic changes have sparked off discussions and investigations regarding the older sectors of the population in Sweden. Ronström (1998), writing about Sweden, is of the opinion that being a senior citizen is a natural consequence of having once been a younger citizen and thus research should concentrate on a more comprehensive perspective rather than specializing in established categories of research such as "children" and "the elderly." The Swedish Government set up an official commission of enquiry known as Senior 2005 and in an interim report on their ongoing deliberations, this commission has coined the phrase "demolish the age stairs" (Sw. *"riv ålderstrappan"*) (SOU 2002:29). Changes in demography and intergenerational interaction are also considered in this report. In addition, there has been another investigation in Sweden, concerning health services and senior citizens (Stockholm Gerontology Research Center, 2001. Sw. *Stiftelsen Stockholms Läns Äldrecentrum*). The results of this enquiry indicate that the increasingly large proportion of senior citizens in the population will probably remain healthier for a longer period of time than was the case for earlier generations, which provides opportunities for the senior citizens of today to continue to participate in society to a greater extent than was possible in earlier times. In yet another investigation (Batljan and Lagergren, 2000), an estimate of the costs for health services was made, whereby it was predicted that these costs would not increase as rapidly as had previously been expected because the prior estimates were based on the assumption that such increased costs would begin at the onset of retirement at 65 years of age. Today, as people remain healthier for longer during the course of their lives, the costs for health services will thus not begin to increase substantially until senior citizens reach a very old age–above 80.

Activities across generational boundaries have also been a specific area where financial incentives for local projects have been provided in recent years through the government's project, Freedom of Choice/ Older People and Public Health (Sw. *Äldreprojektet*).

But despite these efforts, comprehensive and systematic measures to develop and strengthen contacts across generational boundaries have been few and far between in Sweden. Instead, official measures within various areas have targeted different groups, often defined in terms of their age and stage of life course.

THE HISTORICAL PERSPECTIVE

It is an old tradition that the section of the family responsible for the household are to provide care for children and the elderly (Odén, 1993). Most often this "family" consisted not only of relatives but also of ser- vants and others who lived on the homestead. This tradition was formal- ized for a minority group in Swedish society, the free-holder farmers, through the introduction in the 18th century of a contract providing for a life annuity stipulated in an agreement for, or in conjunction with, the transfer of ownership of a homestead (Sw. *undantagskontrakt*). This le- gally binding contract stipulated, for those elderly people who had trans- ferred ownership of their homestead to their children, or others, the pro- vision of such items as corn, meat and kindling.

In Sweden, as in other countries, conflicts between generations have arisen when it has no longer been tenable to retain the established means for ensuring the maintenance of the living conditions for elderly people in the face of new economic, social or demographic pressures. There are a number of examples where legislation was introduced or strengthened during the 19th century, with regard to the protection of the elderly, as pressure increased on the rural system of annuity contracts as a result of successive years of misery, involving crop failure and starvation (Odén, 1985). At the same time, an increasing number of elderly were to be found in urban areas who were no longer able to work and whose chil- dren were not able to take them in, or support them, since they were most often both living in overcrowded conditions and earning only low incomes. The difficulties which were giving rise to conflicts of interest between the generations were eventually resolved through the introduc- tion of the state old-age pension scheme and new approaches to organiz- ing health services and care for the elderly.

Long-term sustainable means for ensuring the quality of life for the el- derly, without placing unreasonable burdens on their children or other relatives, still remains one of the most important prerequisites for good relations between generations, both with regard to family life and society at large. In the light of demographic change, the issue as to the long- term sustainability of such solutions is becoming increasingly conten- sious. In international debates, the contract between generations has become a loaded question. With regard to pensions, it has been claimed that it is no longer obvious that solidarity across generation boundaries can, over time, be taken for granted. The unanimity that originally surrounded the idea that young adult generations are to bear responsibility for dependent children and elderly is not always considered to necessarily extend to that growing group of senior citizens who have left working life behind them in order to concentrate on realizing themselves as individuals.

The following view is stated in Senior 2005 (SOU 2002:29):

> The challenges posed by an aging population imply that society re- quires continued measures for a sustainable development between generations over time. Mutuality across generation boundaries in particular must be strengthened and developed in those areas of importance for the economy and for the power structure in society. Through such mutuality, senior citizens will also be brought into an issue concerning participation in, and responsibility for, political decisions. Notice ought to be drawn to the possibility of promoting long-term meetings and cooperation between people from differ- ent generations in all sections of society. It is necessary to establish structures for this purpose, which should be coordinated to form a foundation for subsequent developments.

It is pointed out in this report that the intergenerational perspective is conspicuous by its absence in Sweden, compared to several other coun- tries where specific programmes exist for activities across generational boundaries.

INTERGENERATIONAL INITIATIVES IN SWEDEN

Contacts across generational boundaries and solidarity between gen- erations are not new issues in Swedish policy with regard to senior citi- zens. For example, solidarity between generations had been the theme for the European Year of Older People 1993 when this was held in Swe- den. In their final report (SOU 1994:39), the Swedish Committee for the European Year of Older People stated that the reason behind the selec- tion of this theme had been the claim that the divisions between genera- tions had probably become wider in Sweden than perhaps in any other

European country. The Committee went on to state that, in retrospect, research has indicated that this claim was to some extent erroneous. The increasing number of senior citizens in Sweden living alone does not necessarily imply increased abandonment and isolation but rather increased independence at an advanced age. The Committee writes that at different points in their life course, younger and older people are the same individuals and they must be a common interest in providing circumstances that are as comfortable as possible for people at different stages of life.

INTERGENERATIONAL INITIATIVES AND "FIERY SPIRITS"

Cultural life provides many opportunities for meetings across generational boundaries and a deeper understanding of age and belonging to a certain generation. However, the fact that cultural policies have so strongly targeted certain groups has meant that these opportunities have not always been grasped. Further, in Sweden there has been an almost complete lack of initiatives to provide intergenerational activities with a foundation, based on tried and tested methods and long-term effects in various areas. Intergenerational activities have generally taken the form of projects, initiated and lead by "fiery spirits" (Sw. *"eldsjälarna"*), and often running out of steam when the time, energy and engagement of such leading lights becomes depleted.

Senior 2005 considers that there are opportunities in cultural policies, being an area where competence and functioning structures already exist, for the long-term development of an intergenerational perspective and therefore that it is a matter of some urgency that appropriate methods and working arrangements be put in place. An initial step in this regard would be to draw greater attention to age as a cultural phenomenon and cultural construction in initiatives involving target groups that are determined by age. Other types of initiatives could include common activities for learning, creating and exchanges across generational boundaries.

SOCIAL ECONOMY

In terms of social economy, there is a need to draw attention to the importance of, and opportunities provided by, the consequences of an aging population. The value arising from, for example, voluntary work provides a considerable amount of social capital to society at large. Although older and middle-aged people at present have a very strong position in the activities of popular associations, their level of active membership in these is at the same time falling off. As a result, activities generating social capital appear to be increasingly concentrated to those people who are already participating in such associations or in voluntary work. The support from public funds for the running of these associations and cultural life in general, including access to various premises, is of considerable importance in making it possible to carry out their activities which promote participation and bring people together. In this regard, it is stated in Senior 2005 that it is considered to be an urgent matter that those various actors concerned in generating social capital be encouraged to find new means to broaden the participation of older people in popular associations and voluntary work. Actors in the public sector, including local authorities, should also be involved in promoting the development of social capital, not least in their own areas of responsibility such as schools and civil defence. Methods and forms of work ought thereby to be developed in order for activities to be more systematically intergenerational.

Exactly as in the case of cultural life, this kind of social capital provides many opportunities for meetings across generational boundaries. Here, too, the building up of a knowledge base and systematic measures are required to be better able to make use of these opportunities. One possible means of promoting activities across generational boundaries is to provide a "premium" for them through financial incentives to local popular associations. A small portion of such incentives could, for example, be earmarked for those popular associations with members drawn largely from younger people or older people in order for them, at some time during the financial year, to take action to break down the age barriers, perhaps in cooperation with some popular associations where most members are drawn from other age groups. However, such an approach does imply some risk with regard to this becoming a degree of unwanted detailed intervention in the affairs of the associations concerned.

Comprehensive measures to develop the local environment or the local community are being carried out by local community groups that have rapidly grown up in Sweden. Research on these local community groups indicates that social capital would appear to be of considerable importance in maintaining strong or reinvigorated local communities. This seems to be particularly true with regard to creating a local identity and local democracy. There were almost 3,900 such groups in May 1999, which may be compared to a total of 1,500 that were in existence seven years earlier. These groups carry out work with regard to everything from new business establishments and the creation of local employment opportunities, together with service industries, homes and roads, to tourism and cultural events. It is "soft" activities that dominate, that is to say, activities that are concerned with quality of life, parties, culture, local meeting places and study groups. In rural areas, these groups are more concerned with creating employment opportunities, stimulating population expansion, telephony/computing and education.

In 1997, it was calculated that 70,000 people were active in the local community groups existing at the time. There were about an equal number of men and women who were active in this way. However, among the contact persons that each group nominates, about two-thirds were male. It is not clear how many older people were active in these groups, but it has been claimed by the Popular Movements Council for Rural Development, the national umbrella body for these local community groups, that there are many people in their 60s and 70s who actively participate in them. There are also many examples of ways in which older people assist in schools. Projects around the country, including such activities as school hosts, assisting with homework, and class granddad activities, are run under the auspices of such organizations as the Red Cross and the pensioners interest organizations, Swedish Pensioners National Organization (PRO) and the Swedish Association for Senior Citizens (SASC). There are also cases where local authorities have initiated projects where older people work in schools on a voluntary basis. However, such activities are not generally considered as part of the obligations of the school but rather an issue concerning pensioners, or possibly an issue of integration in areas where there is a high level of crime and strong segregation between different groups. In the long term, the activities now being carried out by the Association of Class Granddads in School might well make a significant contribution to revitalizing and structuring the form these functions might take. This latter association stresses that these older people are to fill an important function in the school, for example, by assisting in the classroom, during breaks, in the dining hall, and on outings and study visits away from the school.

FINANCIAL SUPPORT

Formerly, many associations were, in the view of Wijkström (2001), very concerned to preserve their independence and adopted a guarded attitude towards the state administration. Today it would appear that the state and local authorities dictate to a growing extent what the associations are to do, that is to say, the activities they wish to see put into practice, while at the same time the popular movements and other voluntary organizations accept this new order of things. Previously, associations were granted financial support because of their very existence, which in itself was considered to be of benefit to society, while today they increasingly are provided with financial resources as a result of what activities they carry out. It is necessary for them to produce something, in the form of a service, in some manner which lightens the burden on the local authority or state. Here it is possible for us to identify a shift in the activities, both in the voluntary section as a whole and within particular associations, what has become a movement "from voice towards service." A growing number of associations are engaged in producing social welfare services, which in itself is not necessarily a negative development, but unfortunately it appears that there has at the same time been a reduction in the space and resources available for activities concerning aspects of democracy and the production of "voice."

Although there has been a long history of intergenerational interventions in Sweden (Boström, 2000), in terms of the considerable level of informal learning that has taken place, and which continues to take place today, the concept of intergenerational programmes is not in common usage. Today, many initiatives continue to be taken throughout the country, for example, on the part of individuals, voluntary organizations and interest groups, such as churches and sports associations.

THE FUTURE

One project that has arisen in response to an identified social need is the "Granddad project." Research (Boström, 2003) indicates that it is possible to measure a mutual delight and satisfaction in the meeting between pupils and class granddads. In October 2003, there were about 200 older men working in this project in various places throughout Sweden.

The responses that have been analysed give expression to the fact that the granddads are largely very satisfied with their work in schools and that they often actively participate to the highest degree in school activities and the sense of solidarity among the staff. The results from research of the granddad programme in Sweden indicate benefits for both students and the elderly men in an intergenerational learning situation.

Bearing in mind demographic, health and economic considerations, the official evaluation, together with all others who have come in contact with the project, have also identified positive effects for society from it.

Other areas of activity will probably embrace future intergenerational measures in a more structured and long-term manner than has been the case so far.

REFERENCES

Batljan, I., & Lagergren, M. (2000). *Kommer det att finnas en hjälpande hand: Bilaga 8 till Långtidsutredningen 1999/2000.* Stockholm: Fritzes.

Boström, A-K. (2000a). Sweden. In A. Hutton-Yeo and T. Ohsako (Eds), *Intergenerational programmes. Public policy and research implications: An international perspective.* Hamburg: UNESCO Institute of Education and Stoke-on-Trent: The Beth Foundation.

Boström, A-K. (2003). *Lifelong learning, intergenerational learning, and social capital: From theory to practice.* Stockholm: Institute of International Education, Stockholm University.

Odén, B. (1985). De äldre i samhället-förr. Arbetsrapport 22 från projektet äldre i samhället-förr, nu och i framtiden.

Odén, B. (1993). Tidsperspektivet. I Odén, B., Svanborg, Alvar., & Tornstam, Lars. Att åldras i Sverige.

Ronström, O. (1998). *Pigga pensionärer och populärkulturer.* Stockholm: Carlssons.

SOU (2002:29). *Riv ålderstrappan! Livslopp i förändring. Diskussionsbetänkande av den parlamentariska äldreberedningen.* Stockholm: Fritzes.

Wijkström, F. (2001). Socialt capital och civilt samhälle i Norden. In L.S. Henriksen og B. Ibsen (Eds), *Frivillighedens udfordringer.* Odense: Odense Universitetsforlag.

A Faith-Based Intergenerational Health and Wellness Program

Mary Duquin, PhD

James McCrea, MPW

David Fetterman, MEd

Sabrina Nash, MEd

SUMMARY. The purpose of this program was to create an intergenerational, faith-based health and wellness program for kinship caregivers and their families (i.e., grandparents and other relatives who are raising children *and* their children's children). The program took place over a 12-week period in a faith-based setting and focused on education in (a) Health, Exercise, Nutrition and Stress Management; (b) Parenting Education; and (c) Religious Practices (such as worship, scripture, and prayer). Each week's session included lunch, which modeled a healthy, easy to prepare, and cost-effective meal. Both quantitative and qualitative measurement techniques were employed. The number of participants completing both pre- and post-tests was small and therefore not valid for statistical tests of significance. Nonetheless, the quantitative findings of the scales viewed in combination with the qualitative findings of the focus groups, participant observation and interviews provide some helpful indicators of the program's outcomes and effectiveness.

Mary Duquin, James McCrea, David Fetterman, and Sabrina Nash are affiliated with the University of Pittsburgh, Pennsylvania.

[Haworth co-indexing entry note]: "A Faith-Based Intergenerational Health and Wellness Program." Duquin, Mary et al. Co-published simultaneously in *Journal of Intergenerational Relationships* (The Haworth Press, Inc.) Vol. 2, No. 3/4, 2004, pp. 105-118; and: *Intergenerational Relationships: Conversations on Practice and Research Across Cultures* (ed: Elizabeth Larkin et al.) The Haworth Press, Inc., 2004, pp. 105-118. Single or multiple copies of this article are available for a fee from The Haworth Document Delivery Service [1-800-HAWORTH, 9:00 a.m. - 5:00 p.m. (EST). E-mail address: docdelivery@haworthpress.com].

Digital Object Identifier: 10.1300/J194v02n03_09

Participants in the health and wellness program reported that they became more aware of resources in the community, used nutritional information provided, noticed positive changes in the home, felt a feeling of connectedness with others in the program, used new stress management techniques, gained a greater understanding of their grandchildren and appreciated the social support the program provided. The experience of providing a faith-based intergenerational health and wellness program was rewarding for caregivers, children and staff. *[Article copies available for a fee from The Haworth Document Delivery Service: 1-800-HAWORTH. E-mail address: <docdelivery@haworthpress.com> Website: <http://www.HaworthPress.com> © 2004 by The Haworth Press, Inc. All rights reserved.]*

KEYWORDS. Health and wellness, intergenerational programs, grandparents, faith-based programs

GRANDPARENTS RAISING GRANDCHILDREN: HEALTH AND WELLNESS ISSUES

Many parents look forward to the golden years of retirement and the role of grandparent. For grandparents living separately from their children it is often that time of life when they can experience many of the joys of visiting grandchildren but little of the day-to-day work and responsibility of raising them. Over the past 30 years, however, due to a variety of serious social problems the number of grandparents taking on the primary responsibility of raising their grandchildren and other young relatives has dramatically increased. Alcohol and drug abuse, abandonment, incarceration, poverty, divorce, family violence, child abuse, teen pregnancy, HIV/AIDS, unemployment, mental illness and parent death are some of the major causes of the growing phenomena of grandparents raising grandchildren. These social problems, in turn, have resulted in many health and wellness problems affecting both grandparents and the children they raise.

As compared to parent-maintained families, grandparent-maintained families are more likely to be impoverished, lack health insurance and face a plethora of health concerns including many problems related to high stress (Landry, 1999). Children raised in such households are more likely to suffer from higher rates of asthma, poor eating and sleeping patterns, high physical disabilities, greater hyperactivity and physical, emotional and social effects of prenatal drug and alcohol abuse and neglect. Grandparents raising grandchildren often suffer from stress-related illnesses such as high blood pressure, depression, diabetes, digestive problems, and heart disease. Many parenting grandparents are isolated from their peers and do not have access to support services, especially in the area of health and wellness (Casper & Bryson, 1998; Kelley, Yorker, Whitley, & Sipe, 2001; Roe & Minkler, 1998).

In 2001, a focus group was conducted with kinship caregivers by Second Chance, Inc., a non-profit social service agency in Allegheny County. Focus group members stressed the need for programs that addressed the health, well-being, and spiritual life of both caregivers and children. The need for health and wellness programs that are holistic in nature, and that include wellness in body, mind and spirit, has been supported by research that shows that people in crisis have religious and spiritual needs that are intimately related to their physical health and that religious beliefs and practices are often important in emotional healing. Research has also shown that religion, as embodied in prayer and scripture, offers a variety of coping methods in times of stress for people from many different religious traditions (Abeles, Ellison, George, Idler, Krause, Levin, Ory, Pargament, Powell, Underwood, & Williams, 1999; Benjamin & Looby, 1998; Koenig, McCollough, & Larson, 2001). By locating a health and wellness program in a faith-based organization it is possible for grandparents to take advantage of the support systems inherent in those faith-based congregations.

A FAITH-BASED HEALTH AND WELLNESS PROGRAM

In the summer of 2002 a grant from the Howard Heinz Endowments supported a faith-based health and wellness program for grandparents and their grandchildren. This program was implemented in Pittsburgh, PA, by the coalition of Generations Together, an intergenerational studies program within the Center for Social and Urban Research of the University of Pittsburgh, the Parish Nurses of Mercy Hospital of Pittsburgh, The Parental Stress Center, Inc., the University of Pittsburgh's Department of Health, Physical, and Recreation Education (DHPRE), and Emory United Methodist Church. Generations Together provided the intergenerational expertise and administrative functions such as identifying the program site and recruiting the grandparents and grandchildren. Parish Nurses provided medical counseling and the spiritual components related to the health and parenting topics within the wellness program. The Parental Stress Center provided parenting education and the DHPRE provided the health and wellness curriculum and staff. Emory Church provided the space for the program including kitchen facilities and staff. Recruitment for the health and wellness program began with a list of grandparenting caregivers compiled by Generations Together, as well as local publicity and announcements at various religious institutions. The publicity for the program stressed the intergenerational nature of the program involving health and wellness education that would benefit both grandparents and grandchildren. Publicity flyers also noted that bus passes, lunch, and babysitting for very young children would be provided. The health and wellness program was conducted once per week on Saturdays for 12 weeks between October and December of 2002.

HOLISTIC HEALTH AND WELLNESS

The health and wellness program as designed was holistic in nature and focused on the development of six interrelated dimensions of wellness. These dimensions of wellness included physical, emotional, social/interpersonal, intellectual, environmental and spiritual wellness. Physical wellness emphasized getting exercise, eating healthy foods, taking steps to prevent injuries, and recognizing symptoms of disease. Emotional wellness included developing a sense of self-esteem, self-confidence, trust and self-control, practicing good stress management skills and being able to identify emotional obstacles in life. Social wellness included having good interpersonal and communication skills, the capacity for intimacy and the ability to develop a strong social support network. Intellectual wellness was characterized by the ability to keep learning, to think critically, to be open to new ideas, and to be a good decision maker and problem solver. Environmental wellness focused on recognizing and taking steps to protect oneself against dangers in the environment that may pose a threat to health. Finally, spiritual wellness involved having guiding moral principles and values that gave meaning to one's life and support in times of crisis. Spiritual wellness was characterized by developing compassion, altruism, forgiveness, and love (Insel & Roth, 2002).

A number of national organizations and programs, including Healthy People 2010, the Center for Disease Control, and the Association for the Advancement of Health Education, have identified areas of health risk for our nation and especially for our nation's children. These risk areas include tobacco use, lack of physical activity, unintentional and inten-

tional injuries, poor nutrition, alcohol and other drug use and HIV/
STDs (Meeks, Heit, & Page, 2002). Hence, the health education curriculum for this program concentrated on developing health knowledge,
healthy behaviors, and responsible decision-making skills. The curriculum also stressed the promotion of healthy relationships, enhancing
protective factors against health risks, and developing resiliency skills.
Health and parenting content areas included stress management, massage, physical activity, nutrition, alcohol, tobacco and drugs, conflict
resolution, community resources and services, safety and violence prevention, healthy expression of emotion, discipline, empathy, children's
self-worth, family roles and rules, resistance skills and decision-making
skills. During the 12-week program period health education alternated
with parenting education every other week.

TYPICAL SATURDAY SCHEDULE

9:30 a.m. Teachers and staff arrived

The staff arrived at the church recreation hall and began preparations
for the education program and lunch.

10:00-10:15 a.m. Gathering–Music

The staff greeted families as grandparents and children arrived.
Lively music, played in the background, set the stage for the movement
and exercise portion of the health and wellness program.

10:15-10:30 a.m. Intergenerational Physical Activity and Massage

Initial discussions with grandparents and grandchildren around the
topic of physical activity revealed that grandchildren were very physically active. Grandparents, however, were not likely to exercise regu-
larly due to chronic health problems, weight problems, lack of energy,
lack of time, and lack of a support group. Thus, each session began with
intergenerational exercises. The group participated in various forms of
exercise, stretching and moving to music. The benefits of exercise and
the importance of integrating physical activity into daily life were emphasized. The topics discussed in this session over the 12 weeks included health benefits of exercise, health-related fitness, skill-related
fitness, barriers to exercise, lifetime physical activity, frequency, intensity, time and type of exercise, physical activity for stress reduction and
options for regular exercise with grandchildren.

Massage has the power to forge healing relationships (Ward, Duquin, & Streetman, 1998). Partner massage was taught early in the program so that grandchildren and grandparents learned the basic techniques of massage for stress reduction and were able to perform a form of clothed chair massage on each other. The use of a brief massage after physical activity became a common practice in this part of the program. Other stress management techniques that were taught included visual imagery, yoga, progressive relaxation, and deep breathing. Information on physical activity, stress management techniques and massage was distributed to participants during health sessions.

10:30-10:45 a.m. Intergenerational Spiritual Reading and Discussion

The group was surveyed to determine what religious faiths were represented among the group participants. The program planners were prepared to draw spiritual readings from any number of religious traditions as represented by the group attending. An initial survey revealed that all attending participants were of the Christian faith. Appropriate religious texts were then selected for inclusion in the curriculum. Scriptural and responsive readings were selected to correspond to the health or parenting topic of the day. The scripture and responsive readings opened a brief discussion of family problems and concerns relating to the topic for the day (e.g., conflict resolution, stress management, or decision-making skills). Handouts of scripture and responsive readings were given to the families.

10:45-11:30 a.m. Intergenerational Health or Parenting Education

Grandparents and grandchildren over the age of seven participated in an interactive, activities-oriented health or family education session. Discussions began with a question and answer session on the topic for the day which elicited the specific problems families were having in that health or parenting area. New strategies for behavior change were explored and practiced in role play situations, discussion groups, and small group activities. For example, when teaching "conflict resolution" grandparents and grandchildren were taken through a process that enabled them to practice calming techniques, learn to deliver I-messages, engage in active listening and participate in brainstorming to find solutions to recurring family conflicts. Handouts on the health or parenting topic were distributed to the grandparents, and families were asked to practice the skills presented in the session during the upcoming week.

11:30-12:00 p.m. Grandparent Support Group and Grandchildren Activities

In this thirty-minute session grandparents and grandchildren met separately with staff members. Grandparents discussed the topic for the day and offered support and advice to other grandparents and discussed topics difficult to talk about in front of the children they were raising. The grandchildren met with staff members and participated in planned recreational and educational activities. These activities were often physically active and enabled the children to develop relationships with the other children and with staff members.

12:00-12:30 p.m. Grace, a Healthy Hot Lunch and Ending Prayer

After saying grace, families and staff ate lunch together. Lunches were designed to be nutritionally balanced, easy to prepare and low cost. One lunch session was devoted to grandparents and children making their own individual pita bread pizzas. Recipes for each meal were given to the families and any leftover food was divided up among the families. Following lunch the group joined hands for an ending prayer. This ending prayer returned to the day's topic and asked for spiritual help in trying to implement, during the week, the lessons learned in the health and wellness session that day.

12:30-12:40 p.m. Grandparent Evaluation

After each session, grandparents completed a brief evaluation form on the interactive health or parenting session for that day.

12:45-1:15 pm Staff Discussion and Planning

Staff met for 30-45 minutes after each session to read the grandparent responses to the lesson and share their impressions of how each part of the program was received by grandparents and grandchildren. Staff then discussed any curriculum or methodological changes that needed to be made. If any specific information was requested by a grandparent the staff discussed who might be able to give that information to the family the following week.

RESULTS

The faith-based health and wellness program was structured to have positive health and relationship benefits for grandparents and the grandchildren they were raising. The curriculum was presented in such a way that participants would both enjoy coming to the sessions and would learn to incorporate knowledge and skills of various health topics including nutrition, exercise, parenting strategies, and stress management techniques in their life.

Grandparents ranged in age from the upper fifties to the upper seventies. As is common with this population, not all grandparents had legal custody of their grandchildren. For this reason, we could not collect any data on the grandchildren in this program since consent from a parent or legal guardian was necessary. However, we were able to use several pre-post instruments on the attending grandparents. Various quantitative and qualitative measurement techniques were used to evaluate change in grandparents as a result of the program. The quantitative measurements included the Adult-Adolescent Parenting Inventory (AAPI-2) (Bavolek, 1987), the Assess Your Stress Scale (Cohen et al., 1983), and the Spiritual Well-Being Scale (SWBS) (Abeles et al., 1999). The qualitative measurements included participant observation, interviews and a summary focus group. The health and wellness program ran for 12 weeks and had varying numbers of participants. During the 12-week session a total of 12 adults and 29 children attended at least one session. Although one grandfather attended twice during the 12 weeks, only grandmothers filled out the pre- and post-survey instruments and participated in the final focus group evaluation. Overall pre- and post-testing participant numbers were too small for meaningful statistical analysis. However, the positive trend in the quantitative scores is mirrored in the responses received in the focus group and in discussions with grandparents and grandchildren over the 12-week period.

Adult-Adolescent Parenting Inventory (N = 2)

The AAPI-2 is a 40-item self-reported questionnaire designed to assess the parenting and child-rearing attitudes of adult and adolescent parent and pre-parent populations. The AAPI-2 provides an index of risk in five "Parenting Constructs" forming the following continua:

```
                                  Scale
                    1   2   3   4   5   6   7   8   9   10
A. Inappropriate Expectations    ─────────────────►  Appropriate Expectations
B. Low Level of Empathy          ─────────────────►  Appropriate Level of Empathy
C. Strong Belief in Value        ─────────────────►  Values Alternatives
   of Corporal Punishment                             to Corporal Punishment
D. Reverses Family Roles         ─────────────────►  Appropriate Family Roles
E. Restricts Power/Independence  ─────────────────►  Values Power/Independence
```

Raw score totals for each respondent were converted into standard scores for reporting on norm tables. The standard scores provided consistency of meaning of the data for different groups of parents. In each construct, the higher the score the more desirable the attitude or behavior with the highest score (10) being the ideal. Similarly, the lower the score the less desirable the attitude and behavior with the lowest score on the scale (1) being the most at-risk attitude or behavior. The AAPI-2 was administered as a pre-test and a post-test.

Of the two grandmothers who completed both the pre-test and post-test, increases are indicated in the following constructs:

	Pre-test	Post-test
Appropriate Expectations	3.00	3.50
Empathy	4.50	6.00
Value of Corporal Punishment	4.00	5.00
Appropriate Family Roles	5.00	4.00
Power/Independence	6.00	8.00

Assess Your Stress Scale (N = 5)

The Assess Your Stress Scale is a 10-item self-reported questionnaire. Each question indicates a particular stressor (e.g., "Do you feel a loss of energy or zest for life?"). Respondents used a 5-point scale to circle the most appropriate response ranging from "Never" to "Nearly Always." Participants completed this scale as a pre-test and a post-test. The mean scores were calculated for each test. A lower score in the post-test than the pre-test indicates a reduction in stress. The post-test showed lower means for 9 of the 10 indicators on the Assess Your Stress Scale.

	Pre	Post
Loss of freedom	3.67	3.20
Stretched beyond capabilities	3.50	3.00
Financial pressures	3.33	3.00
Feeling burdened	3.33	3.00
Lost control of life	3.17	3.00
Trouble sleeping	3.00	2.40
Appetite changes	2.83	2.40
Lack of interest in people/things	2.83	2.80
Physical health suffering	2.83	2.20
Loss of energy/zest for life	2.83	3.00

Spiritual Well-Being Scale (N = 5)

The Spiritual Well-Being Scale (SWBS) is a 20-item self-reported questionnaire that provides a "measure of overall well-being," according to Life Advance, Inc., the designers of the instrument. Scores of 21-40 indicate low spiritual well-being, 41-99 indicate moderate spiritual well-being, and 100-120 indicate high spiritual well-being. Respondents use a 6-point scale to circle the most appropriate response ranging from "Strongly Agree" to "Strongly Disagree." Participants completed the SWBS as a pre-test and a post-test. The mean scores were calculated for each test. A higher score in the post-test than the pre-test indicates an increase in spiritual well-being. The post-test showed a higher mean score (89.00) than the pre-test (81.50).

The increase in mean scores from the pre-test to the post-test indicates an increase in participant spiritual well-being over the course of the 12-week session. We discovered early in the session the importance of spirituality to our participants, expressed in common comments such as, *My faith in God means everything to me.* It is not surprising, then, that the pre-test mean for spiritual well-being indicated "moderate spiritual well-being." The already moderate well-being indicated in the pre-test scores increased in the post-test scores, thus moving closer to "high spiritual well-being." One possible reason for this increase may be found in the key theme of "Connectedness" as indicated in the focus group below. In a fundamental way, spiritual well-being has to do with people feeling connected to each other and to a source of transcendent power. The comments of participants, both in the focus group and in informal conversation, indicated that this sense of connectedness developed over the course of the 12-weeks of the fall session and contributed to the increase in their spiritual well-being.

Focus Group (N = 4)

To complement the paper and pencil instruments, a focus group consisting of four grandmothers was conducted on the last day of the program. This focus group enabled program participants to share and expand on outcomes not revealed via the standardized tests. Group members were asked to reflect on the successes and disappointments of the program; how the program affected them and their families; and what they might change if they were planning the next 12-week session. The final item in the focus group asked them to complete the sentence: *The most helpful thing that I learned during this program was . . .* Responses to that question suggested some of the important outcomes that emerged from the program.

- *I have learned that I am not alone. A lot of grandparents are in the same predicament.*
- *I feel great about us helping each other.*
- *I like hearing what other people think and discussing problems.*
- *I learned from the role-play and the interactions with the kids. I leaned to understand how my grandchild feels. I saw a side of my grandchild that I had not known before. My attitudes toward my grandchild have changed in positive ways.*
- *The interactions with the kids helped me to better understand how kids feel. I am more aware that they keep a lot bundled up.*
- *My grandson and I can get along with God's help with many things going on.*
- *I am more sensitive to the pressures kids are feeling.*
- *I am more aware of the resources that are available and where to find them, for example, tutoring programs.*

Several themes emerged from the focus group. Grandparents spoke about the support and connectedness they found in the program, the enthusiasm they and their grandchildren felt for the program, the positive effects of the program on home life and the implementation of knowledge and skills they acquired in the program.

Connectedness. Being connected to other people who understand and care is important for a sense of wellness. In addition, many grandparents consider being connected to a source of divine strength as a key to coping with stress. Grandparents illustrated these sentiments when they said things like:

- *If this were not a faith-based program, I would not be here.*
- *I need God for everything that I do.*
- *When I listen to others speak of their concerns I feel some of the pressure coming off.*
- *I look forward to coming. The program is my release.*
- *We are not alone. We are not alone. That's a good feeling. I like it.*

Positive impact on the home. The focus group revealed that the program had a positive impact on home life and interactions between grandparents and their grandchildren.

- *Siblings are fighting less at home.*
- *Children are offering to help more around the house.*

- *Kids are opening up more.*
- *Kids are coming out of their shell.*
- *I have a new understanding of my grandchildren and have changed in my attitude and approach to discipline.*
- *My grandson used massage therapy techniques on his ill grandfather to make him feel better.*
- *When a stressful family event occurred in our home, my grandchild reminded me of something that we learned at the Saturday session by saying, "Remember the Saturday People and what they taught us."*

Program components that contributed to this outcome included the following: learning new strategies to cope with stress; learning active listening skills; learning and participating in therapeutic massage; role-playing; parenting education classes; and healthy meal preparation.

Beginning of transfer of learning. A short-term outcome of this program was to teach new skills to the participants. For example, meals that were low cost and easy to prepare were served each week. In addition each family was given a detailed description of ingredients and menus for the meal so that they could be replicated in their homes. Several of the families actually prepared these meals at home and reported their success upon their return to the group. Grandparents reported other examples of the transfer of learning.

- *There is less sibling fighting at home.*
- *There is an increase in family cooperativeness.*
- *Kids are reading more and volunteering to read at school.*
- *There is better communication between grandparent and grandchildren.*

Enthusiasm for participation. Grandparents reported that some grandchildren couldn't wait to come to a Saturday session because they so enjoyed it. The grandchildren were ready and waiting before their grandmother was. One grandchild found the program so meaningful that he came by himself on a day when his grandparent was unable to attend. Other grandchildren eagerly and without coaching from anybody told their school teachers about what they were doing and learning at Saturday sessions. Grandparents too seemed to enjoy the program.

- *I've never been treated so well. You make me feel like a Queen.*
- *12 weeks wasn't long enough. I would have liked to see it be a longer time period.*

CONCLUSIONS

These findings, though based on small numbers, indicate that the program had a positive impact on the participants. More research is needed in future offerings of this program to determine the extent to which a direct connection can be made between the wellness sessions and the perceived positive impacts experienced by the families.

The primary problem encountered in providing this health and wellness program for parenting grandparents and their children was underestimating the commitment of the time and effort on the part of the families that was needed to attend consecutive weekly sessions over a 12-week period. Although overall participation in the program was high, consistent attendance from week to week by the same families was low. A survey conducted with 61 relative caregivers after the program considered a variety of ways to restructure the program including reducing the number of weekly sessions, holding the sessions after church on Sundays, or providing the content within existing health and wellness programs operating within religious institutions or existing grandparent support groups. These suggestions will be tried in future offerings of the program.

Overall, the first attempt to provide a faith-based intergenerational health and wellness program was rewarding for caregivers, children and program staff. Since the need for health and wellness education for grandparents and their grandchildren is still evident, the challenge is to find a venue and method of delivery that is convenient and comfortable for these busy and stressed grandparents and their children.

REFERENCES

AAPI-2 Family Development Resources, Inc. (2001). Park City, UT: Family Development Resources, Inc. 1-800-688-5822.

Abeles, R., Ellison, C., George, L., Idler, E., Krause, N., Levin, J., Ory, M., Pargament, K., Powell, L., Underwood, L., & Williams, D. (1999). *Multidimensional Measurement of Religiousness/Spirituality for Use in Health Research: A Report of the Felzer Institute/National Institute on Aging Working Group.* Washington, DC: The Felzer Institute.

Assess Your Stress Senior Connections. (1999). San Mateo, CA: STAR, Support and Training for Assessing Results. 1-800-548-3656.

Bavolek, S. J. (1987). In: Corcoran K. & Fischer J. *Measures for Clinical Practice: A Sourcebook.* New York: Free Press (415-418).

Benjamin, P., & Looby, J. (1998). Defining the Nature of Spirituality in the Context of Maslow's and Roger's Theories. *Counseling & Values, 42*(2), 92-101.

Casper, L. M., & Bryson, K. R. (1998). *Co-resident Grandparents and Their Grandchildren: Grandparent Maintained Families.* (Population Division Working Paper No. 26). Washington, DC: U.S. Census Bureau.

Cohen, S., Karmack, T., & Mermelstein, R. (1983). A Global Measure of Perceived Stress. *Journal of Health and Social Behavior, 24,* 385-396.

Ellison, C. W., & Smith, J. (1991). Toward an Integrative Measure of Health and Well-Being. *Journal of Psychology & Theology, 19*(1), 35-48.

Horowitz, M., Wilner, N., & Alvarez, W. (1979). Impact of Event Scale: A Measure of Subjective Stress. *Psychosomatic Medicine, 41*(3), 209-218.

Insel, P., & Roth, W. (2002). *Core Concepts in Health.* Boston, MA: McGraw Hill.

Kelley, S. J., Yorker, B. C., Whitley, D. M., & Sipe, T. A. (2001). A Multimodal Intervention for *Grandparents Raising Grandchildren*: Results of an Exploratory Study. *Child Welfare, 80*(1), 27-51.

Koenig, H. G., McCollough, M. E., & Larson, D. B. (2001). *Handbook of Religion and Health.* New York, NY: Oxford University Press.

Landry, L. (1999). Research into Action: Recommended Intervention Strategies for Grandparent Caregivers. *Family Relations, 48*(4), 381-390.

Meeks, L., Heit, P., & Page, R. (2003). *Comprehensive School Health Education.* Boston, MA: McGraw Hill.

Myers, J. E., Sweeney, T. J., & Witmer, J. M. (2000). The Wheel of Wellness Counseling for Wellness: A Holistic Model for Treatment Planning. *Journal of Counseling & Development, 78,* 251-266.

Roe, K. M., & Minkler, M. (1998). Grandparents Raising Grandchildren: Challenges and Responses. *Generations, 22*(4), 8.

Ward, C. R., Duquin, M. E., & Streetman, H. (1998). Effects of Intergenerational Massage on Future Caregivers' Attitudes Toward Aging, the Elderly, and Caring for the Elderly. *Educational Gerontology, 24*(1), 35-48.

Ware, J. E., & Gandek, B. (1998). Overview of the SF-36 Health Survey and the International Quality of Life (IQOLA) Project. *Journal of Clinical Epidemiology, 51,* 903-912.

Futures Festivals:
An Intergenerational Strategy
for Promoting Community Participation

Matthew Kaplan, PhD
Frank Higdon, PhD
Nancy Crago, PhD
Lucinda Robbins, MPA

SUMMARY. This paper describes a special events strategy for mobilizing community residents of all ages to take part in a community visioning process. Through locally initiated special events–called "Futures Festivals"–community residents come together to share their concerns and hopes for their community. Planning for these events is driven by a

---

Matthew Kaplan is Associate Professor, Intergenerational Programs & Aging, Department of Agricultural and Extension Education, Penn State University.

Frank Higdon is Senior Lecturer in Community Development, Community and Economic Development Graduate Program, Penn State University.

Nancy Crago is Family and Consumer Science Educator, Penn State Cooperative Extension, Allegheny County.

Lucinda Robbins is Community Development Educator, Penn State Cooperative Extension, Fayette County.

Address correspondence to: Matthew Kaplan, Dept. of Agricultural and Extension Education, Penn State University, 315 Ag Admin Building, State College, PA 16802 (E-mail: msk15@psu.edu).

[Haworth co-indexing entry note]: "Futures Festivals: An Intergenerational Strategy for Promoting Community Participation." Kaplan, Matthew et al. Co-published simultaneously in *Journal of Intergenerational Relationships* (The Haworth Press, Inc.) Vol. 2, No. 3/4, 2004, pp. 119-146; and: *Intergenerational Relationships: Conversations on Practice and Research Across Cultures* (ed: Elizabeth Larkin et al.) The Haworth Press, Inc., 2004, pp. 119-146. Single or multiple copies of this article are available for a fee from The Haworth Document Delivery Service [1-800-HAWORTH, 9:00 a.m. - 5:00 p.m. (EST). E-mail address: docdelivery@haworthpress.com].

collaborative process involving representatives of local community organizations and agencies. The rationale for this intergenerational model is twofold; people of different age groups often have limited opportunities to communicate with one another, and the viewpoints of youth and seniors are frequently overlooked in the community planning process. This paper profiles two Futures Festival events and other preliminary organizing taking place in western Pennsylvania communities during the summer of 2002. Findings suggest that Futures Festivals can be effective tools for broadening the circle of community residents and other stakeholders engaged in critical dialogue about community issues. *[Article copies available for a fee from The Haworth Document Delivery Service: 1-800-HAWORTH. E-mail address: <docdelivery@haworthpress.com> Website: <http://www.HaworthPress.com> © 2004 by The Haworth Press, Inc. All rights reserved.]*

KEYWORDS. Community participation, Futures Festival, intergenerational, visioning

INTERGENERATIONAL ENGAGEMENT AND COMMUNITY DEVELOPMENT

Intergenerational Programming–Roots and Rationale

Over the past 25 years, there has been rapid growth in the number and diversity of intergenerational programs across the country. As defined by the International Consortium for Intergenerational Programs, these are "social vehicles that create purposeful and ongoing exchange of resources and learning among older and younger generations." They are found in a variety of community settings, including schools, community organizations, retirement communities, hospitals, and places of worship. The focus is usually on establishing connections between people who are 21 and under and people who are 60 and over, with the intention of benefiting one or both age groups. Intergenerational programs represent a set of practical, effective strategies for enriching the lives of young people and older adults, promoting family cohesion, and strengthening community support systems (Henkin and Kingson, 1998/99; Stearns, 1989).

At the root of this program activity is a conceptual framework that attributes societal significance to intergenerational programs and practices. For example, we are in the midst of what has been termed a "longevity revolution," a dramatic increase in the size of the older adult population.[1] From an "intergenerational perspective," the aging society phenomena is seen as presenting an "opportunity to be seized" (Freedman, 1999); intergenerational programs serve as vehicles for mobilizing the talents, skills, energy and resources of older adults (as well as young people) in service to people of other generations (Henkin and Kingson, 1998/99).

Intergenerational programs are also often justified on the basis of providing an effective countermeasure to patterns of residential and social segregation of age groups (Newman et al., 1997; Stearns, 1989). Various negative consequences have been associated with the trend toward increased intergenerational segregation, including a decline in senior adults' life satisfaction, an increase in negative stereotypes toward the aged and aging among younger people, and a reduction in the extent and quality of the social networks of children and senior adults (Crites, 1989; Henkin and Kingson, 1998/99; Kalish, 1969; Newman et al., 1997).

In the intergenerational programming literature, the rationale used to justify intergenerational programs has traditionally generally been derived from human development theory. This theoretical approach suggests that children, teens and young adults need nurturers, positive role models, a sense of identity, a secure value system, recognition of their worth and a sense of their place in history. Likewise, adult development theory suggests that older adults need to nurture, a sense of purpose, and recognition of their worth. Certainly, intergenerational programs do fulfill many needs for both groups, yet the significance of intergenerational programming goes beyond impact on the participants. Largely ignored in the intergenerational literature are the community development aspects to these programs.

INTERGENERATIONAL PROGRAMMING AND COMMUNITY DEVELOPMENT

When conceptualizing the intersection between intergenerational programming and community development, it is helpful to employ an "empowerment" theoretical framework. Rappaport (1984) defines empowerment as "a process: the mechanism by which people, organizations, and communities gain mastery over their lives" (p. 3). In the context of intergenerational programs, empowerment means that participants take an active, directive role in program development and implementation. Throughout the process, participants gain knowledge about key community issues and the underlying organizational and political dynamics that affect their quality of life. Participants also develop leadership and other skills to enact desired change–change within themselves, change in their organizations, and change in their communities. For intergenerational initiatives with community improvement goals, an empowerment framework might mean that participants are at the helm in terms of choosing issues on which to focus, defining community change objectives, and deciding upon organizing tools and tactics.

When older and younger members of a community are brought together to explore local issues and work together to improve local conditions, there are community quality of life as well as human development implications. In this context, some intergenerational programs are designed to help participating youth and older adults learn about each other's community concerns and this, in turn, provides a focal point for stimulating intergenerational collaboration and joint involvement in community affairs (Kaplan, 1997).

Here are some examples of intergenerational programs intentionally designed to promote community study and improvement:

- "Hidden Treasure: Our Heritage–New Horizons"–developed at the Oklahoma State University in 1981: The emphasis is on studying and preserving local history (Generations United, 1994).
- "Youth and Elderly Against Crime" program–established by Dade County Public Schools (Florida): Senior adults and older school-aged children work together to develop antiviolence bills which they present to state legislators and for which they seek political support (Friedman, 1999).
- Neighborhoods-2000–developed at the Center for Human Environments (City University of New York) in 1988: Fifth and sixth grade students and senior volunteers work together on a series of community exploration activities such as the neighborhood "walk about-talkabout" activity and landuse mapping (Kaplan, 1994).

Benefits afforded to participants of such intergenerational programs include:

- an enhanced understanding of societal problems,
- a greater sense of "belonging" to the community,
- a better sense of local history and how this history contributes to residents' current feelings about community pride and identity, and

- more of a sense that others value their views and (potential) contributions to the community.

Interest in intergenerational approaches to community development also emerges from the community development side of the equation. Community development projects have traditionally focused on a particular locality with an emphasis on creating or increasing the "capacity" of the local community to plan and act upon a basic change strategy (Hyman, McKnight, and Higdon, 2001). Key to this process of building community capacity is the creation of communication channels between citizens and local leaders in the public, private and non-profit sectors. All too often, community development projects are organized, planned and implemented by professionals or working age volunteers with an interest in a particular local issue. When the number and diversity of participants is broadened to include people across the age continuum, the planning groups' perspectives and ideas for viable alternative visions of a particular community development project or neighborhood plan are also likely to be broadened.

If we consider the complexity and depth of many community problems, it does not make sense to exclude any age groups when trying to figure out solutions. Why remove the time, talent, and experience of any age group when seeking to address society's most pressing needs? Also, why deny anyone the opportunity to contribute to the civic vitality of their communities? An intergenerational perspective could readily be brought to bear on problems traditionally seen as being related only to youth (e.g., "youth vandalism") or older adults (e.g., the loneliness experienced by many homebound seniors). In a broader, intergenerational context, by looking at the full range of recreational opportunities available to *all* residents, and examining what this means for building community relationships and support systems, it would likely be considered everyone's business if it is found that there are not enough positive recreational outlets for any one age group.

An intergenerational approach to community development is characterized by intensive dialogue about how people of all ages experience the local community. As conversants articulate their personal narratives of local history and experience, they learn of collective histories and shared concerns about the quality of life in their communities. Such realization helps to transcend interpersonal barriers, whether they are erected on the basis of age, cultural identity, or some other characteristic.

FUTURES FESTIVALS IN WESTERN PENNSYLVANIA

The remainder of this paper will highlight and provide mini-case studies of a unique intergenerational community visioning model called "Futures Festivals." This approach was developed by the Center for Human Environments at the City University of New York Graduate Center, and piloted in Long Island City (New York) and Mount Vernon (New York) in the late 1980s, as a means for bringing community residents of all ages together to share their views and visions for their communities. Through murals, models, photographs, theatrical displays, and other communications media, community residents and public officials share their ideas about community development. Festival participants get the chance to answer (and learn how others answer) the all-important question: "What would you like to see in the future of your community?"

In the fall of 2001, a group of interested Penn State University faculty, Penn State Cooperative Extension staff, and community leaders agreed that the Futures Festival model, as described in an Extension community development publication (Kaplan, 2001), would be a useful tool for promoting an age-inclusive community participation process in two communities in the southwestern section of Pennsylvania, one an urban community in the south end of Pittsburgh and the other a rural community in Fayette County. These areas were chosen, in part, due to the availability of local Extension educators with community development skills and staff support offered by the newly created University Center for Community Engagement and Partnerships at the Penn State McKeesport Campus, located south of Pittsburgh (UCCEP).

Before describing and discussing these events, we provide some generic information about Futures Festival methodology and lay out several points about the community-building significance of this approach.

What Is a Futures Festival?

There are various ways to conduct a Futures Festival. They can be organized as separate events or incorporated into other events (such as annual fairs) for which strong local traditions already exist. In either case, it takes a team effort to conduct a successful Futures Festival event. At the core of the team, there is usually an official event coordinator and a home base for operations. The event planning process generally takes place over a two- to four-month period of time and involves the basic steps outlined below.

Step #1: Organize an event coordination team

> Members of the event coordination team are responsible for: recruiting participants, exhibitors, and presenters; publicizing the event to the media; and coordinating, facilitating, and evaluating activities on the day of the event. Team members might include human service professionals working with children, youth and older adults; planning professionals working at the community, county, and municipal levels; and volunteers with skills in environmental design and development, community history, photography, public affairs.

Step #2: Determine event location and date

> One of the first tasks is to determine event location and date. Futures Festival events are typically conducted in public parks or large indoor facilities.

Step #3: Recruit exhibitors/presenters and generate community interest and excitement

> The planning process requires time to pull together local groups and incorporate stakeholder interests. Strategies for publicizing event-planning meetings and the event itself include putting up postings on local bulletin boards, writing articles for community organization newsletters, conducting presentations at meetings of various school and community organizations, and drawing upon personal social networks to reach key local educators, community organization administrators, and other professionals with community ties. Here are some examples of event activities and exhibits:

> a. *Mural painting or model building of the "ideal neighborhood":* Intergenerational groups of community residents work together to create murals or build models that depict their desires for the future of their neighborhood.
> b. *Theatrical displays:* Local groups and organizations develop short skits to dramatize quality-of-life concerns, highlight ideas for new community resources, arouse feelings about places of sentimental value, and promote a sense of civic awareness and responsibility.
> c. *Photography exhibits:* Photos (old and new) and drawings of favorite landmarks and other locations of sentimental value are displayed.

d. *Display plans for new facilities:* County, regional, and municipal planning officials display sketches and models of planned facilities and request feedback on these plans.

The Futures Festival does not end with the event. Organizers are encouraged to take actions after the event to keep residents interested and involved. One simple post-event strategy involves writing a press release to highlight the community concerns expressed at the Futures Festival. This media coverage typically conveys the "human interest" angle that is a vital yet often ignored part of community development. Ideally, members of the event planning group will continue to meet to plan additional events and programs through which local youth and seniors can continue to share and work collaboratively to enact their community visions. For more information on how Futures Festival events are organized, see Kaplan (2001).

In terms of the community-building significance of Futures Festivals, event organizers have the opportunity to generate an alternative planning vision within the community and, by skillful follow-up activities, can use the enthusiasm and knowledge generated by the event to influence the planning agenda of more dominant economic and political institutions in the community. This process can be viewed broadly as a grassroots, participatory development technique (Prokopy and Castelloe, 1999) and more specifically as a form of "popular education" in which young and older residents are engaged by a facilitator in a grassroots search for community-specific knowledge and social change (Castelloe and Watson, 1999).[2]

The role of the community development practitioner in this process is to allow seniors and youth to engage in an open dialogue of mutual understanding and learning. In this way, the Futures Festival participants are able to become "actors" in a democratic planning process as opposed to being acted upon or directed by established political and economic institutions. This process can also be seen as a form of "action research" where local groups learn to understand their personal experience in the context of reflective learning about broader trends and changing realities (Lewin, 1948). Participation in a Futures Festival event encourages residents of all ages to reflect on their current situation and to consider modes of direct action to change that reality. From this perspective, community visioning can facilitate a process of "creative empowerment" in a multigenerational project setting.

Futures Festivals provide a venue for articulating indigenous expressions of community concern and vision. The method is flexible and can be implemented in a wide range of community and cultural contexts.

The Fayette County Futures Festival (Fayette County, PA)

Background

Fayette County is a distressed Appalachian area that began to suffer economic and population losses in the 1940s from which it has not fully recovered. Although the population is mostly rural and homogenous (more than 95% of residents are Caucasian), the social welfare statistics most closely resemble Philadelphia County with high rates of infant mortality, teen pregnancy, disability and health problems, and crime and delinquency. Education levels are low and much of the available employment is concentrated in low-paying, service sector jobs. About 18% of Fayette County residents live in poverty, with more than one quarter of families with small children living in poverty. In addition, Fayette County has a rapidly aging population; more than 18% of the residents are over the age of 65 and the median age is 40 years. In the face of its economic troubles, however, Fayette County refused to lie down. In the past ten years, concerted actions with community support have resulted in greater educational achievement, increased employment opportunities, and rising income levels. Planning and investment in the health care sector have resulted in greater prenatal care, lower rates of disease, and increased health opportunities. Furthermore, areas of the county have been designated a Federal Enterprise Community, and public and private investments are leading to increased opportunities for education, work, and community development.

Process

The Fayette County Futures Festival was planned by representatives of five agencies over a 31/2 week period of time. The Penn State Cooperative Extension Community Development Educator in Fayette County initiated the event planning process by pulling together a small planning group which included directors of three key local development organizations, the Redevelopment Authority of the City of Uniontown, Uniontown Downtown Business District Authority, and Fayette Enterprise Community/Fayette Forward. The planning team decided to hold the Futures Festival event as part of the Fayette County Family Fun Fest.

An entire tent was devoted to the Futures Festival which consisted of the following three activities:

- *"Test Your Knowledge" Quiz Show:* Participants were given a series of questions about Fayette County's resources and rich heritage.
- *"Where Is This Place?":* Participants were asked to identify the name and location of the sites pictured in over 40 photos. The person who identified the most pictures correctly won a basket of exotic foods.
- *"Design the Ideal Community" Mural Painting:* Working in small groups, participants were asked to paint their images of the "ideal" community on 24" × 36" canvas boards.

Outcomes

The Fayette County Futures Festival drew approximately 300 people, with a majority of the participants attending as families. According to comments made by the participants at the event, many became more aware of the community's rich natural and cultural resources. Those who took part in the "Where Is This Place?" activity made comments such as: "That's so beautiful," "That's really in Fayette County?" and "Where are these places? Are they all in Fayette County?"

During the debriefing meeting after the event, members of the event planning group assigned significance to such statements; they indicate how little many local residents know about their community. At this meeting, for example, an entire discussion took place focused on how few people could answer the question, "Who wrote the Marshall Plan?" General George C. Marshall, a native of Uniontown (in Fayette County), is memorialized by a Marshall statue, a Marshall Park, and a Marshall highway; George Marshall even won the Nobel Peace prize.

Planning team members also gained some insight as to *how* to promote more awareness of the area's rich history and heritage. According to the coordinator of the "Where Is This Place?" exhibit, the images that drew the most attention were those that provided hints of activities that participants can engage in such as rafting. This suggests that in developing a campaign designed to enhance appreciation of the various significant sites of Fayette County, it might help to emphasize the activities that can be done at these sites.

The objective of stimulating intergenerational dialogue about the community was only partially realized. The "Where Is This Place?" activity yielded a fair amount of intensive discussion between family members of different age groups, particularly when one family member–usually the oldest–was able to identify and say a few words about the sites pictured in the photos (Figure 1).

Efforts to encourage participants of various age groups to share their hopes and visions for the future of their communities were less successful, however. The mural painting activity, which was intended to be an intergenerational activity, ended up being a youth activity. Consistent with most activities traditionally conducted at the Fayette County Family Fun Fest event, children and youth did the activity, in this case mural painting, with the parents and grandparents standing behind and watching. Furthermore, the visioning component of the event did not emerge as planned; of the nine murals painted at the event, only one had any elements of something new (i.e., a tree house). Again, this might be a function of the overall event, which was focused on fun activities rather than community reflection.

Reflections

There were some negative as well as positive aspects associated with linking the Fayette County Futures Festival to the Fayette County Fam-

FIGURE 1. Senior Adult as Resource–The "Where Is This Place?" Exhibit and Activity, Fayette County Futures Festival (July 2002)

Photo: Mary Garrity

ily Fun Fest event. On the positive side, this made it easy to work out basic logistics such as location, timing, and food, thus making it possible to conduct the Futures Festival event with very little advance preparation (3 1/2) weeks instead of 2-4 months). Yet, there was also a drawback; the people who traditionally come to the Family Fun Fest event tend to expect fun activities for the children, rather than to engage in dialogue and reflection about community places and issues. To address this problem in future years, the Futures Festival planning team plans to work more closely with Family Fun Fest organizers to ensure that the public is informed about the goals and objectives of the Futures Festival. Planning team members also discussed starting the planning process earlier next year, thus allowing more organizations to be brought in as part of the event-planning team. This also provides time to correct an unintentional omission in the planning process noted above, i.e., the lack of involvement of youth and older adults in the event planning meetings.

Also, as noted in Table 1, and the ensuing discussion comparing this event's mural painting activity to the one organized as part of the Lincoln Place event, a lengthened planning process has implications for generating more intergenerational dialogue and more reflection about future development possibilities.

To reflect further on the limited attention that event participants paid to community development possibilities, it is relevant to note that there is very little mobility in Fayette County. Almost 92% of Fayette County residents in 2000 lived in Fayette County in 1995, and most of these individuals are native-born Americans (99.4%), born in Pennsylvania (87.5%). This lack of mobility combined with the isolation of an insular community leads not only to strong community ties but also to limited visions of development possibilities.

The Lincoln Place Community Pride Festival (Pittsburgh, PA)

Background

Lincoln Place is located on the southeastern tip of the City of Pittsburgh. This quiet residential neighborhood, one of four city communities tucked into the wooded hillsides that make up the 31st Ward, has a population of approximately 3,800 people. It features several churches, a community park, an elementary school, a child care center, a couple of convenience stores, and a dance studio. Lincoln Place residents often refer to their community as the "forgotten" neighborhood. There are people living in Pittsburgh who have never heard of Lincoln Place, and

Lincoln Place residents have the perception that they are often over-looked when authorities make decisions about which neighborhoods will receive city services. Yet, the suburban atmosphere makes it a desirable and affordable place to live for city-employed teachers, fire-fighters and policeman who must reside within the city limits as well as other middle income persons working in construction, production, management-related, and service professions. One challenge facing this community is figuring out how to make it an active, viable community for the residents who span three generations. Many of the older, long-time residents (19.5% of the residents are 65 and over) articulate a strong sense of community identity and pride, but have concerns that such sentiments do not extend to newer residents. Part of the problem is that there are no organizations or organizing efforts that serve to build a sense of inclusiveness on the part of newer residents in the community.

Process

Staff members from Penn State Cooperative Extension and Penn State McKeesport-UCCEP worked with members of a local church congregation to organize this Futures Festival event. Whereas the church members initially saw themselves as holding the festival "for the community" and did not seem to fully recognize the importance of including other groups in the planning of the festival, a common goal was soon established for broadening the base of local participants in the organizing committee. Over the course of a three-month planning process, the planning committee grew to over 25 community residents, project team members and local sponsors.

The planning group decided to name the event the "Lincoln Place Community Pride Festival." There were two reasons for this. First, it was felt that the critical issue facing the neighborhood was the need to build a greater sense of local pride in the area. Second, there was concern that people would not respond well to the concept of a "futures festival." One person on the planning committee stated, "We can't call it 'futures festival.' It's too abstract. People won't know what it means." Though the ultimate goal was still to initiate a visioning process, it was decided to focus on the past and the present in order to first "get people on the same page," a starting point for launching a visioning process.

The Festival was held in two adjacent spaces; one was a big community room in the Lincoln Place Presbyterian Church and the other space was the public parking lot behind the church. Activities/exhibits included the following:

- *Lincoln Place History:* A subcommittee of local residents, infor-
mally called the local "historians," put together a display of vin-
tage photos, maps, and news stories.
- *Now and Then:* This display consisted of the juxtaposition of historical and current photographs of six sites in the community.
- *Dancing–Then and Now:* Children and young and older adults taking dance classes at Mary Ann's Dance Studio jointly performed a
series of dances from different eras.
- *Design the Ideal Community Mural Painting:* Using water-based
paint and brushes, older and younger participants worked side by
side to create three large murals (4′ × 6′) which portrayed collective visions of the community.
- *Time Travel:* This small exhibit included various items from 30+
years ago–e.g., a first generation television set, old dolls, toys, and
books.
- *Tour of the Indian Cemetery:* A series of tours were conducted of
this site which is a centerpiece of a fair amount of local folklore.
- *Tree Planting Ceremony:* A crab apple tree, donated by Penn State
Cooperative Extension and the Southwestern Pennsylvania Community Tree Association, was planted on the grounds of the nearby
elementary school as a symbol of community unity.

Outcomes

The Lincoln Place Community Pride Festival was attended by approximately 300 residents. Most participants arrived in "extended family" clusters of parents, toddlers and children, and grandparents, though
there was an assembly of older adults arriving in pairs and in small
groups. The most significant intergenerational contact occurred during
the painting of the "Design the Ideal Community" murals. Muralists of
ages 3-80 worked together on constructing three large murals. The most
popular items, resounding with muralists of all age groups, were a diner,
a multi-program recreation center, and a camp site/nature preserve. All
three of these elements have in common the characteristic that they provide safe, comfortable places where people can congregate with their
friends. Several of the suggestions for community facilities were age
specific. For example, a couple of teenage boys championed the cause
of inserting a WWW Federation (wrestling) facility. The murals were
kept intact and have been displayed at the City-County Building in
downtown Pittsburgh (Figure 2).

Several activities at the Lincoln Place event were viewed as being part of the exclusive domains of younger or older participants. For example, the older participants tended to gravitate toward the display of photos depicting the community in the past. These images provoked a great deal of discussion and reminiscence among these older adults. In fact, one observer noted that the lively interaction between the seniors reminded him of seeing a group of children trading baseball cards. Although the younger participants at first did not appear interested in the historical photo display, they did ultimately exhibit a keen interest, particularly after a neighborhood history trivia game was initiated in which prizes were awarded to youth who could answer questions about the photos. This turnaround in interest level suggests the importance of careful activity planning.

At the post-event debriefing meeting, Festival organizers judged the event a "success" in terms of bringing an unprecedented number of people and organizations together for an afternoon of enjoyment, celebration of the past and creative visioning of the future. Of particular note was how the event and the event planning process encouraged local community organizations to be more collaborative and community-fo-

FIGURE 2. Envisioning Lincoln Place's Future. Mural Created at the Lincoln Place Futures Festival (July 2002)

Photo: UCCEP

cused in their operations. For example, administrators of the Holmstead & Mifflin Township Historical Society[3] noted that they will make a greater effort to participate in community events, particularly those at which they are likely to meet community residents who are great sources of historical information and photographs.

Reflections

One of the main limitations of this event was the way it was laid out physically. The historical photo displays and food for sale were located inside the Lincoln Place Presbyterian Church community room. The other exhibits and activities took place outdoors, in the parking lot behind the church. As noted above, the photos drew an extensive amount of interest on the part of local senior adults, some of whom stayed indoors for most of the event and missed the mural painting, the dancing display, and other activities taking place outdoors. With more careful planning, exhibits and activities could be arranged in a manner which facilitates a greater level of intergenerational interaction.

Comparing Futures Festival Events

Though both Futures Festival events drew approximately 300 people, there were fundamental differences, primarily in terms of length of the pre-event organizing period, the number of organizations involved in the planning teams, how the events were organized (e.g., whether part of a larger event or as a stand-alone event), and in the activities and exhibits chosen by event organizers to highlight local residents' concerns. Yet, as one similarity between both events, they both included a "Design the Ideal Neighborhood" mural-painting activity.

Table 1 illustrates some of the process and outcome differences in the mural activities enacted in both events. Compared to the mural painting activity at the Lincoln Place event, the one at the Fayette County event yielded more completed murals (9 versus 3), murals with fewer innovative ideas about community development (there were 0-1 versus 4-8 items per mural representing ideas for new community elements), and more limited plans for using the murals after the event. (The Lincoln Place murals were kept intact and displayed at the City-County Building in downtown Pittsburgh, whereas no such plans were made for the Fayette murals.) There was also a fundamental difference in the age composition of the muralists; in Fayette county the participating muralists consisted predominantly of children and youth, whereas the Lincoln Place muralist groups included adults as well as children and youth.

Several of these differences in mural outcomes can be attributed to differences in the planning process which took place for both events. The 11-week planning period for the Lincoln Place event provided time for event organizers to enlarge the event planning group (and this made it possible to enlist several facilitators to stimulate discussion between muralists), engage in detailed review of the underlying intent and operating procedure for each of the planned activities (this helped ensure that event organizers had a common understanding about the event emphasis on promoting intergenerational communication where possible), and to begin discussions about what would take place after the event (e.g., arranging for post-event display of the murals).

In contrast, the 3 1/2-week planning period for the Fayette County event did not provide event organizers with ample opportunity to fully discuss each activity and explore ways to facilitate multigenerational participation and intergenerational communication. The truncated planning process necessitated an emphasis on making quick, efficient decisions rather than on expanding the planning group to include more stakeholders in the planning process. After contrasting both event planning processes, results suggest that the time spent on preliminary orga-

TABLE 1. Comparisons Between Futures Festival Events

Name of Event	Fayette County Futures Festival	Lincoln Place Community Festival
Some basic characteristics of the event	–About 300 participants –F.F. organized as part of another event –Planning process: 3 1/2 weeks –Planning team: 4 orgs.	–About 300 participants –F.F. organized as a stand-alone event –Planning process: 11 weeks –Planning team: 8-10 orgs.
Name of mural-painting activity	"Design the Ideal Community"	"Design the Ideal Community"
# of murals developed	9	3
Avg. # of participants for each mural	3	10
# of new (futures-oriented) items	0-1 per mural	4-8 per mural
Level of i.g. communication (Mural-painting)	Little (mostly children and youth)	Some (mixed-age groups)
Plans for future use of the murals	As "art"	A "statement" of community desires (and "art")

nizing pays dividends in terms of being able to reach out to a broader spectrum of the community and obtain input in organizing activities and framing issues on which to focus at a Futures Festival event.

In the section below, we describe a community needs assessment strategy called "stakeholder analysis" which can be a very valuable tool for systematically broadening the segments of the community that are brought into preliminary planning process for Futures Festival events. It is also an effective strategy for identifying issues of local concern.

"STAKEHOLDER ANALYSIS" AS A PRELUDE TO ORGANIZING FUTURES FESTIVALS

Background

While the Futures Festival events noted above were being planned, staff from UCCEP (Penn State-McKeesport Campus), CEDEV (Penn State-University Park) and Penn State Cooperative Extension were using a "stakeholder analysis" strategy aimed at examining the feasibility of organizing additional Futures Festival events in several areas of the Mon Valley, located south of Pittsburgh along the Monongahela River.[4] Stakeholders are the people, groups and institutions in a community that have a genuine interest in the development of a project or program. A stakeholder analysis identifies the projects' key stakeholders, assesses their interests and evaluates how their interests affect the project's chances of acceptance and success (Allen and Kilvington, 2001). As a result of this community assessment process, three of the Mon Valley communities–McKeesport, Duquesne and Braddock–were identified as prime sites to conduct future Futures Festival and other intergenerational community visioning initiatives.[5]

Stakeholder Analysis

The stakeholder analysis process has three main stages: (1) identify major stakeholder groups; (2) determine interests, importance and influence; and (3) establish strategies for involvement. At all stages, the project team attempts to capture a wide range of opinions of the local community.

Identifying Stakeholder Groups

The project team used a key informant approach to identify major stakeholders in the community (youth, elderly groups, ethnic groups, social service and business groups). Key public and non-profit participants (or informants), identified with the help of UCCEP staff, were interviewed using a semi-structured interview protocol that allowed them to voice their concerns, hopes and ideas in regard to intergenerational communication. As part of the interview, participants were asked to identify up to five other members of the community who might have an interest in an intergenerational program. This "snowball" sampling technique allowed the project team to quickly build a sample of community contacts and identify an initial set of community stakeholders in the project. A partial listing of stakeholder groups includes public housing residents and management; YWCA, Boys and Girls Club and other youth recreation organizations; Social Service Agencies; school district officials; middle and high school students; business owners; local government officials; and members of the Weed and Seed program (federal youth program). In total, there were 35 informants from the entire three-community area.

Stakeholder Interests and Concerns

Below are some of the interest statements coming from our preliminary stakeholder contacts. Each generalized statement is followed by the percentage of contacts mentioning it directly and a listing of the stakeholder groups who identified it.

1. *Younger residents are leaving the area* because of unemployment, crime and lack of youth-oriented activities. (53%: public housing; youth organizations; social services agencies; local officials; retired residents; school district officials)
2. *Violence is an increasing problem among local youth* and the fear of violence is causing divisions between younger and older community residents. (40%; youth organizations; college students; middle and high school students; retired residents)
3. *The community continues to be "close-knit" despite a continued migration of families into and out of the area.* The feeling of being a close-knit community is strongest among older residents. (33%; youth organizations; retired residents; local government officials; school district officials)
4. *Racism is perceived as a major problem in the community.* There are divisions between and within racial groups and this has fueled political conflict, resentment and misunderstanding within neigh-

borhoods. (33%; public housing; social service agencies; youth organizations; retired residents)

5. *Drug use is becoming more prevalent* among area residents–especially among the youth. (33%; youth organizations; high school students; business owners)
6. *Local team sports continues to be an important outlet for youth and a source of local pride.* There are concerns about the availability and access to the sports organizations that exist in the community. (13%; public housing residents; high school students)

The image one gets from this sampling of community voices is that of an urban community struggling to retain its youth in the face of persistent racism, rising unemployment, violence, and drug abuse. In spite of these problems, residents still see their community as "close-knit" although changing rapidly as migration continues to change local demographic patterns. While this "snapshot" of local stakeholder interests and concerns is incomplete, it does give us some indication of the problems facing the community and moreover, a more realistic sense of some of the issues that might be addressed through a Futures Festival visioning process. For example:

- Given the positive feelings many residents express about the close ties they have within the community–is it possible to find a common cultural, historical or emotional "link" with which older, younger, long-time and newer residents can identify?
- Considering the negative feelings expressed about racism, violence and drug abuse–is it possible to find a festival location where everyone would feel welcome and safe to attend?
- Since many local contacts realized the community was losing its youth (and future workers, business owners, voters and volunteers)–could one possible theme among festival organizers be the need to create a "youth-friendly" community?
- Given the importance many people place on local sports teams–would it be possible to weave sports (local sports heroes, clinics, contests) into this local festival as a way to build interest among parents and their children?
- Considering the prevalence of youth problems in the area–is there a pool of senior adults that can be drawn upon to listen to the concerns of local youth and to engage them in constructive activities?

These initial observations and "questions" are only suggestive of a number of complex forces interacting within the community. Furthermore, they only represent a starting point–a baseline for understanding how local residents might begin to successfully organize an intergenerational visioning event in their community. The challenge for community organizers is to help facilitate a process that allows generational groups to foster or rediscover feelings of mutual trust and a shared sense of purpose that commonly exist within "healthy" communities.

EVALUATING FUTURES FESTIVALS

In terms of evaluating Futures Festival events, a distinction needs to be made between assessing impact on those who attend/participate in the festival itself–a one day experience–and impact on those involved in the festival planning process–a 1-4 month process. To assess the former, one or two members of the event coordination team could readily circulate and conduct brief interviews with participants before they leave. The interview could revolve around one basic question, "What did you learn from your experiences today?" Respondents could be further prompted to describe what they learned about the community, what they learned about the needs and concerns of local residents, and how they feel about their role in the community as a result of this new knowledge.

To assess changes in planning team members' perspectives, concerns, and visions for the target community, one strategy is to have them fill out a questionnaire, such as the one presented in Appendix 1, at the beginning of the planning process and again at the debriefing meeting after the event. This particular questionnaire is designed to tap into a number of variables, including community development issues of concern, perceptions of the community concerns of other residents, and views about the value of working with age-diverse groups and promoting intergenerational dialogue on issues of common concern. Insofar as members of the event planning team tend to be community leaders (or potential leaders), a significant influence on how they view the community and its residents, and work to improve the community, can have a far-reaching influence on future community planning processes and outcomes.

Also, considering that some communities may want to establish a tradition of conducting annual Futures Festivals events, to help inform the planning and follow-up process each year, it would be useful to keep a careful record of each Features Festival event, noting the date, collaborating agencies, number of participants, number and nature of exhibits and activities offered, and the ideas expressed for community development and change during the course of each festival.

CONCLUSIONS

There is a paradox inherent in the idea of organizing a community participation "event." No one community event, in itself, could generate a sustainable amount of public awareness, interest, and participation in community affairs. Hence, the Futures Festival approach, at best, needs to be viewed as a beginning, to be followed by additional efforts aimed at broadening the circle of community residents and other stakeholders, extending the dialogue, and promoting an ongoing sense of civic involvement and responsibility. In part, attention needs to be paid to the question of how to extend and strengthen the planning process. In this context, the needs assessment tool of "stakeholder analysis" is presented as a strategy for ensuring a longer, more in-depth, and more systematically conducted pre-event organizing phase. It represents a promising strategy for broadening the circle of participants, and helping them frame the community development issues on which they will focus.

It is also paradoxical to expect that a singular event can engender intergenerational trust and relationship formation. Intergenerational relationships take time and numerous engagement opportunities to form. Before intimacy can be established, there needs to be a period of communication that allows for safe and surface-level contact (Angelis, 1996; Bressler, In Press). Over time and across numerous meeting opportunities, a sense of rapport is achieved, where participants feel more comfortable with personal disclosure (e.g., of neighborhood fears), and trust each other enough to commit to joint action based on similar concerns. Thus, from an intergenerational relations framework as well as from a community participation perspective, it is important to involve youth and older adults early in the event planning process and to work to create interaction opportunities that extend across the periods of pre-event planning to post-event follow-up.

A fundamental lesson learned from both Futures Festival events that were organized is that a "community visioning" process readily includes a focus on collective histories as well as on indigenous visions for future community development. Whereas the originators of the Futures Festival concept focused almost predominantly on the goal of centering people's attention on the future, it soon became clear that local planning teams for both events wanted to discuss community life as it was and as it is, as well as how it could be. Activities and exhibits such as the "Test Your Knowledge" trivia game (Fayette County) and the historical photos exhibit (Lincoln Place) emphasized each area's historical circumstances. After reflecting on this for some time, we now conclude that this emphasis on sharing common histories is an important part of the process, one that can serve as a nice complement for activities and exhibits focused on stimulating dialogue about what people would like to see in the future. Though the event in Fayette County did not stimulate much activity focused on articulating a community vision for the future, we view this as an indication that the community is in the very early stages of a visioning process rather than as a sign of failure of the Futures Festival intervention that was conducted.

Although this article focuses on intergenerational community events organized in the U.S. (Pennsylvania), the organizing and visioning processes are likely to have utility in a wide range of geographic and cultural contexts. Certainly, the local development concerns, local traditions, and the organizations and practices in place for making development decisions are likely to vary across communities and countries. Yet, the idea of broadening the dialogue about community development to include residents of all ages is a theme that should resonate with all sorts of populations. Concern about the future is universal, as is the human desire to contribute to efforts to enhance quality of life. The Futures Festival approach can be modified to fit into all sorts of community celebrations and festivals as found throughout the world, including those that emphasize cultural traditions and historical roots. What the Futures Festival concept adds is a chance to reflect on the role of such traditions and related values when looking forward into the future of the planned community.

In communities that are increasingly composed of younger and older residents from different racial and ethnic groups, the challenge becomes *how* to bring these diverse elements together and facilitate a worthwhile community participation and visioning process. We feel that the Futures Festival model represents a promising approach for extending the community participation arena to include young people and older adults. It also seems to be a potentially effective strategy for providing community development professionals with an additional means for finding out what community residents of all ages know and care about their communities.

However, as noted above, the Futures Festival method is, at best, a beginning point for promoting community participation and intergenerational relationship building. We advocate working to broaden the community intervention platform to include community education and service activity options other than the Futures Festival. One such model is "neighborhood reminiscence," developed by the Netherlands Institute of Care and Welfare as a means for facilitating youth awareness of the community memories and stories of older neighborhood residents (Mercken, 2003). One of the benefits of working with a larger arsenal of intergenerational community participation strategies is that it becomes possible to reach out to a larger number of community institutions and involve a larger, even more diversified audience.

NOTES

1. Whereas in 1900, 4 percent of the population, three million people, were age 65 or older, in 2000, nearly 13 percent of the population, 35 million people, reached this milestone. By 2030, it is estimated that 20 percent of the population, over 70 million people, will be over age 65 (Federal Interagency Forum, 2000).

2. Popular education, as pioneered by Freire (1970), can be viewed as a series of iterative stages in which a project facilitator helps participants to: (1) explore individual experiences; (2) link those experiences with others in the community; (3) make connections between experience and outside knowledge; (4) use the skills and knowledge they have gained; and (5) take action steps to achieve common goals (Arnold et al., 1991). Participants learn from one another by sharing personal experiences and perspectives about the community.

3. This organization was launched in 2001 with the mission of preserving and promoting the history of the original Mifflin Township (established in 1788); it includes 14 western Pennsylvania communities including Lincoln Place.

4. This activity was supported by a small internal Penn State grant secured by the Community and Economic Development Program (CEDEV).

5. The Mon Valley is best known as the former industrial district of the Pittsburgh region. While Mon Valley communities thrived in the early 20th century, they have struggled economically and socially since the collapse of the steel industry in the 1970s and '80s. In recent decades, many of these communities have seen large, steady declines in jobs, housing stock and population. At the same time, there have been significant increases in the number of youth, elderly and minority residents. For example, between 1990 and 2000 the City of McKeesport saw the total population decrease by 8.2% and minority population increase by 7.3%.

REFERENCES

Angelis, J. (1996). Intergenerational communication: The process of getting acquainted. _The Southwest Journal of Aging 12_(1/2), 43-46.

Arnold, R., Burke, B., James, C., Martin, D. & Thomas, B. (1991). _Educating for a change_. Ontario, CA: Doris Marshall Institute for Education and Action.

Bressler, J. (In Press). *Connecting generations, strengthening communities: Handbook for intergenerational programming*. Philadelphia, PA: Center for Intergenerational Learning, Temple University.

Castelloe, P. & Watson, T. (1999). Participatory education as a community practice method: A case example from a Head Start program. *Journal of Community Practice, 6*(1): 71-89.

Crites, M.S. (1989). Child development and intergenerational programming. In S. Newman & S.W. Brummel (eds). *Intergenerational programs: Imperatives, strategies, impacts, trends*. Binghamton, NY: Haworth Press.

Federal Interagency Forum on Aging-Related Statistics (2000). *Older Americans 2000: Key indicators of well-being*. Washington, DC: Government Institutes.

Freedman, M. (1999). *Primetime: How Baby Boomers will revolutionize retirement and transform America*. New York: Public Affairs.

Freire, P. (1970). *Pedagogy of the oppressed*. New York: Herder and Herder.

Friedman, B.M. (1999). *Connecting generations: Integrating aging education and intergenerational programs with elementary and middle grades curricula*. Needham Heights, MA: Allyn & Bacon.

Generations United (1994). *Young and old serving together: Meeting community needs through intergenerational partnerships*. Washington, DC: CWLA.

Henkin, N. & Kingson, E. (1998/99). Keeping the promise: Intergenerational strategies for strengthening the social compact. *Generations, 22*(4). [Special issue.]

Hyman, D., McKnight, J. & Higdon, F. (2001). *Doing democracy: Conflict and consensus strategies for citizens, organizations and communities*. North Chelmford, MA: Erudition Press.

Kalish, R.A. (1969). The old and the new as generation gap allies. *The Gerontologist, 9*(2), 83-89.

Kaplan, M. (2001). The futures festival: An intergenerational approach to community participation. [Web-based curriculum] *http://intergenerational.cas.psu.edu/Futures.pdf*. State College, PA: Penn State Cooperative Extension.

Kaplan, M. (1997). Intergenerational community service projects: Implications for promoting intergenerational unity, community activism and cultural continuity. In *Journal of Gerontological Social Work, 28*(3), 211-228.

Kaplan, M. (1994). *Side-by-side: Exploring your neighborhood through intergenerational activities*. San Francisco: MIG Communications.

Lewin, K. (1948). *Resolving social conflicts: Selected papers on group dynamics*. New York: Harper and Brothers.

Mercken, C. (2003). Neighborhood-reminiscence: Integrating generations and cultures in the Netherlands. In *Journal of Intergenerational Relationships: Programs, Policy, and Research, 1*(1), 81-94.

Newman, S., Ward, C.R., Smith, T.B. & Wilson, J. (1997). *Intergenerational programs: Past, present and future*. Bristol, PA: Taylor & Francis.

Prokopy, J. & Castelloe, P. (1999). Participatory development: Approaches from the global south and the United States. *Journal of the Community Development Society 30*(2), 213-231.

Rappaport, J. (1984). Studies in empowerment: Introduction to the issue. *Prevention in Human Services, 3*, 1-7.

Rosebrook, V. & Murray, T. (1999). "Intergenerational Interactions." Paper presented at the National Association for the Education of Young Children, New Orleans, Louisiana.

Stearns, P.N. (1989). Historical trends in intergenerational contacts. In S. Newman & S.W. Brummel (eds). *Intergenerational programs: Imperatives, strategies, impacts, trends.* Binghamton, NY: Haworth Press.

Will, A. & Kilvington, M. (2001). *Stakeholder analysis.* Manaaki Whenua Landcare Research Institute: Lincoln, New Zealand. *www.landcareresearch.co.nz/* November 2001.

APPENDIX 1. Pre- and Post-Event Questionnaire Tools for "Futures Festival" Events

Name of Event_____

*Name:*_____

*Date:*_____

*Pre*_____   *Post*_____

Contact:_____

Introduction: The_____is a special event that will take place in your community/area. To help us learn how to best organize this and similar future events, we are requesting that you fill out the following survey. Your answers will give us a sense of the issues that local people care about most. It takes about 10-15 minutes. We thank you in advance for participating in this survey.

Date: _____   County in which you reside: _____

Age Category: [circle one]   15-24   25-34   35-44   45-54   55-64   65-74   75+

1. If your community/area has a name, what is it called?

2. How long have you lived in your current community/area?

3. How do you feel about living in this community/area?

4. (a) Do you think there is anything in this community/area that should be changed?
   Yes___ No ___
   (b) If yes, what kinds of changes would you like to see?

5. What about the community/area do you think residents care about most?

6. Who do you think is responsible for deciding what will be built or changed in your community/area?

7. (a) If somebody wants to start a community/area project such as making a garden on a vacant lot or getting rid of an illegal dumping site, what is the first thing that person should do?

   (b) State the additional actions that person should take to set up a community garden project or get rid of an illegal dumping site?

8. How easy or hard is it to do things, such as building a garden or improving housing conditions, which make a community/area better? **[Circle the number for your answer.]**

1	2	3	4	5	9
Very Hard				Very Easy	Don't Know

9. How interested are you in helping to make your community/area better?

1	2	3	4	5	9
Not Interested at All				Very Interested	Don't Know

10. (a) Are there any community/area improvement activities in which you would like to get involved?
    Yes __ No __

    (b) If yes, what are they? If no, why not?

11. List the three local development issues which you feel are most important in influencing quality of life in your community/area.

12. (a) How important do you think is to have young people and older adults talk to each other about community/area issues?

1	2	3	4	5	9
Not Important at All				Very Important	Don't Know

    (b) Please explain your answer:

13. What are some examples of local issues that **both** young people and older adults care about?

APPENDIX 1 (continued)

14. How did you find out about the Futures Festival? [Check all that apply.]

_____ Brochure/Flyer   _____ Newspaper
_____ Extension newsletter   _____ Radio
_____ Friend   _____ Other: _____

Additional Questions to Be Asked **AFTER the Futures Festival**

---

15. (a) Did you learn anything about your community/area from the Futures Festival?
    Yes __ No ___

    (b) If yes, what?

16. (a) Did you get any ideas about things you can do to improve your community/area?
    Yes ___ No___

    (b) If yes, what?

17. How do you think the Futures Festival could be conducted differently to make it more enjoyable?

18. (a) To what extent did your participation in the Futures Festival affect how you view **young people**?

        1   2   3   4   5   9
        None   A Great Deal   Don't Know

    (b) Please explain your answer:

19. (a) To what extent did your participation in the Futures Festival affect how you view **older adults**?

        1   2   3   4   5   9
        None   A Great Deal   Don't Know

    (b) Please explain your answer:

20. How do you feel about the idea of having additional Futures Festival events in your area?

        1   2   3   4   5   9
        Strongly   Strongly in   Don't Know
        Against It   Favor of It

21. List two specific things you learned about the community/area and its residents from your participation in the Futures Festival event

    (1)

    (2)

22. Answer this question **if you are currently employed**.

    (a) What is your job title? _____

    (b) To what extent did your participation in the Futures Festival provide information that will help enhance your job performance?

        1   2   3   4   5   9
        None   A Great Deal   Don't Know

    (c) Please explain your answer:

Terms for Intergenerational Relations Among the Tumbuka of Northern Malawi

Lupenga Mphande

SUMMARY. Culturally enshrined ideas about generational relations affect language, the use of language, and linguistic conventions for expressing these ideas. Generation terms (or age-set terms) distinguish people in the social group according to their age and sex. The age set is a formally organized group of youths, or men or women which has collectively passed through a series of stages each of which has distinctive status, ceremonial, military or other activities. Membership of the group frequently involves ritual in initiation, accompanied by special teaching of the community's law and customs, instructions in sexual matters, and, in some societies, physical initiation that is the mark of attainment of maturity. But how is the system of intergenerational relationship manifested in a particular social group? How do the members of each generation use language differently? How does language treat the generations differently? How do such differences affect our perceptions, attitudes and behavior in everyday life? How do language and behavior reflect unity of the generation groups and their relationship to each other? In this paper we are going to examine the social, cultural, and linguistic characteristics that focus on features common to members of a particular

---

Lupenga Mphande is Associate Professor of African and African American Studies, Ohio State University, 486 University Hall, Columbus, OH 43210 (E-mail: mphande.1@osu.edu).

[Haworth co-indexing entry note]: "Terms for Intergenerational Relations Among the Tumbuka of Northern Malawi." Mphande, Lupenga. Co-published simultaneously in *Journal of Intergenerational Relationships* (The Haworth Press, Inc.) Vol. 2, No. 3/4, 2004, pp. 147-170; and: *Intergenerational Relationships: Conversations on Practice and Research Across Cultures* (ed: Elizabeth Larkin et al.) The Haworth Press, Inc., 2004, pp. 147-170. Single or multiple copies of this article are available for a fee from The Haworth Document Delivery Service [1-800-HAWORTH, 9:00 a.m. - 5:00 p.m. (EST). E-mail address: docdelivery@haworthpress.com].

Digital Object Identifier: 10.1300/J194v02n03_11

generation and account for its relationship to other generations. We will do this by looking at the Tumbuka of northern Malawi, and examining their social organization and the system of terms and social behavior that is employed in addressing and referring to members of a particular generation. The learning of generation-type language by children and cross-cultural aspects of these questions will be considered. *[Article copies available for a fee from The Haworth Document Delivery Service: 1-800-HAWORTH. E-mail address: <docdelivery@haworthpress.com> Website: <http://www.HaworthPress.com> © 2004 by The Haworth Press, Inc. All rights reserved.]*

KEYWORDS. Generational relations, kinship terms, age sets, social groups, social organizations, customs and rituals, language and generational relations, marriage and kinship, community law

Recently, partly as a consequence of the disruptive socioeconomic and political changes in the capitalist world and the renewed concern over their effects on the notion of "family," there is new interest to interrogate the role of the social network and ethnicity in society. In the face of a changing world, people naturally seek security through the certainty of their community values and social interrelationships. Community, thus, provides its citizens with a sense of brotherhood in the sterility of technology and modernity, and against competing groups in a global capitalist structure. But what is community, and how is it constituted? Anderson (1991) argues that communities are not a natural cultural residue left over from the past, but rather a deliberately imagined construct for the pursuit of specific present-day interests of the group or groups of individuals.

The definition of community is important for any discussion on the handing over of traditional values from one generation to the next, and the inter-relationship between the generations. In Africa, where such values are not encoded in print or encrusted in a maze of regal edicts, a clarification of these intergenerational relationships is even more urgent than in the Western world (Crandall, 2000). African societies practice the rites of initiation, circumcision, and language arts where the young need to be trained, apprenticed, and supervised by the older generation, and where the presence of and supervision by elders ensures prestige, continuity and stability in society. How are communities and their social values constructed? How are generations conceived, manifested, and memorialized? How are relations between citizens, and between generations, regulated and with what consequences? Are generations, or the concept of generations, recreated for political expediency, or are they organic to the society's cultural fabric? If so, what are the social mechanisms for their construction and operation? In this article I will examine answers to these questions by looking at language in order to unveil the underlying social structure. I take the view that culturally enshrined ideas about generation affect language and the use of language and that linguistic conventions for expression of generation differences reinforce these ideas. The citizens of the community on basis of gender and generation will exhibit the structure and usage patterns in language. Since each generation is set apart in terms of time and social space, each will use language differently, and in turn the language will treat them differently, and this will affect their perception, attitude and behavior in everyday life. I will do this by examining the structure and usage of the ChiTumbuka kinship lexicon. I take the assumption that the kinship lexicon and its equivalent in the social rule regulates the social relationship between generations among the Tumbuka in the sense that the social structure of a group is likely to be mirrored in its kinship terminology. The first part of the paper gives a brief outline of the location and social organization of a specific Tumbuka clan, and poses the question of how individuals are related to other members in that community. The second part presents the data collected, and the third part analyzes the social and linguistic implications of the kinship terms.

The Rev. Cullen Young, one of the pioneer Scottish missionaries in the then British Central Africa, was struck by the kinship system of the Tumbuka people among whom he worked: "this misty multitude of loosely knit clans . . . [where] the ancestral name was still the bond of union between individuals" (Young, 1923: 28). Young, however, cautioned his overzealous contemporaries who might stray where he had treaded: "incidents in the succession will be made clearer if it is realized at once that 'succession from father to son' does not mean what it does in Britain" (Young, 1923: 81). It appears Young's warning was heeded, for after him nobody ventured again into the study of the intricate kinship system of the Tumbuka until now, so that there is a lacuna in our knowledge about the Tumbuka social structure and its operation. In this paper I want to examine the Tumbuka system of classifying individuals by looking at the interface between language and culture. Who is a person's kin, and how is the structure of the kin lexicon relevant to understanding the social relationship rules in Tumbuka society? In what way does the social rule in that society provide a linearization of lexical items in the language? How are generation-typed language learned by children among the Tumbuka and what are its cross-cultural aspects? These, and others, will be the central questions that this paper will address.

It was with the curiosity whetted by Cullen Young's observation above that I ventured to look again at that "multitude of loosely knit clans" of the Tumbuka people in an attempt to examine the strains that still hold these clans together. In particular, I wanted to examine the structure of ChiTumbuka lexicon and investigate whether there is a social rule that regulates marriage between clans among the Tumbuka, and if so, to find the equivalents of such a rule. In this regard I took the assumption (taken by other researchers in the field) that if such a social rule does exist then it may be reflected in the kinship terms of the language in the sense that the social structure of a group is likely to be mirrored in its kinship terminology, and that, ideally, we can look for the social rule without necessary recourse to lexical encoding. Furthermore, I took the assumption that everybody in the social group shares the underlying linguistic and cultural components for organizing and analyzing the language and social relationships, as kinship is embodied in a bilateral family relationship that is active in productive activities. Besides, social organization can change while language does not.

I think Levi-Strauss is right in saying that if social relations are to be understood or learned, then they must be specified by the linguistic terms describing them, as no Ego can be fully appreciated except in relation to all the other members in a class (1963:42). Although Levi-Strauss' "theory" is so basic a principle that it should presuppose no real cultural content, it is still important to caution against the assumption that what is defined as a key to the set of relations in one culture necessarily assumes a universal function in all cultures (Salzmann, 2004). Clifford Geertz points out that each social group should be studied in its own cultural setting because only in this way can one hope to understand the kind of symbolism the group uses and the way in which it goes about making sense of the world (Geertz, 1973:83).

The original Tumbuka are generally considered to be descendants of the Twa, a Khoi San group that inhabited northern Malawi long before the migration of Bantu peoples from the northeast began to arrive. Today the Twa have virtually vanished, except in folklore, and even their influence on present-day ChiTumbuka language is yet to be systematically studied. The people called Tumbuka today occupy a territory of approximately 20,000 square miles in extent. They are basically subsistence agriculturists, and live by cultivating crops and practicing animal husbandry. They live in a communal existence where food is produced through cooperative labor (Chipeta, 1982). The homestead is the main unit of traditional economy, with the division of labor regulated by sex and age. The data in this paper was collected at Thoza in the Mzimba district of northern Malawi. This site was chosen in preference to other sites because of the author's personal knowledge of the area and its clan's social and cultural background, being his place of birth and upbringing.

Thoza has about eleven villages, covering an area of about five miles in radius. A "village" is here to be understood as a collection of homesteads regarded as a distinct unit, and of such a size that its inhabitants can all be personally acquainted. The village, therefore, defines where one stands, what is proper, and what should be. Villages differ in who lives there (e.g., clans), the way houses are built, the way people marry and socially relate to each other, the way fields are laid out, the way chiefs become chiefs, the intricate set of responsibilities, and obligations that bear on community members.

The village as a social and cultural force has endured in Tumbukaland that continues to suffer from the migrant labor system and economic exploitation in the Southern Africa region. The average population of a village would be about three hundred. The village I studied has four hundred residents, all knit together in clusters or clans of family units or bands. "Family unit" is here loosely defined as comprising of Ego, and all male Ego's affine, and families of Ego's siblings–in other words, a group of people who trace their patrilineal descent to a common ancestor. The village clan thus consists of several such family units, as shown in Table 1.

TABLE 1. The Mphande Clan

O Mphande
1 Banda, Yalelo
2 Banda, Njolinjo
3 Phiri, Kwalila
4 Phiri, Gwamba
5 Saka
6 Chirwa
7 Mwale
8 Nyongo
9 Honde
10 Mkandawire

Note that units like Banda-Yalelo, and Banda-Njolinjo are different families and should not be confused. Although Malawi is predominantly matrilineal and matrilocal, the Tumbuka have patrilineal and patrilocal marriage practices. This means that, among the Tumbuka, women move from their natal homes to their husband's villages. The names of the family units would be used as last names of all members of that unit. The nuclear family unit in this village consists of the Mphandes, which is the largest group, and each family unit with a different clan name is related to the other in the village through them. They are the only family in the village who relate to the other family units directly. This is mainly because a female member of the nuclear Mphande clan first introduced each of the other family units into the village. For example, most of the other family units other than the Mphandes originate from unsuccessful marriages of the female member of the clan. In that case the female member is allowed to return to her original home with her children who would be allowed to establish themselves as a new family unit, related to the nuclear clan through their mother.

In only one instance (the Banda-Njolinjo case) was a family unit introduced into the village by the husband and wife together. A Banda-Njolinjo, who had married a female member of the nuclear clan, decided he didn't want to live with his own paternal people and came to establish himself in his wife's village. However, I treat this case similar to the other cases, i.e., as a case where a family unit has been introduced into the village through the female member of the nuclear clan. Whether she came back alone with her children or was accompanied by her husband is, for our present purposes, irrelevant.

What is important to remember is that the various family units are not related to each other directly but through the centrally placed nuclear clan. Put graphically, the village would look like that shown in Figure 1.

The nuclear family unit has about eighty members in its fold, but on the average each clan has about thirty-five members. The population breakdown is shown in Figure 2.

Each couple lives in their own dwelling unit, and if a man is married to more than one woman, each wife has to be provided with a separate dwelling unit. Of the two men practicing polygamy, one is married in levirate: that is, married to a former wife of a deceased relative. The ten widows are the women who have decided to stay in the village but remain single after their husbands' death. The oldest man in the village is about eighty-eight years old, and the oldest woman is about the same age. It must be pointed out in the foregoing that the ancestral name, e.g., Mphande, denotes clan membership. As stated before, because this is a

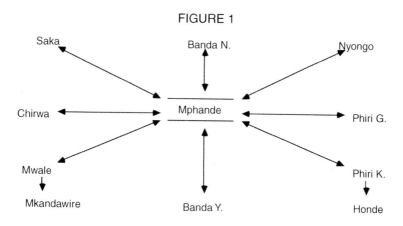

FIGURE 1

TABLE 2. Marriageable Population

Total marriageable population	400
Population nuclear clan	80
Couples: men	138
women	142
Men married to two wives	2
Number of couples in nuclear clan	23
Widows	10
Widowers	1
Girls (marriageable age: 12 years and above)	60
Boys (marriageable age: 15 years and above)	40
Women who come from the village	0

patrilocal society, the women leave their folks to come and live with their husbands, and it is also patrilineal society because descent is through the male. Therefore the members of this clan are related only through males because only male members are found in the village, the female members having married elsewhere.

There are two men having two wives in the Thoza village, and the wives are then called co-wives, and are usually ranked in the order of their marriage to their common spouse. Typically, the first wife has got authority over the other wives and over the husbands' immediate wealth and property. This is the social structure found at Thoza, the network of social relations in which members of the village were involved. Language has to clarify these social relations for members.

The relationship between language and social structure and behavior has fascinated researchers for a long time. Language is part of the culture; it is the primary means of communication (Bonvillain, 1993). But so too are customary acts of behavior. Taboo (an inhibited expression), for example, can be either behavioral or linguistic, and the protective sanctions are much the same. Although what they were actually saying is the source of much debate, in their work Sapir and Whorf, leading American anthropologists in the twentieth century, seemed to suggest that people are prisoners of language because it determines the way they think. Today, however, language and culture are taken as resources that the society draws upon for behavior.

Such a view is most apparent in the study of vocabulary, which has attracted a lot of attention of linguists and anthropologists. Words are taken as a label of aspects of culture, and are thus the cultural index of the cultural world of society. If a language has no term for something, it may mean that thing is probably not important in that culture. On the other hand, if a language has a set of names for something then maybe that thing reflects some cultural essence of the people. Underlying a word is relationship with other words, and the goal of analysis is to discover vocabulary sets that carry the underlying semantic component of the language and a people's culture.

Human beings use space in a patterned way; they have a core area or residence that forms one's immediate environment, a home or community encompassing several groups within which the individual wanders at certain times for certain purposes, and a territory or outer limits which the individual's group will defend from outsiders. Occasional population gathering for community rites dramatically reinforces the demarcation of the second area, the community. If we accept the view that the human community is the basic unit for society and culture, then we should also configure the ways in which human beings act out their various roles within the framework of the community during their lifetime. Community is where culture, the body of learned behavior, is transmitted, where people are trained in tasks appropriate to their age and sex, and inducted into new phases of their life by rites of passage. These activities are performed through institutions that regulate functional activities that relate human beings to each other. But in order for individuals to act their functional roles and hand over the heritage to the next generation they have to have prior knowledge about those roles, and that is why instruction becomes very important in society.

But what is generation? Generation is a single stage in a family history, the average period (usually 25 to 30 years) in which children grow up to become full adults. It is also experience handed down from generation to generation. The generation gap is the difference in attitude or lack of understanding between young people and older people. Rites of passage are stages in the life circle, usually marked off by similar biological crises, such as birth, puberty, procreation, old age, and death. These stages are also categories of particular social roles to be learned and enacted. When human beings pass from one stage of life to another, especially when such transition is marked by a biological life crisis, the change may involve a cultural event known as the rite of passage. Such rites function to regulate a smooth transfer from one role to another. They are social events that may or may not coincide with related biological events. Rites of passage come in three phases: separation of individual from the old status, transition, and reincorporation into a new status. Rites teach and induct, and also compel some persons into new roles while confirming others in old ones. Rites of passage turn boys into men, with the hope of marrying. But the hope of marrying implies that the individual has to be clear how he or she relates to others in society: who are kin and who are not–in short, which individual is a potential spouse, and who is not.

What is kinship? Benedict Anderson defines what he calls imagined community as emerging out of a creative response of peoples' need to organize the world in which they live, and that this involves a certain amount of imagination because the community to which it refers extends well beyond the social network of any one individual, yet assumes that there are those beyond this network who share a similar worldview (Anderson, 1991). This means that different cultures will have different models for reflecting their relationships, and these models of social behavior will be reflected in their languages. Kinship is reinforced by events that pull people together from several social networks, since kin ties extend over several social groups. A funeral, for example, obliges close relatives to gather and mourn, including siblings, parents, children, and mates of the deceased, as well as great-grandparents and great-grandchildren. Funeral, therefore, is a rite of passage more for the survivors than for the deceased since it is the living whose status changes from wife to widow, or child to orphan, etc. Thus rites of passage function not only to move individuals through their life cycles but also to identify the actual spatial context of behavior and the levels of the community. In the induction that is life, the individual has to muster an intricate network of kin and social relationships, and it is language that aids him in this important task by making apparent the various social interconnections. In the kinship system everybody in the community shares underlying components or uniformity for organizing and analyzing the language and social relationships.

Right from birth, the presence of the older generation in a child's life ensures cohesion in the community. In terms of sustenance, the child is a rather passive individual, the food being provided by the mother and caregivers who continue to pour adoration on the child. Among the Tumbuka, this is a period of intense maternal attention–breast-feeding is usually two years, the child sleeps with the mother but moves to the grandmother after weaning. The resident grandparents play such an important role in the child's upbringing through caregiving chores, instruction, and education through storytelling. The child is generally in cooperative mood at this stage, and parents find it easy to train the child without applying physical punishment–the parents never 'work against the child,' and the child negotiates smooth transition to the world outside the household. Language plays a crucial instrument in navigating the way to the child's social and physical environment. In the subsequent training, the child is trained through participation, whether it be hunting or cultivation, emulating older members of the community, always working together in peer groups that foster solidarity and brotherhood/sisterhood. This type of training also reinforces intergenerational interaction because, in all cultural practices, such as initiation, language arts and rites of passage, the youth is trained, apprenticed, and supervised by the older generation. This supervision and presence of elders gives the youth prestige and stability, and help keep the community together.

Some scholars (Whorf, 1956; Leach, 1976) have argued that language and culture determine even what part of our environment is edible. Thus, from this perspective, language does more than provide us with a classification of things; it actually moulds our environment, placing each individual at the centre of a social space that is ordered in a logical and reassuring way. This is a real chicken and egg problem because it's very likely that cultural practice informs native exegesis of linguistic meaning. In Figure 2, for example, do verbal categories set social space in terms of distance from Ego independently of social rules, or do we say that social rules provide a linearization of lexical items?

The succeeding columns of words indicate categories that are progressively more remote from Ego. Thus verbal categorization will have some correspondence to the way in which human beings are categorized with regard, for example, to sexual relations and generation. Those who

FIGURE 2

(a)	Ego	**-dumbu/-kulu/ng'una**	**-vyala-**	**zengezgani**	**-ntu**
	[Ego.....	sister/brother	cousin	neighbour	stranger]
(b)	Ego	**-ʋeto**	**-ʋeto**	**nyama**	**lwani**
	[Ego.....	pet	livestock	'game'	wild]

are in mutually incestuous categories for a male ego (e.g., 'true sisters') and those who are kin but do not belong to mutually incestuous categories (e.g., 'clan sisters') will belong to a category where marriage with Ego is either prohibited or strongly disapproved. The category of neighbors (e.g., friends) who are not kin is the one from which Ego will ordinarily be expected to obtain a spouse, and distant strangers who are known to exist but with whom Ego's kin have established no social relationship of any kind are a possible set of equivalents with wild animals, i.e., of possible danger or enemies. In the set of relationships the language must reassure those individuals with potentially tense relations so that they feel some protective distance from each other. It is against this background and understanding of the social norms of exogamy and endogamy that marriages in the Thoza community take place.

MARRIAGE AND KINSHIP

If social relations are to be understood or learned then they must be specified by linguistic terms describing them, as no Ego can be fully appreciated except in relation to all the other members in a class. Boas (1940) and Chomsky (1968, 1976) have asserted that neither language nor culture rise to the consciousness: it is precisely because we are unaware of the linguistic and cultural structures that we are unlikely to revise them at will or invent 'ad hoc' explanation of their nature and opera- tion.

There are basically three features or social institutions that make people conscious of themselves as members of a particular generation: language (kinship terms), social structure (presence of members of other generations in their midst) and cultural expression (ritual and oral performance). When people migrate they may eventually lose their mother tongue and adopt a new language, and they also lose the basic means of cultural expression and kin networking. Thus, if you adopt English as your new language, then you start talking about "cross cousins twice removed," or "step brother," a phenomena that is meaningless in the indigenous social system. Similarly, among the Tumbuka a child cannot be described as "orphan" when one of the parents is still alive! In Africa today urbanization has brought with it the construction of day care centers and old people's homes that have resulted in the physical separation of generations and impoverishment of society in some fundamental ways. The presence of parents is a trough of cultural treasure as they are the bearers of society's mores, values and specialized knowledge (i.e., medicinal).

In this age of materialism, there is a disconnect between parents and children because the parents are constantly preoccupied with issues of survival and professional development, and no attention is given to the children. This lack of parental attention and supervision forces children to turn to their peers for guidance and solidarity, but the peers are not mature enough to give guidance to the young generation, and this can lead to drug use, reckless partying, violence, gang membership, etc. In the traditional African extended family system these problems are avoided by the constant presence of the older generation in the life of youths, and the coincidence between the peer network and family social network. The urban community tendency to abandon old people to 'old people's' homes' is also an unnatural inversion of the social order: how can you have young people without the balance of old people? Besides, how do you expect old people to impart societal knowledge and values to the younger generation from whom they are physically separated? Surrendering children to day care centers and latchkey programs means that children are being prematurely weaned and disconnected from their cultural umbilical cord, leaving a vacuum in the child's natural development at a critical stage of life, and this can lead to permanent impartment of society. But since nature abhors the vacuum, quickly other forces will step in to fill the gap, usually with children learning from children without supervision from older generations, with dire consequences for the whole society.

Intergenerational relation is crucial for the survival of society, and this interaction takes many forms. Young people go as age-grade when seeking potential spouses, but elders have to approve their desire for marriage. Before two young people can marry, the bridegroom's party must pay the bride's party a minimum of five head of cattle. In "capture" marriage and any form of marriage not duly sanctioned by the two parties in official contracts, the bridegroom's party is automatically fined an additional two heads of cattle. Once a young person has found a possible spouse, one member of the intermediate age-grade is usually authorized by the elders to negotiate a marriage contract, and this is also considered as part of the ongoing training for that intermediate age-grade. The subsequent wedding is another forum for the meeting and cooperation of the generations: young boys tend to the cows for the bride price and wedding feast while young girls help in the preparation for the wedding by participating in singing and dancing, fetching water and firewood, preparing millet and flour, and cooking; young men and women are the main celebrants, mind clothes and costumes to be worn by the bride and groom, and accompany the bride and the groom; men and women are engaged in feasting and beer drinking, and exchanging gifts with their counterparts.

It is important to note that women have a unique value in traditional society as the source of man's posterity. The reproductive function is regulated by marriage, which ensures that men relinquish their sisters in exchange for those of other men, following that unmistakable mark of humanity–the incest prohibition. Marriage directly establishes official relationships between the kin of the bride and groom; ideally it also pro-duces offsprings and hence provides the ideological principle of 'de-scent,' that is, socially recognized common or 'blood relationship.' Marriage thus gives rise to the central or focal social unit of a man, his sister, his wife and their child. See Diagram 1.

Although among the Tumbuka descent through the father is stressed, and children take their identity from him rather than their mother, they are also matrilaterally related by 'blood' through the mother, and we saw how several clans came to settle in the Thoza village claiming this

DIAGRAM 1

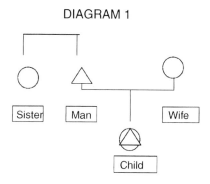

N.B. in kinship diagrams, triangles represent males and circles females. Ties between siblings (brothers and sisters) are represented by l‾‾‾‾l and marriage by l——l
In the diagram above, child is ◯ or △.

relationship. Their patrilineal affiliation makes them, in addition, affines of their mothers.

Another way to explain the difference between kinship and affinity among the Tumbuka is to refer to, say, 'mother' (-mama) as a kins-woman, and 'mother-in-law' (-pongozi) as an affine, and imply, 'inter alia,' that the corresponding norms of behaviour vary. Thus it is clear, in this type of kinship, that, by definition, kins are related by descent, and affines by marriage. Because of the patrilineal and patrilocal nature of their society, the Tumbuka take the former as more important than the latter–but, of course, different cultures stress one relationship at the ex-pense of the others. When rejected by father's kins, sometimes a man turns to his mother's patrilineal clan, appealing to their common matri-lineal relationship. In a situation where a man is dependent on his wife's support, the affinal rather than the blood relationship may be empha-sized.

In its widest sense descent simply means to be related through a com-mon ancestor. Whatever groups are formed by one or the other process of perpetuation, the members of a group will be related to each other by *common descent*; they will be descended from a common ancestor in ei-ther the male line as is the case with the Tumbuka (patrilineal), or the fe-male line as is the case with the neighbouring Chewa (matrilineal), or through links of both sexes (cognatically). Such a group is a *descent group*.

In a binary set of relationships among the Tumbuka, therefore, the re-lation between maternal uncle and nephew (whether it be intimate or formal) is to the relation between brother and sister as the relation be-tween father and son is to that between husband and wife. If one knows one pair of relations, Levi-Strauss says, then it is possible, as in any analogy, to figure out the other (1963:42). The key to the relation is therefore the appropriate unit of analysis which he says "is the most ele-mentary form of kinship that exists. It is, properly speaking, the unit of kinship" (p. 46). Under this analysis a married couple is treated as a sim-ple unit within the kinship system.

Many other researchers have worked in this field of ethnoscience or componential analysis of kinship terminology. Although I acknowledge the strength of the position taken by Lounsbury (1956), Egan (1968), Goodenough (1970) and Burling (2000)–that kinship terminology is a linguistic system and that as such it is likely to reflect such social phe-nomena as marriage, residence, descent, succession, and inheritance–in this paper I argue that language cannot do this independently and that the social rule is the one that provides a linearization of lexical items. I further subscribe to the view of cognitive anthropologists that the correspondence between a community's social structure and its kinship terminology is likely to be found in the structural principles underlying the social phenomena and the semantic principles underlying the kinship terminology, because both are conceptual and, therefore, of the same logical order. F. G. Lounsbury, however, cautions that a formal analysis of a society's kinship terminology should be used "only as a tool for getting at the structure of non-linguistic behaviour within the family and kindred in that society" (Lounsbury 1956:189). My analysis of Tumbuka terminology presented in this paper is intended as further contribution to this growing literature.

TERMS OF CLASSIFICATION OF INDIVIDUALS

A list of twenty most frequently used terms was drawn up after a pilot survey and through my own intuition as a member of the culture. The assumption was that terms are a label of aspects of culture and are thus the social index of the relationships in society. Thus, if a language has a set of kinship terms which are frequently used it must be because they reflect some social essence of the members of the group. These groups were then used in the research where two hundred individual members of the clan were asked to name kins they would include under the term.

Following is an explanation of symbols used in this paper (see Diagram 2).

ANALYSIS

Semantic analysis of kinship terminology has focused on the problem of understanding the meaning of kinship terms, in particular the question of whether a given term is to be understood as applying to all members of a class of relatives, or whether it applies specially to a particular subclass and is then extended to others. The first category can be defined as *simple* class, definable in terms of specific properties common to all its members. The second category is *focus* class, to be described in terms of features common to a focal subclass, but with reduction and equivalent rules which account for the extension of the term to

DIAGRAM 2

F = father M = mother   S = son   D = daughter   C = child,

W = wife   H = husband Z = sister B = brother P = parent.

Thumbuka Kinship Terms

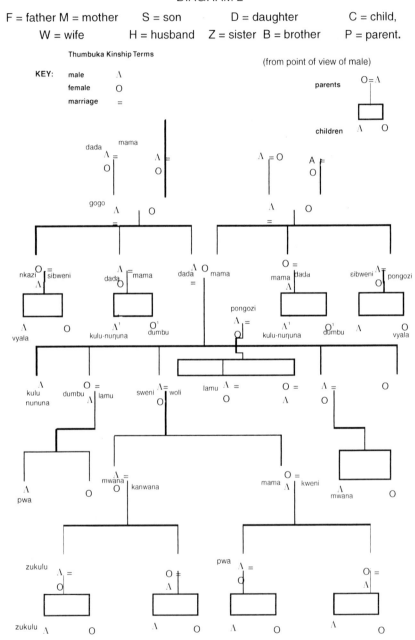

Terms	Focal Types	Extended Types
1. -kulu -nu°una	B/Z (older) B/Z (younger)	FBS, MZS, FBD, WZH, WBW, HBW, FFBSS, FMZSS, FFBSD, FMZSD, FFZDS, FMZDS, FMBDS, FFZDD, FMBDD, FFBDD, FFZSD, FFBSS, MFZSS, MFZSD, MFZDS, MFZDD, etc.
2. -dumbu	B/Z (of any age but of opposite sex)	FBD, MZS, FFBSS, FFZDS, FMZSS, FMBDS, FBD, MZD, FMZSD, FMBDD, FFZDD, MFZSD, etc.
3. -woli	W	
4. -sweni	H	
5. -lamu	WB/WZ ZH/BW	WDC, WFBC, FZDH, MBDH, FZSW, WFZC, WNBC, HFZS, FBSW, MZSW, WMZC, FBDH, MZDH, HFBS, HMZS, etc.
6. -Vyala	FZC/MBC	FZS, MBS, FZD, MBD, FFZCC, MBZCC.
7. -dada	F	FB, MH, MZH, FFBS, FMZS, MMZS, MFZS, FFZDH, FMBDH, MMBDH, MFZDH, etc.
8. -mama	M	MZ, FW, FBW, MMBD, MFZD, FFBSW, FMZSW, MFZSW, etc.
9. -nkhazi	FZ	FFBD, FFZD, FMBD, FMZD, FMDD, FFZSW, etc.
10. -sibweni	MB	FZH, FFZS, MFBS, FFBDH, etc.
11. -pongozi	WP/HP	WFZ, WFB, WMZ, MFBSW, WFFZS, WFFZD, HFFBS, HFB, HFZ, etc.
12. -ana	C	BC, WZC, ZC, FWCC, MHCC, FBCC, MZSS, MBDS, FBCCH, FZDDH, FWCC, WZC, HBC, MHCC, MZCC, MBCC, etc.
13. -pwa	ZC	FZCC, MZDC, FBDC, etc.
14. -khweni	DH	FBCCH, MZCCH, FZCCH, BCH, ZCH
15. -Kamwana	SSW	FBCCW, MZCCW, FWCCW, MHCCW, FZCCW, MBCCW, BCW, ZCW
16. -gogo	PP	FFB, MFB, FMB, MMB, FMZ, MFZ, MMZ, FFZ, FFW, MFW, FMW, MMH, HFF, HFM, HMF, HMM, WFF, WFM, WMM, FFF, WMF, FMF, MFF, MMF, FMM, MFM, FFM, MMM, FFZH, FMZH, MMZH, FFBW, FMBW, MFBW, MMBW, etc.
17. -zukulu	CC	CCW, CCC, BCCC, ZCCC, BCC, ZCC, CCH, etc.

other relatives. We are thus using Ego as the referent point, standing in the middle and looking around at all his kin.

Is the social organization of the Thoza clan described earlier reflected in its terminology for kin, i.e., the system of terms employed in addressing and referring to kinfolk and affines? If it is, how does it do so? In a characteristic feature of classificatory kinship terminologies, a few pri-

mary terms such as 'parent,' 'child,' and 'sibling' elegantly and economically categorize a large array of distinct and, in principle, distingui-
shable relatives. Kinship terminology and behaviour may reflect unity
of the sibling, lineage, and generation groups.

The *generation* terms (or age-set terms) distinguish people in the clan
according to their age and sex. The age set is a formally organized group
of youths, or men or women which has collectively passed through a series of stages each of which has distinctive status, ceremonial, military
or other activities. Membership of the group frequently involve ritual in
initiation, accompanied by special teaching of the community's law and
customs, instructions in sexual matters, and, in some societies, physical
initiation which is the mark of attainment of maturity.

As regards the sibling and lineage groups, descent is one criterion
used to distinguish kin on a focal type scale. *Mu-* and *a-* are prefixes in
the language used for singular and plural, respectively. The prefix *mu-*
is unmarked in ChiTumbuka, and is used to denote 'succeeding' or
'younger' (e.g., *mu-dumbu*, 'younger sister'), and the plural prefix *a-* is
marked and denotes 'preceding' or 'older' (e.g., *a-dumbu*, 'older sister').
Originally the single/plural distinction was only a grammatical distinction of number. However, through a complex series of historical, social
and linguistic process, the singular and plural pronouns have evolved to
bear a pragmatic distinction: second person pronominal choice, besides
fulfilling a deistic distinction, establishes a perceived relationship between the speaker and the addressee. Such a relationship is founded on
variables such as class, age, power, distance, respect, intimacy or solidarity (McLaughlin, 1987:1). As these variables change, so too can the
use of singular and plural pronouns so that, for example, a younger person may call an older person by the singular term *iwe* instead of the expected plural *imwe* to show annoyance or to inflict intended insult.

Similarly, on the extended type scale, Ego still treats those descending from people born before his father, mother, grandfather, etc., as
a-dumbu if they are female. However a person may use *a-dumbu* to a
person who, although 'young' in descent, may be older in age, or may
use it to a younger person to show affection. The compilation of these
terms is based on ordinary use, and the metaphorical use above would
not be ordinary in the sense intended here.

Most of the terms in this clan are confined to kin types of a single
generation, either that of Ego's parents, or his own, or his children's. *A-
dada*, and *a-gogo* thus belong to the ascending generation, while *mwana*
and *mu-zukulu* belong to the descending generation. Grandparent-

grandchild marriage is not allowed among the Tumbuka, but there is a joking relationship between these two generations which is reflected even in the kinship terminology. The word for grandchild is *mu-zukulu*, and this term is commonly used with *mu-nyane* (my compeer). A granddaughter is called by her grandfather *mu-woli* (wife), and a woman similarly calls her grandson *mu-sweni* (husband). Therefore, generation seems to be one important criterion by which the Tumbuka categorize their kins.

However, there are other ways of analyzing the data on Tumbuka kinship terminology, apart from the generation and descent dimensions discussed in the preceding paragraphs. There is, for example, *reciprocity*, which refers to terms used by a related Ego and alter to refer to one another. In part, this dimension has a sexual aspect in that it separates terms for male relatives from those of female relatives:

a-**kulu**´	↔	mu-**nuŋuna**	(same sex)
mu-**dumbu**	↔	mu-**dumbu**	(opposite sex)
mu-**vyala**	↔	mu-**vyala**	(neutral)
mu-**lamu**	↔	mu-**lamu**	(neutral)
a-**sibweni**	↔	mu-**pwa**	(neutral)
a-**pongozi**	↔	mu-**kweni**	(male)
a-**pongozi**	↔	mu-**kamwana**	(female)
a-**dada**´	↔	mwana	(neutral)
a-**mama**	↔	mwana	(neutral)
a-**gogo**´	↔	mu-**zukulu**	(neutral)

Another approach we could use to analyzing the data would have been the bound form usage. This refers to the use of kin terms with forms which enhance their semantic standing, as shown in Table 3.

I did not include this category of the bound form type in Table 3 because they are secondary rather than primary kin terms. Besides, they highlight the problems of translating kin terms from one social organization to another. For instance, you cannot really find terms in this language which are equivalents of say the English step-child, step-mother, foster-parents, etc. This bound form usage would therefore be a doubtful methodological, base to use in describing the kinship terms in this language.

TABLE 3

Term	Description
mwana- mulanda	orphan, both parents dead
mwana-siwa	orphan, one parent dead
mwana-musangapo	step-child

This leaves us with kinship terms categorized on the basis of sex and the marriage roles distinctions. I think the most important criteria for analyzing these terms is the sex of the referent. Terms like *a-sibweni, a-dada* refer only to males, while *a-nkazi, a-mama, mu-dumbu* refer only to females. Table 4 illustrates this point.

Several comments can be made about the semantic system of Tumbuka kinship terminology as illustrated in Table 4. First, the system has terms that are sexually neutral, because its function is to highlight reproductive status. Hence, secondly, there are more terms for women than for men, both with respect to their status in the betrothal stage and in the reproductive stage; *mu-lolokazi* links these stages. Males appear to be placed outside this system after marriage in the terms. Thirdly, if a person is temporarily or permanently out of the system of reproduction (*chi-wuya, mu-chekulu*), or is not placed in it for the purpose of discourse (*muntu*), the terms neutralize the sex/reproductive status. Therefore, the major parameters are reproductive or non-reproductive, then female versus male, and 'before' reproduction versus 'during' reproduction, as illustrated in Table 5.

If the main function of the kinship terms in this language is to distinguish between the marriage roles of the female members of the clan as we have seen, then we still have to explain how these kin terms regulate the relationship between the female members of the clan and their male counterparts. To do this we have to demarcate kinship terminology from kinship as a social status, and examine the relationship between them. We can say that the boundary of the lexicon is established on a basis constant with the fact that Ego's kinsmen belong in the lexicon, while kin of Ego's kin belong outside the lexical field.

But since the lexical kinship domain is not coterminous with socially salient kinship domain, a further question arises: what is the meaning of the lexical boundary? This question recoils back to our main concern in this paper, i.e., the rules that determine these boundaries. We have examined several kinship feature: generation, descent, marriage, etc., and all are coterminous with the lexical kinship domain, so, for one thing,

TABLE 4

Neutral	Female	Male	Description
a. mwana			child
b. mwaniche	1. mwanakazi	mwanalume	suckling baby, female/male
c. nthumbilwa			newly weaned child
Betrothal stage:			
	2. musungwana	musepuka	girl at the age to look after younger children/boy herdsboy
	3. mwali		girl at puberty
	4. ntombi	munyamata	girl eligible for marriage proposal young man (undergone puberty)
	5. mbeta	jaha	girl proposed marriage/candidate for marriage
	6. mu-lolokazi		newlywed wife
	7. wo-mama	ba-dada	ladies, i.e., plural address women/gentlemen, i.e., plural honorary address men
d. Chiwuya			divorced or widowed
e. mu-chekulu			old person
f. mu-ntu			person, probably unknown to speaker
Reproductive stage:			
	6. mlolokazi		newlywed wife
	8. nchembele doda		woman who has given birth/man with children
	9. nchembale-mbeta		woman, divorced with children staying with parents eligible for re-marriage proposal
	10. mama	dada	mother, or honorary address to any woman/father honorary address

the boundary of the lexical field is the boundary of the incest taboo. The lexicon is thus 'exogamous,' and tells Ego which people are suitable candidates as spouses. *A-nkazi, mu-pwa, a-gogo, mu-zukulu, mu-dumbu*, and their mothers and daughters are thus off-limits for the male Ego.

However, we have left out two female kinship terms for the male Ego: *mu-lamu* and *a-pongozi*. The *mu-lamu* category of kins, like that

TABLE 5

Terms	Age	Sex	Marriage Status	Ever Married	Now Married
mu-**ntu**					
mu-**anakazi**					
mu-**analume**					
mu-**ana**	0-9	F/M	S	–	–
chivuza	0-1/2	"	S	–	–
mu-**aniche**	0-2	"	"	–	–
nthumbilwa	2-9	"	"	–	–
mu-**sepuka**	9-13	M	"	–	–
mu-**sungwana**	9-13	F	"	–	–
mu-**ali**	puberty	F	"	–	–
nthombi	mature	"	"	–	–
mu-**nyamata**	"	M			
jaha	"	M	"	–	–
mbeta nchembele-	"	F	"	–	–
mbeta	"	F	"	+	–
mu-**lolokazi**	"	F	Wed		+
chi-**uya**	"	"	Divorced	+	–
mu-**chekulu**	old	F/M			

of *mu-vyala* and *a-gogo*, has got a joking social relationship with Ego, whereas the *apongozi* kinship is based on avoidance social relationship. *Mulamu* includes Ego's brother's wife (or husband's brother) and wife's sisters (or sister's husband). Among the Tumbuka, Ego can marry brother's wife in levirate, and in polygamous cases there are people married to their wives' sisters. Therefore the *mulamu* term picks out from the social group those relations who would be suitable wives.

The term *a-pongozi* is more complicated because it is based on avoidance social behaviour. *A-pongozi* includes two important or focal relations: HP/WP and MBW. It is interesting that these two groups of people should be terminologically equated because, although marriage between Ego and children of HP/WP is permitted, that between Ego and children of MBW is prohibited. There is no parallel or cross-cousin marriage among the Tumbuka. In fact when FZ returns from her marriage and resettles in the village with her children then there is usually a terminological shift: her female children cease to be *mu-vyala* and become *mu-dumbu*. Since *mu-dumbu* is based on sexual distinction while *mu-vyala* is not, this shift can only be done to prohibit any contemplation of cross-cousin marriage.

But Ego can marry children of MBW's kin, on the same linguistic basis we examined earlier, that 'my' kin's kin is outside the lexical kinship field. If Ego can marry children of kin of MBW, that now equates MBW with WP, and hence resolves the apparent complication.

The operation of the marriage rule also affects the genealogical and economic structures of Tumbuka society, the details of which are outside the scope of this paper. Suffice it to say that genealogically, marriage is prohibited within the same clan. Ego's spouse does not really belong to Ego's clan, and that's the other reason why wives retain their maiden names. This makes them free to choose to remarry Ego's kin after Ego's death, and male Egos are free to marry their spouse's sister.

Economically it is an advantage if new members are recruited into the clan. If marriage was permitted within the clan this would *not* necessarily increase the numerical strength of the clan–an important consideration in a communal existence. Therefore the social and economic demands, reflected in the linguistic structure, compel the clansmen to recruit members from outside their clan (Stockard, 2002).

By having features like 'elder' brother, 'younger' father, 'younger' uncle, etc., the language simplifies the social structure giving important guidelines on matters of descent, inheritance and succession. This means that even if somebody else is the current village headman, there is no confusion at all as to who is the real 'spiritual' head of the clan–the linguistic network of kin terms will provide the answer at any one time.

In conclusion, it is clear from my analysis that by using kinship as a connection between known cultural realities (genealogy) and language forms (kin terms), i.e., as a base for studying semantics, it is possible to uncover social boundaries that provide a linearization of lexical items, and it is my opinion that among the Tumbuka these social boundaries are based on descent, inheritance, succession, the communal economic fabric, 'generation' terms and reproductive status. In this paper I have examined in detail only the marriage dimension.

I have also demonstrated how a clan, one of the principal building blocks in the ethnicity structure, is constructed and functions in its linguistic and social modes. These conclusions are important at a time when genocide, globalization, and violence has made scholars scramble to explain the phenomenon of community and its set of values.

REFERENCES

Anderson, B. 1991. *Imagined communities: Reflection on the origin and spread of nationalism.* New York: Verso [first published by Verso 1983].

Boas, F. 1940. *Race, language and culture,* New York: Macmillan.

Bonvillain, N. 1993. *Language, culture, and communication.* Englewood Cliffs: Prentice Hall.

Burling, R. 2000. *Learning a field language.* Prospect heights, IL: Waveland Press (first published 1984).

Chipeta, C. 1984. *Economics of indigenous labour.* New York: Vantage Press.

Chomsky, N. 1968. *Language and the mind.* New York: Harcourt & World.

Crandall, David, P. 2000. *The place of stunted ironwood trees: A year in the lives of the cattle-herding Himba of Namibia.* New York: Continuum.

Egan, F. 1968. "One hundred years of ethnology and social anthropology." In *One hundred years of anthropology,* edited by J. O. Brew. Cambridge, MA.

Geertz, C. 1973. *The interpretation of culture.* New York: Basic Books.

Goodenough, W. H. 1951. *Property, kin, and community on Truk.* New Haven: Yale University Press.

Jones, W. J. 1990. *German kinship terms* (750-1500). New York: W de Gruyter.

Leach, E. 1976. *Culture and communication.* Cambridge: Cambridge University Press.

Leedy, L. c1995. *Who is who in my family?* New York: Holiday House.

Levi-Strauss, C. 1963. *Structural anthropology.* New York: Basic Books

Lounsbury, F. G. 1956. "A semantic analysis of the Pawnee kinship usage." In *Language* 32:158-94.

McLaughlin, F. 1987. "Use of singular/plural among Senegalese urban population." Unpublished paper.

Salzmann, Z. 2004. *Language, culture and society.* Westview Press.

Stockard, J. E. 2002. *Marriage in culture: Practice and meaning across diverse societies.* San Diego: Hartcourt.

Whorf, B. L. 1956. *Language and thought, and reality; selected writings of Benjamin Lee Whorf.* John B. Carroll, ed. New York: Technology Press of MIT.

Young, C. 1923. *Notes on the speech and history of the Tumbuka-Henga peoples.* Livingstonia: Livingstonia Press.

Transformations over Time
in Generational Relationships in Africa

Choja Oduaran, PhD
Akpovire Oduaran, PhD

SUMMARY. Generational transformations over historical time and space in Africa have featured a mixture of the "good" and the "bad." The valuable interactions and relationships that endured in our traditional communities typify the good. The bad, on the other hand, is typified by the alterations that our cultures have witnessed as a result of profound and, sometimes, negatively influencing foreign contacts that have put in jeopardy whatever we had cherished in our generational relationships in the past. However, it is obvious that Africa cannot remain in the past in a globalizing and modernizing world. We live in the present, and therefore our peoples must engage in the deconstruction, reconstruction and transformation of whatever could help them maintain some degree of cultural development. *[Article copies available for a fee from The Haworth Document Delivery Service: 1-800-HAWORTH. E-mail address: <docdelivery@haworthpress. com> Website: <http://www.HaworthPress.com> © 2004 by The Haworth Press, Inc. All rights reserved.]*

Choja Oduaran is affiliated with the Department of Educational Foundations, University of Botswana, Gaborone.

Akpovire Oduaran is affiliated with the Department of Adult Education, University of Botswana, Gaborone.

[Haworth co-indexing entry note]: "Transformations over Time in Generational Relationships in Africa." Oduaran, Choja, and Akpovire Oduaran. Co-published simultaneously in *Journal of Intergenerational Relationships* (The Haworth Press, Inc.) Vol. 2, No. 3/4, 2004, pp. 171-185; and: *Intergenerational Relationships: Conversations on Practice and Research Across Cultures* (ed: Elizabeth Larkin et al.) The Haworth Press, Inc., 2004, pp. 171-185. Single or multiple copies of this article are available for a fee from The Haworth Document Delivery Service [1-800-HAWORTH, 9:00 a.m. - 5:00 p.m. (EST). E-mail address: docdelivery@haworthpress.com].

http://www.haworthpress.com/web/JIR
© 2004 by The Haworth Press, Inc. All rights reserved.
Digital Object Identifier: 10.1300/J194v02n03_12

KEYWORDS. Generational, community relationships, familial relationships, Africa

INTRODUCTION

A transformative approach to the discourse of generational relationships in Africa over historical space and time can almost automatically liberate us from the "sin" of what Carlos Fuentes (quoted in Jenks, 1993, p. 120) once defined as "historical ignorance." For as Carlos Fuen- tes said:

> *If we are ignorant of the past, we will be obliged to declare that everything durable in our societies was constructed by ghosts; and consequently we ourselves are nothing more than the souls of the departed. Without the culture of tradition we would not have the tradition of culture. We would be orphans of the imagination.*

> *–Carlos Fuentes (quoted in Jenks, 1993, p. 120)*

Fortunately, as far as the African discourse of generational relationships is concerned, we may not become orphans of our imagination. For generational relationships in traditional Sub-Saharan Africa had been well constructed and transmitted with some degree of dexterity before the nascent altercation that seems to be rendering what we had inherited over the years almost diminutive and worthless in complete surrender to the so-called modernism and, now postmodernism (Jenks, 1993). Therefore, what we seek to do in this paper is to explore very briefly and, perhaps, superficially the transformations that might have occurred over time in Africa's generational relationships. Thus far, the literature search has not yielded any serious attempt to conduct the kind of exploration intended in this discourse. Much of what is available in terms of scholarship on generational relationships in Sub-Saharan Africa are descriptive surveys of the so-called contemporary generational relationships in particular locations in Africa (Gush, 2002; Hoffman, 2003; Oduaran, 2003). This paper is therefore very important and timely for the major reason that it attempts to highlight generational relationships in Sub-Saharan Africa over historical space and location. It might have the added advantage of not only filling a yawning gap in the literature on the subject in Africa but also that of giving some lead towards future directions in the advocacy for recognizable and effective foundation-lay-

ing activities that could strengthen generational relationships in the continent. Whatever gaps might emerge from this exercise should offer further opportunities for explorations, productive criticisms and meaningful debates.

CONCEPTS

Two major concepts would be operationalised here in order to make
the discourse more meaningful. The first of such concepts is generational relationships, and the second is that of cultural reproduction in
which Sub-Saharan Africa's generational relationships are located.

Generational Relationships

The direction of the debate and scholarship on generational relationships seem to suggest that we are still "locked" up in scholastic paradox.
For the way some scholars use the concept seem to suggest to us that we
will soon be drawn into very serious disciplinary boundary contestation
with scholars in the fields of social welfare, social work and education.
Sometimes, we wonder if generational relationships, as a concept, can
safely adopt the nomenclature of social welfare and education. We
doubt very much. That is not to say that generational relationships cannot manifest the features of either sister disciplines by the manner of its
operation. At the same time, we believe that generational relationships
should and could carve out a niche for itself as it begins to develop and
become a veritable caveat for resolving serious relationship issues in the
private or individual and public and community domains. Without
wanting to rehash all the advantages and, perhaps, limitations of conjec-
turing a stand alone definition of generational relationships, we are
adopting in this discourse the proposition already made by Oduaran
(2003, p. 28) to the effect that we uphold in whatever definitions of generational relationships anyone might choose to adopt the following features:

- involvement of all generations, irrespective of age, gender, race,
location and socioeconomic status;
- uniting effectively in the process of generating, promoting, and
utilizing ideas, knowledge, skills, attitudes and values in an interactive way; and

- applying the outcomes of such unification and interactions to the improvement of self and the community.

That is how we shall conceptualize generational relationships in this paper and the outline discussion beginning from the pre-colonial running through the colonial and to the present times.

Cultural Reproduction

As already pointed out, generational relationships in Sub-Saharan Africa may be said to be clearly and squarely located in cultural reproduction. However, what is cultural reproduction?

Cultural reproduction, as a concept, was first used and developed by the French sociologist and cultural theorist Pierre Bourdieu in the early 1970s (Jenks, 1993, pp. 1-3). At that point in time, the concept was used frequently and mainly to emphasize the emergent quality of experience of everyday life–usually through a spectrum of interpretations. As Jenks (1993, p. 1) observed, the concept serves the purpose of helping us to articulate the dynamic process that gives meaning to utter contingency of, on the one hand, the stasis and determinacy of social structures and, on the other, the innovation and agency inherent in the practice of social action.

The concept of cultural reproduction is being adopted in this discussion because a discourse in generational relationships in Sub-Saharan Africa cannot be divorced so easily from the African culture itself. As Malinowski (1944, p. 17) posited, culture mostly consists of ". . . inherited artifacts, goods, technical process, ideas, habits and values." For Jenks (1993, p. 3), culture, as a process, tends to be emergent, forthcoming and continuous in the way it reproduces itself together with its entire social processes tacitly reflected on the grounds and parallel context of social action.

We probably know that cultural reproduction helps communities to meet certain needs. For Africans, cultural reproduction enables our communities to contemplate the necessity and complementarity of continuity and change in social experience. When applied to generational relationships in Sub-Saharan Africa, it guarantees the continuous cherishing of the values our peoples attach to wisdom and the high esteem in which they hold the elderly. For the elderly represent our rich past. Indeed, the elderly are the custodians of our history and culture. Our culture emphasizes communal existence, and any problem that confronted anyone member of our community is assumed as one that confronted all. Fortunately, the cultural reproductive nature of generational relationships in Sub-Saharan Africa does not take the form of reproduction as copying or imitating. Far from that, it takes the form of regeneration and synthesis as future generations seek to improve on practices that were in existence.

SCOPE OF THE DISCUSSION

Even though good scholarship demands it, the presentation and discussion of generational relationships and transformations in Africa from historical perspective is presently undoubtedly hampered by a dearth of relevant written records. It is also limited by the absence of reliable data, and this will probably remain unattainable for a long time to come, and this is especially for the pre-colonial era. This also means that African generational relationships research is yet in dire need of valid historical reconstructions of what prevailed in the past. When research and scholarship get to attain this academic apogee, we can then hope to generate sufficient theoretical and conceptual models of the impact of social change on generational relationships and practices in the present age and time. When that time comes, we would be able to table for debate the contrast between the past and the present in terms of gap.

Moreover, the transformative nature of generational relationships in Africa cannot be constructed perfectly through what Parsons (quoted in Malinowski, 1944, pp. 14-17) once described as *"mosaic atomism."* This is so because Africa is so diverse and vast that one cannot easily take a few cases of what is happening and proceed from there to generalize for the entire continent. It is also not possible to isolate the myriads of traditional communities and exhaustively examine the cultivation of generational relationships over historical time and space in an exploratory discourse of this nature. However, among the discontinuities one may identify in African cultures, there are common grounds and commonalities, and it is in such foundations we premise our discussion. For example, discontinuities are characterized by the distinct and different colonial heritages. They are also characterized by differing geographic facts and effects, socioeconomic and political systems together with political upheavals in different African modern states. For the common grounds and commonalities, it is possible for us to draw attention to the fact that even though the 1884/85 Berlin Conference allowed the partition of African peoples speaking the same language and sharing the same culture between different European colonial powers, such people have continued to identify themselves as having originated from the same ancestors. For example, the Yoruba who are mostly found in Nigeria and to some extent in the Benin Republic and those of them in diaspora in Brazil and the Caribbean have continued to cherish their unity, love and common heritage. Similarly, the Setswana-speaking peoples that are geographically located in Botswana and South Africa have continued to cherish their common heritage, love and unity to date. Such are the similarities that these groups and others share that it is quite possible to generalize with some degree of correctness about the performance of generational relationships among different African groups. So then, we are able to make some tentative description and discussion of what has happened and continues to happen in some English-speaking African modern nation states, beginning from pre-colonial times and terminating in the present. To that extent, our discussion must have some limitations that are possibly obliterated by the fact that the linguistic divisions among Africans are simply colonial artifacts that can easily be nullified by the similarities of our cultures, whether we are Lusophone, French and English-speaking Africans in the Sub-Saharan African region.

GENERATIONAL RELATIONSHIPS IN TRADITIONAL AFRICA

By traditional Africa, we refer to what happened in our communities before colonial rule was introduced. Today, traditional communities are best represented by our indigenous peoples and their communities. Indigenous peoples are defined by Beauclerk, Narby and Townsend (1998, p. 3) as human groups whose ethnic characteristics, cultural traditions and methods of using resources and technology distinguish them from the majority of people in the nation state. Although this kind of community is already being subjected to the whims and caprices of the so-called modernity and thereby made vulnerable, the indigenous peoples in Africa still cherish and keep all that had held their societies together in terms of relationships among cohorts of human groups within them. They share many things together, and among such things are problems and challenges, wealth, land, sustainable use of resources and kinship. Those were the kinds of things that shaped generational relationships in traditional Africa.

In traditional Africa, the different cohorts of generations were constituted along the lines of:

- Those who are physically alive;
- Those who are departed but whose souls and spirits are very much alive; and
- Those who are yet to be born.

Among those who are physically alive, the cohort was arranged according to age-grade groupings but at a macro level–the young, the adults and the elderly. By far the most revered and respected among these groups was the elderly. We had already alluded to the reason as to why this is the case. In Africa, ancestral worship was strongly upheld prior to the coming in of other cultures. Prior to that time, the elderly were respected for they were presumably nearer the ancestors. They were not only community custodians of wisdom but they were the pivot of the spiritual and judicial systems. It was widely believed that to disrespect the elderly was to invite the wrath of the gods of the land. Anyone who chose then to disrespect the elderly was to have himself/herself to blame. The elderly were the traditional philosophers who handed down orally the patterns of relationships and interactions. Generational relationships relied so strongly on African cultural philosophies. Hoffman (2003, pp. 173-174) has reported on one of such cultural philosophies known as "ubuntu" in South Africa and, indeed, its equivalents among other diverse traditional communities. For example, among the Urhobo ethnic group in the Delta State of Nigeria, "ubuntu" is verbalized as "ekwogbe." As Hoffman (2003, p. 174) points out, "ubuntu" represents the philosophy of human solidarity and this embraces co-operation, compassion, communalism, respect and the emphasis placed on dignity in social relationships and practices. In other words, generational relationships in traditional communities were constructed and cultivated in the people's ways of living. Consequently, generational relationships in Africa could be said to be firmly rooted in the spiritual, philosophical, sociocultural, and experiential manifestations of living among the Zulus of South Africa, for example. In all these aspects, traditional, religious and metaphysical beliefs play primary roles in the way the young, adult and elderly persons interacted and related in the sacred, material and spiritual existence of our peoples.

Generational relationships in pre-colonial or traditional Africa, especially among the Edos and the Urhobos of Edo and Delta States of Nigeria, respectively, took the form of social action for it depended largely on its African context and the generation of competence in the way people related and interacted. It also took the form of an original, coherent, intelligent, reliable, accepted and, sometimes, unspoken social structure. At that time, generational relationships were an integral whole of the African culture and in that context, it featured unwritten charters of actions and activities for different social groupings of African communities whose beliefs, customs and values continuously struggle with some- what stronger external influences.

The primary objective of the generational relationships was how to cultivate and nurture the social equilibrium of the community in the first place. Secondly, there was a strong desire to keep in focus the kinship relationships that existed for they helped in ensuring that the socioeconomic inability of a kinswoman or kinsman did not ruin his/her emotional stability. Moreover, the anchorage on the ancestors and lineages also ensured that people understood their roots.

Generational relationships in traditional Africa relied on the use of moonlight stories, ancestral worship, art forms and then proverbs for effectiveness. In other words, the mode of operation relied on existing social structures and methodologies of delivering indigenous knowledge. Let us take for the sake of illustration the use of proverbs as a method for generational exchange. Among Africans in the pre-colonial existence, proverbs were considered as veritable means of communication. Proverbs, in agreement with the views of Kaplan (2002, pp. 39-40) quoting Farghal (1995), reflect our culture and have served, from time immemorial, as the linguistic means of expressing our ideals, values, beliefs or convictions and everything that we hold dear to ourselves as individuals and to our communities. We conceptualize in this instance only proverbs that do not convey what has been described as stereotypical and defamatory notions about groups of people based on the notions of ethnicity, age, religion or any other kind of characteristic (Nuessel, 2000, quoted in Kaplan, 2002, p. 40). Proverbs were expertly used in driving home the virtue of good behavior, cooperation and understanding among members of the community.

At the level of individuals, it was not possible to allow a profound degree of individualism to prevail. For example, traditional communities among the Urhobo ethnic group in the Delta State of Nigeria did not give room for anyone to want to live by himself or herself all alone. There must be someone always wanting to find out if you were doing okay even in what some may today term as personal and private matters. In those communities and many others yet unresearched in terms of generational relationships, the systems and structures were fairly stable before external contacts came along to influence them in different ways. Among the Urhobos of Nigeria, it is no longer "fashionable" to allow the elderly of a given family complete responsibility for the upbringing of grandchildren.

THE COLONIAL LEGACY

The first of such contacts was, first of all, from the broad and, sometimes, militant Islamic forays from the Arab world, beginning from the 11th century A.D. From about 1460 A.D., the explorations of the continent by curious European explorers had paved the way for Christian missionaries from the West to venture into "unknown" lands. Both external influences were significant in eventually working covertly or overtly to modify, or reshape, the structure, focus and processes of generational relationships in Sub-Saharan Africa.

The tacit effect the coming of external cultures had on generational relationships in Sub-Saharan Africa was both symptomatic and reflective of what Jenks (1995, p. 5) has termed as "high culture." In that case, external interventions from the Arab and then the Western worlds unchallengingly, so it seemed, took the African culture as the "low" culture that needed to be salvaged by the so-called more sophisticated and/or civilized "high" culture of the Arab and Western worlds. African cultures, in the frameworks and operations of these explorers and religious crusaders, were deemed as "stagnant, primitive, less developed and largely unhelpful" (Jenks, 1995, pp. 5-7). At that point in time, few people saw anything good in the traditional cultures, especially their utility in terms of strengthening generational relationships. At that point in time, African generational relationships became a hapless cultural item that needed to be panel beaten to suit the ideals and purposes of the "civilizing" external cultures. African cultures were evaluated against the so-called universal standard offered by Western culture. So where did African generational relationships stand in both the colonial arrangements?

Generational relationships under the colonial system were largely Western. It is perhaps natural under colonial arrangements to find that the institutions and systems of the "guest" ruler would be enthroned upon the institutions and systems of those who had been colonized. With the establishment of European political rule in almost all of Sub-Saharan Africa after the partition of Africa in 1884/1885, newer welfare systems and systems of generational relationships were introduced. We began to have several welfare institutions, especially in the British ruled colonies. We began to have remand homes, foster homes and old people's homes. With the coming of old people's homes, the elderly were isolated from the rest of the communities and they were looked upon as another kind of species that must be removed from their grandchildren and great grandchildren. Luckily, the practice was then predominant in urban areas. The rural communities continued to hold to whatever was left of the rich past but that they did with some success. For as people began to acquire Western education, all the Western value systems were also passed on and societies got more urbanized and somewhat impersonal. The media of mass communication that came along at that time also helped in subtle ways to entrench Western values, interests and tastes. At that point in time, one could not say that there were still much of the traditional exchanges among the children, adults and the elderly that had existed before the intervention. It was at that point in time that the elderly suddenly became, as Hoffman (2003) puts it, dreary in outlook as a consequence of the aging process, and belief systems began to emerge that ascribed to the elderly magical powers. It was common at that point in time to ascribed to the elderly some kind of "unsubstantiated" linkage to witchcraft and wizardry and power to place a curse upon any erring member of the community. Thus, it could be assumed that the educational, social and modern communication systems that were introduced into Africa did alter to some extent the values attached to generational relationships.

POST-COLONIAL GENERATIONAL RELATIONSHIPS

By post-colonial generational relationships we imply the exchanges that took place in the years immediately preceding independence and the years immediately after. For from about 1950 Sub-Saharan Africa began to witness vigorous movements for independence. Political independence had meant the management of our social and economic affairs as best as we could. Unfortunately, it had not been possible to glean from the literature any profound transformations in terms of generational relationships that tended to revive what we had lost to the coming of foreign rule and influences. Rather, the political elites sought to entrench whatever they had inherited. What then followed were more moves towards Western civilization, value systems and urbanization. Indeed, it was fashionable then to be Western in outlook, habits, tastes, interests and values. What that meant was that the institutions and systems introduced during the colonial rule became even more entrenched. It should not be surprising then that it was only in recent times that political leaders are now beginning to talk about the African renaissance that is intended to bring to the fore everything that was good in our past. Hopefully, generational relationships that prevailed before the introduction of colonial rule may be rejuvenated as a major strand in Africa's indigenous knowledge and social systems.

CONTEMPORARY TRANSFORMATIONS IN GENERATIONAL RELATIONSHIPS

Sub-Saharan Africa is part of the modern world. The modern world itself is industrial, expansionist, capitalistic and bureaucratic. It is industrial because it is committed to the domination of humankind over nature; expansionist because it is committed to "growth" foisted on the flag post of the division of labor from a stable, contained, simple society to heterogeneous, diffuse organismistic urbanized societies; capitalistic because it seeks to accrue profit; and bureaucratic because it attempts to handle and control all aspects of being through rational process (Jenks, 1993, pp. 126-127). That observation implies for Africa the fact that generational relationships are being influenced by industrialization and urbanization, expansionism, capitalism and bureaucracy. How could this be the case?

Industrialization and urbanization have drawn Africans away from compliance with and reverence of nature and the primary role the extended family system usually played in generational relationships (Itoe Hampson, 1982, p. 1). Industrialization has drawn Africans to the side effects of manufacturing processes wherein, as Jenks (1993, p. 123) observed, the benevolence of a few industrialists continue to cause some of the other or less privileged Africans to see themselves as paupers whilst taming the so-called wild and irrelevant African cultures that needed to be whipped into strict compliance.

Expansionism practices of the industrialists often cause the fragmentation of the hapless poor who is forced to consume the products of industrialization together with the accompanying culture.

It is also true that capitalistic existence has tended to dash into pieces the hitherto caring attitudes of the African. Most people, especially the educated, have been compelled by circumstances probably beyond their control to embrace egalitarianism or elitism as well as profit-making tendencies in which relationships are objectified and commercialized.

Bureaucratic existence seeks to treat and control all aspects of being through rational process (Jenks, 1993, p. 127). Under that kind of arrangement, people, ideas, or relationships must be properly and appropriately processed so that they can be produced in a tangible, object form. We had argued earlier that this kind of productive object- ification of personal and community existence had collectively cultivated and foisted upon us all the new emphasis on individualism in which people tend to be personal or individualistic, selfish and protective. Under that dispensation, generational relationships begin to be quantified and valued in terms of the costs that such relationships might involve. Under arrangement, the youth, the adult and the elderly are further driven apart so much so that we now have to learn new principles in relating to one another. For example, an elderly grandparent cannot simply "jump" on the road nowadays to visit with the children or grandchildren for that matter without having given notice of such visits and then requiring approval from those being visited. That had never been part of Sub-Saharan African cultures.

In the modern African societies, traditional knowledge and social influence, especially in the urban centers, are fast declining in importance. As Gush (2002, p. 243) has rightly observed, older people are no longer the source of authority they used to be. This is even more so because there is less need for and less value that continue to be attached to traditional knowledge and skills in the nascent globalizing African economies and societies. Exposure to the Western media of mass communication and the new information communication technologies have meant that people should look up to the West for their social, cultural, economic and political "salvation."

Although contemporary generational relationships have not yielded much information as to the level of improvements one may quickly observe in Africa, we can propose some aspects in which they seem to be operating with some degree of success. Africa is pursuing the appreciation and adoption of the concept of African renaissance that would emphasize generational relationships and the African concept of sharing, caring and mutual respect among all generations. The non-governmental sectors are ingeniously putting emphasis on generational contacts in terms of bringing together the youth and elderly in social and religious programs requiring exchanges.

In the educational and medical sectors, researches dealing with the issues of aging and generational relationships are being sponsored by African universities and other institutions. Gush (2002, p. 244) has reported in South Africa the challenging operations of the South African Community Agency for Social Enquiry, the Center for Gerontology at the University of Cape Town and the Human Sciences Research Council that are funded by the government. Then, it is common to find in Sub-Saharan Africa education policies that have at their base lifelong learning within whose contexts the elderly and the young learn together in the same programs, especially literacy, continuing education and distance learning programs.

It is also common to find in Africa, multipurpose centers where old people and the young are provided health care and relaxation facilities. There are also youth centers where the elderly are employed to play advisory roles.

By far the most successful areas in generational relationships in Africa seem to be in the aspects of familial initiatives. Within that context, it is common to find grandparents still assisting in the raising of grandchildren and this is very common in the rural areas. The practice is also observable in the urban areas where the high cost of hiring house helps compel the young couples to invite their parents to help in the raising of the young ones until such a time that can afford to place the children in day care or nurseries.

Grandparenting is very much valued in contemporary Africa. Grandparenting is presently imposed upon us by the combined effects of the HIV/AIDS pandemic that is ravaging our continent. Then that is made worst by several civil wars that have decimated the populations in several places, for example, Rwanda, Sierra Leone and Sudan. The death of actual parents have meant that the elderly would have to be compulsory saddled with responsibilities of raising the grandchildren that have been left behind. Perhaps, the cries of a continent that is undergoing the trauma of the decapitating effects of HIV/AIDS and poverty are best heard in the hands of elderly persons watching and attending to dying children and grandchildren at the risk of also dying for the reason that they do not even know how best to protect themselves from being infected.

CONSTRUCTION, DECONSTRUCTION, RECONSTRUCTION AND TRANSFORMATION OF FUTURE GENERATIONAL RELATIONSHIPS IN AFRICA

Today, because of internal migration from rural to urban centers where cultures merge in what has been described as multiculturalism and previous cultural identities repudiated in the "warm" embrace of the so-called "township" culture, it becomes difficult to really predict the future of generational relationships in Africa. This is so because Africa is "trapped" in the appeal to modernism. Of course, it could not do otherwise. Modernization is largely typified by Westernization, enculturation in Western cultures, change of tastes and choices. Africa is also engaged in nation building that often requires intensive integration and therefore the need to bring together what Joseph (1998, p. 58) termed as "culturally and socially discrete groups" into the national mainstream in order to promote more effective governments so that new states could implement their policies and promote development. So then, it is easy for anyone to suspect that the processes of internal migration, modernization and nation building may in a way influence negatively the strengthening of generational relationships if they are not properly conceptualized and implemented. If they are not properly managed, they can even further fragment generational relationships in Africa.

CONCLUSION

Generational transformations over historical time and space in Africa have featured a mixture of the "good" and the "bad." The valuable interactions and relationships that endured in our traditional communities typify the good. The bad, on the other hand, is typified by the alterations that our cultures have witnessed as a result of profound and, sometimes, negatively influencing foreign contacts that have put in jeopardy whatever we had cherished in our generational relationships in the past. However, it is obvious that Africa cannot remain in the past in a globalizing and modernizing world. We live in the present, and therefore our peoples must engage in the deconstruction, reconstruction and transformation of whatever could help them maintain some degree of cultural development. Whatever that is valuable in our culture would have to be ingrained in the modern conceptualization of generational relationships. It is only by doing this that we can partly cultivate and nurture generational relationships in responding to what Amilcar Cabral once perceived as African indigenous culture. That indigenous culture is an heritage of the common people, and Amilcar Cabral had posited that:

> ... *the people are only able to create and develop their culture and keep it alive despite continual and organized repression of their cultural life because they continue to resist culturally even when their politico-military resistance is destroyed.*

–*Amilcar Cabral (quoted by Joseph, 1998, p. 67)*

When and if you apply the Western standards of evaluating the performance of generational relationships to Africa, it would seem that we are yet to get off the ground. Yet, we have in place somewhat "invisible" structures and unwritten philosophies that should take Africa ashore in generational relationships, policies, programs and practices. That time may not have come at the moment, but we see a silver lining in the dark cloud that seems to be hovering around us. We have a hope. We have the needed faith.

REFERENCES

Beauclerk, J., Narby, J. & Townsend, J. (1988), *Indigenous peoples: a field guide for development*. Oxford: Oxfam Pub.

Gush, C. (2002), 'Intergenerational initiatives in South Africa: reflecting and aiding a society in transition,' in: Kaplan, M. et al. (eds.), *Linking lifetimes: a global view of intergenerational exchange*. New York: University Press of America Inc.

Hoffman, J. (2003), "What motivates intergenerational practices in South Africa," *Journal of intergenerational relationships: programs, policy and research*, Vol. 1, No. 1.

Itoe Hampson, S. J. (1982), *Old age: A study of aging in Zimbabwe*. Gweru: Mambo Press.

Jenks, C. (1993), 'Introduction: the analytical bases of cultural reproduction theory,' in: Jenks, C. (ed.), *Cultural reproduction*. London and New York: Routledge.

Joseph, S. (1998), *Interrogating cultures: critical perspectives on contemporary social theory*. New Delhi: Sage Publications.

Kaplan, M. S. (2002), 'Employing proverbs to explore intergenerational relations across cultures,' in: Kaplan, M., Henkin, N. and Kusano, A. (eds.), *Linking lifetimes: a global view of intergenerational exchange*. New York: University Press of America, Inc.

Malinowski, B. (1944), *A scientific theory of culture*. North Carolina: Chapel Hill.

Oduaran, A. (2003), "Intergenerational practices and possibilities related to the HIV/AIDS pandemic in Botswana and Nigeria," *Journal of intergenerational relationships: programs, policy and research*, Vol. 1, No. 2.

Where We Are Now
with Intergenerational Developments:
An English Perspective

Norma Raynes, PhD

SUMMARY. Intergenerational programs are beginning to burgeon in England. They are relatively recent in their development. The systemic absence of connectiveness between policy developments and services relating to older people and those relating to children and young people is identified. The key strategic players are described. Questions about future developments and research are discussed. *[Article copies available for a fee from The Haworth Document Delivery Service: 1-800-HAWORTH. E-mail address: <docdelivery@haworthpress.com> Website: <http://www.HaworthPress. com> © 2004 by The Haworth Press, Inc. All rights reserved.]*

KEYWORDS. Intergenerational programs, NGOs, English health policy

INTRODUCTION

The development of intergenerational programmes and practice in England began later than those in the USA. Its inception appears, too, to

Norma Raynes is Professor of Social Care, University of Salford, Salford M6 6PU, England (E-mail: n.v.raynes@salford.ac.uk).

[Haworth co-indexing entry note]: "Where We Are Now with Intergenerational Developments: An English Perspective." Raynes, Norma. Co-published simultaneously in *Journal of Intergenerational Relationships* (The Haworth Press, Inc.) Vol. 2, No. 3/4, 2004, pp. 187-195; and: *Intergenerational Relationships: Conversations on Practice and Research Across Cultures* (ed: Elizabeth Larkin et al.) The Haworth Press, Inc., 2004, pp. 187-195. Single or multiple copies of this article are available for a fee from The Haworth Document Delivery Service [1-800-HAWORTH, 9:00 a.m. - 5:00 p.m. (EST). E-mail address: docdelivery@ haworthpress.com].

http://www.haworthpress.com/web/JIR
© 2004 by The Haworth Press, Inc. All rights reserved.
Digital Object Identifier: 10.1300/J194v02n03_13

have been from very different starting points from those in the USA, from whence have emerged the considerable US developments (Newman 1997). In England there is no intergenerational government policy as such, although the term is slowly beginning to appear in government documents. The focus of the various agencies involved in older people and children's issues has not on the whole included intergenerational development as a key theme. Significantly, there is no collaboration between those concerned with older people's issues and those focusing on children's services.

In this paper an overview of the English national policy and agencies involved in services for older people is given first, followed by one for children's services. Intergenerational programme and other related developments are then described. Finally current national policy concerns are identified as the context in which the commonality of needs of older and younger people in England could be raised to enable more coherent and collaborative development of intergenerational work in England.

OLDER PEOPLE: POLICIES AND NGOs

Policies relating to older people are developed at national level for England primarily in the Department of Health and implemented by local authorities. The latter have the prime responsibility for ensuring the well-being of older people, as they do other members of the community and for delivering the services which are described as providing care in the community. These services enable older people to go on living in their own homes and where this is not possible to live in a residential care home or a nursing home. Places in the latter are purchased by the local authority on behalf of the older person and fee contributions are contingent on the level of income of the older person. Increasingly the older person services have become concentrated on what are called high intensity care packages, where there is a high dependency level and focus on personal social care rather than domestic care inputs (Help the Aged 2002).

Policy is also made within the context of the NHS which relates directly to services for older people. The implementation of these policies necessarily involves social services departments which sit within the local authority structures. Most recently the NHS published its National Service Framework for Older People (DOH 2001). This sets standards of the care of older people whether they live at home, in residential care or are being cared for in hospital. This framework contained 8 standards which had to be implemented by those organisations providing health care for older people within the NHS. Standard 8 focuses on the promotion of an active healthy life in older age. It is to be implemented locally with a coordinated programme of action led by the NHS with support from local councils. Local champions were to be established who would drive through the implementation of this and the other seven standards in the National Service Framework. The presence of local champions has varied across the country as has their activity and influence (Manthorpe 2004). A common assessment system is being introduced in England which it is hoped will reduce some of the duplication which currently characterizes access to services for older people. Other means have been established to enable local authorities and health services to work together and pool resources.

NGOs

In England there are many NGOs acting as advocates for older people and providing services. At the national level these are voluntary organisations which are not for profit agencies. They include, for example, Age Concern England, Help the Aged, The National Pensioners' Convention, the Association of Retired Persons, Counsel and Care and the Beth Johnson Foundation. These work in parallel and there appears to be not a great deal of collaboration between them certainly in relation to the development of intergenerational programmes. Alongside these NGOs sits Better Government for Older People. This originated as a government initiative started in 1998 (Hayden and Boaz 2000). In effect it was a three-year experiment within local authorities' partly funded by central government money to establish ways to make services more sensitive to the needs of older people and more joined up and directly involving older people in the development of these. After its central government funding ceased, BGOP became a self-funding organisation promoting joined up working in local settings.

Whilst there is no legislation fixing a retirement age in England, custom and practice has developed so that in most organisations older people are required to retire in England if they are women at the age of 60 and if they are men at the age of 65. These ages are those at which the current state pensions are awarded. This practice, which is still widespread and to be found in contracts of employment in most large organisations in England, is being reviewed. In England, as elsewhere in the UK, the government will be required to implement the European Directive on Age Discrimination in 2006. The government is currently consulting about its proposals to address this issue. Current practice will become discriminatory with the adoption of the EU Directive.

CHILDREN: POLICIES AND NGOs

In 2003 children's services in England remained fragmented. Health, social care, education and childcare are the responsibilities of separate government departments and local agencies and also involve private and not for profit providers. At the national level in England, until recently, the Department for Education and Science had responsibility for education and the Department of Health for children's health and childcare, both in the sense of day care provision and children who are looked after by the state and child protection issues. Since 2000, changes have been made to bring all of the childcare-related policies under the same umbrella as those relating to education of children. In 2004 the social care and education policy are to be brought together in one government department which is the Department for Education and Science. A Children Bill published in 2004 will result in the appointment of a children's commissioner for England and in every local authority a director of children's services. He or she will take responsibility for children's social services and education. Councils will be required to join together services for children which currently are run by different parts of local government and beyond this by the health services. There will be a duty to collaborate placed upon the various organisations involved in working for children.

CHILDCARE

The complexity of provision in relation to childcare is compounded by the variety of different providers and provision at the local level. As successive governments have focused attention and resources in the area the driver has been an attempt to get mothers back to work. Childcare is still seen in England as a personal responsibility, not a service to be funded by either national or local government.

A number of NGOs have both lobbied the government and provided policy development leads and in some cases services. These include in England, the Daycare Trust, Barnardos, Thomas Coram Foundation, Save the Children Fund and Kids Club Network. Research relating to these policy issues has had a clear focus in a number of universities' dedicated research centres.

DEVELOPMENTS IN INTERGENERATIONAL PROGRAMMES AND RELATED ACTIVITIES

We can certainly see a significant growth in the amount of intergenerational organisations and programmes in England. This growth has been captured in the *Intergenerational Directory* published in England, at the Centre for Intergenerational Practice at the Beth Johnson Foundation in December of 2003 (Centre for Intergenerational Practice 2003). A leading role has been taken by this Foundation in highlighting both intergenerational programmes and their relevance to health and well-being of both older people and children. The Centre for Intergenerational Practice was established in 2001. It has two aims. These are:

- The development of intergenerational practice in the UK;
- The promotion of intergenerational practice as an effective tool in promoting sustainable communities and reducing social exclusion.

The goals of the Centre are to:

- Support those involved in intergenerational work;
- Develop the understanding of intergenerational work;
- Influence decision makers to incorporate intergenerational initiatives into their policies and funding guidelines.

To achieve these goals the centre carries out a number of activities. These include hosting a network which is UK wide and which provides a newsletter and hosting a series of national seminars and biannual national conferences to promote the development of intergenerational policy, practice and research. It also has a Website. It provides the secretariat for the international intergenerational body, ICIP. It has funded and supported research in the field. This includes a seven-year mentoring project (Ellis 2003) and a review of intergenerational programmes in the UK (Granville 2002). The Foundation has also supported innovative developments in a number of other local intergenerational projects. Its Website <www.centreorip.org.uk> is a key source of information for anyone in England seeking to develop their understanding of intergenerational projects and development.

Other initiatives have occurred, some developing at a national level in England and others at local levels. An example of the former is the Age Concern England Active Age Unit which supports Trans Age action programme. This supports a number of its own local programmes across the country most of which are school based. It is now producing a newsletter about these programmes. Starting locally and growing into a potential national organization is the Education Business Development Partnership which is a franchised school-based intergenerational mentoring programme which began in one city in England, Salford, and which has now been rolled out into a number of different local authorities. The growth of stand alone programmes has been noticeable. A simple comparison of Granville's 2002 report, with the directory published by the Centre for Intergenerational Practice in December 2003, makes that clear. These programmes cover a wide range of different activities. They are located in different settings in different parts of the country. They all have in common the bringing together of older people and young people outside their family settings into shared activities for their mutual benefit. They include, for example, an arts organization (Langford and Mayo 2001) which is based in Tower Hamlets London. This was started ten years ago and is run by local artists. By contrast the National Association for the Providers of Activities for Older People (NAPA) has developed intergenerational programmes in residential care homes for older people across the country. A sheltered housing scheme which is part of a national housing association, the Mersey Valley Housing Programme, began a wide range of intergenerational activities in the community involving older people and schools in Salford. Operating currently in one other local authority, Trafford, in the Northwest of England is a school-based programme. This is the subject of a research and development programme designed to test a model and evaluate the effects of the programme on all the stakeholders with a view to rolling it out nationally.

All this activity (with the exception of Intergen) is being carried out outside academic bases. Again this contrasts with the American experience and with the development of policy and practice relating to children's education and social services in England.

FUTURE DIRECTIONS: DEMOGRAPHY, POLICY, PRACTICE AND RESEARCH

Concern about older people has been moving up the policy agenda mainly on account of the demographic pressures which are now well known. The growth in the numbers over the age of 60 is clearly shown in Figure 1. In 2003, for the first time the numbers of people in this age group exceeded the number of young people under the age of 16. For the most part the construction of this information has been in negative terms with older people being seen as a burden and drain rather than a resource (Audit Commission 2004).

Recent work has highlighted the isolation of older people in both city centres and rural communities (Scharf et al. 2002). The exclusion of older people from many activities in their local neighbourhoods has been recognised. Thus government concerns with social exclusion and the regeneration of inner city communities has recently recognised the existence of older people as part of the community whose needs have to be addressed. The need to deal with these issues and the importance of seeing older people as a potential resource has been identified in a recent report by the Audit Commission (2004). The building of sustainable communities is a central policy concern at the national level in England.

The conjunction of growing numbers of older people, the beginning of a debate which sees them as a resource as well as consumers, combined with the need to regenerate communities may well offer a convergence of interests in which intergenerational programmes can thrive. However, to enable this to happen there will need to be a coming together of NGOs concerned with older people and with children so that their common interests can be identified. As Directors for Children's Services are to be appointed in local authorities so are Directors for Older People's services. This could lead to further separation of interests. However, it provides an opportunity for those developing intergen-

FIGURE 1. Age Profile of the Population over 60 in England

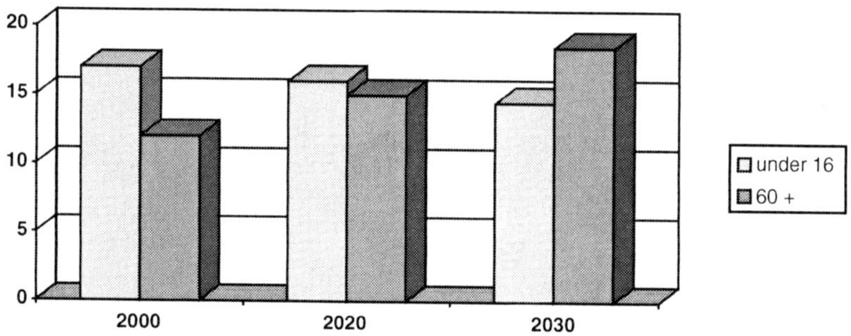

Key: Light Grey = under 16, Dark Grey = 60 and over

erational programmes to identify possible shared resources and avenues for collaboration. Such matters as safe streets and communities, leisure amenities, education and lifelong learning are, at a minimum, shared areas of interest for the development and promotion of independence for young and old members of communities.

It may be that in England the time for intergenerational activity and programmes has come to play a role in the development of cohesion for communities, healthy life promotion of older people and lifelong education.

There is a clear need for a national lead to enable this to happen. It could be that the Centre for Intergenerational Practice in the Beth Johnson Foundation takes this role. If the existing developments are to flourish and have an impact on policy, there is a strong argument also that some research is required to support this. At a minimum a taxonomy and definitions are needed and an evaluation of process and outcome. Whilst research from other countries, notably the USA, is of use, the particular circumstances and organisation of older people's services and children's services in England underline the need for nationally based research. The context and policy issues are different from those in the USA and from those elsewhere in Europe. Knowledge generated in England can be shared with colleagues in practice, research and policy elsewhere to the mutual benefit of all concerned and the promotion of effective intergenerational practice. For this to be of wider value it will be important for those involved in intergenerational research to better understand the policy contexts and service structures which exist for the benefit of older and younger members of other countries.

As yet the similarities in terms of the needs of younger and older members of our society identified by Newman and Smith (1997) have not emerged in the policy arena in England. No signs signal the coming together in a common cause of the old and the young to lobby in England, for funding at the local or national level or to promote policies in which their common interests can be addressed. However, it would now seem that the policy issues surrounding sustainable communities in England are fruitful ground in which to ensure the further growth of intergenerational programmes and organisations to benefit both older and younger members of these communities in England.

REFERENCES

Audit Commission. (2004) *Older People–Independence and Well-being.* London: Audit Commission

Centre for Intergenerational Practice. (2003) *Intergenerational Directory,* Stoke-on-Trent: Beth Johnson Foundation

DOH. (2001) *National Service Framework for Older People.* London: HMSO

Ellis, S.W. (2003) *The Intergenerational Programme Mentoring Project: Final Research Report.* Stoke on Trent: The Beth Johnson Foundation

Granville, G. (2002) *A Review of Intergenerational Practice in the UK.* Stoke on Trent: The Beth Johnson Foundation

Hayden, C., Boaz, A. (2000) *Making a Difference: Better Government for Older People Programme Evaluation Report.* Warwick: The University of Warwick, Local Government Centre

Help the Aged. (2002) *Nothing Personal: Rationing Social Care for Older People.* London: Help the Aged

Langford, S., Mayo, S. (2001) *Sharing the Experience. How to Set Up and Run Arts Projects Linking Young and Older People.* London: Magic Me

Manthorpe, J. (2004) *Championing Older People–Making a Difference.* London: Better Government for Older People

Newman, S., Smith B., (1997) Developmental theories as the basis for intergenerational programs. In (Eds) Newman, S., Ward, C.R., Smith, T.B., Wilson, J.O., McCrea, J.M. *Intergenerational Programs.* Washington, DC: Taylor and Francis, pp. 3-19

Newman, S., Ward, C.R., Smith, T.B.,Wilson, J.O., McCrea, J.M. (1997) *Intergenerational Programs: Past, Present and Future.* Washington, DC: Taylor and Francis

Scharf, T., Phillipson, C., Smith, A.E., Kingston, P. (2002) Older people in deprived Areas: perceptions of the neighbourhood. *Quality in Ageing.* 3, 2 pp. 11-21

"... the (unbearable) 'in-betweenness' of being[1] ...":
A Postmodern Exploration of Intergenerational Practices in Africa: A Framework Towards Programming

Jaco Hoffman

SUMMARY. It seems that there are no clear and mutually exclusive categories of modernity and traditionalism in modern Africa. Modernity still includes forms of traditionalism and at the same time modernity creates its own traditions in what Kaphagawani terms as C4–Contemporary Confluence of Cultures on the Continent of Africa.

We need to position ourselves somewhere between the over-romanticized idea of a golden era in the past and an overly pessimistic view of the family as a disappearing primary care institution; between the "warm, loving, caring, socially-oriented ..." African generations and the "cold technology-oriented" Western generations. This search for a *relative social reality* will be dealt with by a narrative/discursive approach. This framework should, for a start, aim towards intergenerational pro-

---

Jaco Hoffman is affiliated with the University of Pretoria, PO Box 967, Witbank 1035, Mpumalanga, Republic of South Africa.

[Haworth co-indexing entry note]: "'... the (unbearable) 'in-betweenness' of being ...': A Postmodern Exploration of Intergenerational Practices in Africa: A Framework Towards Programming." Hoffman, Jaco. Co-published simultaneously in *Journal of Intergenerational Relationships* (The Haworth Press, Inc.) Vol. 2, No. 3/4, 2004, pp. 197-213; and: *Intergenerational Relationships: Conversations on Practice and Research Across Cultures* (ed: Elizabeth Larkin et al.) The Haworth Press, Inc., 2004, pp. 197-213. Single or multiple copies of this article are available for a fee from The Haworth Document Delivery Service [1-800-HAWORTH. 9:00 a.m. - 5:00 p.m. (EST). E-mail address: docdelivery@haworthpress.com].

Digital Object Identifier: 10.1300/J194v02n03_14

grammes with at least one of three outcomes: transmission of positive values, relevant imageries and a developmental approach.

KEYWORDS. Modernity, postmodernity, intergenerational practices

The dialogue between two selves never ends. The pendulum swings between revulsion and attraction, between the dreams and the reality of a living past and the aspirations, the imperatives of modern living. Ambivalence. . . . The two selves are apt by turns to fight, quarrel, despise each other, hug each other, concede each other's roles. (Mphahlele in Obee, 1999)

It seems that there are no clear and mutually exclusive categories of modernity and traditionalism in modern Africa–modernity still includes forms of traditionalism and at the same time modernity creates its own traditions in what Kaphagawani (1998: 205) terms as *C4*–Contemporary Confluence of Cultures on the Continent of Africa. The consequent result then is what Mbiti (1985: 219) refers to as *". . . posed between two positions: the traditional solidarity which supplied for him land, customs, ethics, rites of passage, customary law, religious participation and a historical depth; and a modern way of life which for him has not yet acquired any solidarity."*

We need to position ourselves somewhere between the over-romanticized idea of a golden era in the past and an overly pessimistic view of the family as a disappearing primary care institution; between the "warm, loving, caring, socially-oriented . . ." African generations and the "cold technology-oriented . . ." Western generations (cf. Watts, 1989: 75).

We somehow need to get beyond the linear dialectical "imposed" opposites of orthodox modernization theory and appreciate the subjective experiences (stories) of different generations as well as the multiplicity of their everyday lives.

This search for a *relative social reality* will probably be best dealt with by a narrative/discursive approach: a micro-level, qualitative approach through which the lived experiences and self-representations–past and present–of people "generationed" together could be explored.

Together/interconnected/interdependent within colors, cohorts, a country and a continent is our quest for a *relative social reality* in order to somehow move towards the exploration of a basic framework *within which intergenerational programmes could be planned and implemented*.[2] Such a framework should, for a start, aim towards intergenerational programmes with at least one of three outcomes: transmission of positive values, relevant imageries and a developmental approach.

Herewith, thus, a few images/poems/narratives/discourses from Africa–particularly South Africa–about the (sometimes even unbearable) "in-betweenness" of being "generationed" together:[3]

TOWARDS THE TRANSMISSION OF VALUES

Between Black and White: Towards Cross-Cultural Values

In a complex society like South Africa, with her rainbow-colored nation, it is perhaps only through formal intergenerational programming (albeit artificial) that cultural boundaries would eventually be crossed towards tolerance and understanding. It is significant that Antjie Krog opens her excellent book, *A Change of Tongue* (2003: 1), by exploring the past ten years (1994-2004) of democracy and change in South Africa through an intergenerational narrative:

> *THE GUNSHOT CRACKS. They lean into the curve. Out from among the white boys shifts the figure of a black child, upright, his fingertips effortlessly upwards at every stride. Down the straight he is way ahead, running with the compelling grace of a top athlete. The pavilion crowd is on its feet. The black schools yelling wildly and pressing up against the railings in front. The white parents cheering, one tossing a hat into the air, and at the finish line a white track official bent almost double by her encouraging screeches.*
>
> *'Why is everybody happy?' I ask a man in a tracksuit next to me. He is wearing a floppy army hat and takkies. The sunburn on his forehead leads me to suspect that he is a farmer.*
>
> *'The blacks are happy because it is a black kid beating the whites. The whites are happy because the winning black kid is from a white school and was trained by them.'*
>
> *It is the Kroonstad district athletics meeting. The programme is running exactly as scheduled. Announcements are made in Afri-*

kaans and Sesotho. Most of the track officials are black, and everybody looks very much at home with the rituals of measuring distance and keeping time, flags, starting guns and walkie-talkies.

'It was not always so', says the man in the tracksuit, 'but we have come a long way.'. . .

. . . 'It was really terrible that first year. . . . To have athletics with black schools, I mean. We were so scared, I cannot tell you! Each white primary school was put in a league with four black schools and a couple of black farm schools for preliminary trails. The white school was told to organize the event, prepare the track and field, provide refreshments, act as main officials and bring the black teachers up to speed.'

He shakes his head as if he cannot believe it himself. 'Although we had a lot of power in the beginning, we told the kids: bring your parents, bring your grandparents, bring your unemployed uncle, tell your auntie to take off from work that morning. Bring everybody along so that the blacks don't engulf us. We must make sure that at least we are a factor, a presence to be reckoned with, otherwise they might sommer let their own children win everything.

'So I told them . . .'

An announcement cuts him off: a new record. The twelve-year-old record for the 200 metres has been broken by a black kid. When the record time is announced, the farmer nods his head and raises his eyebrows. 'That's good. An excellent time.' He writes it down with a Bic pen in his programme . . .

In a cross-cultural programme with an intergenerational emphasis (*Project Masibambisani–Let us help each other to carry*) in Witbank, South Africa, black and white older persons worked together for the sake of the poorest of the poor children in the community. These older persons from the Witbank Society for the Aged in partnership with the Mpumalanga Department of Education and local teachers, identified six of the most disadvantaged primary schools in both urban and deep rural areas–a major shortcoming in all these schools was the lack of educational aids to enhance a stimulating learning environment.

The older persons consequently implemented the project by collecting used and remnant materials (plastic bottles, fabric off-cuts, old X-rays, toothpaste caps, etc.), recycled and creatively adapted them to be used as educational aids within the learning areas of Curriculum 2005: The old plastic bottles became puppets for Communication and Language Learning; the toothpaste caps became counters to be used in the outcome area of Numeracy and Mathematics, etc.

One of the black teachers remarked: *"The old people helped us to carry, so that we, the teachers, can fly . . ."*

A white older person (a cancer patient) remarked: *"This was therapy!"*

Formal intergenerational programmes within the school system should not only address developmental issues but also gently open up towards and touch on sensitive interracial relationships.

> *The quest for a new white humanity will begin to emerge from a voluntary engagement by those caught in the culture of whiteness of their own making. . . . On balance, white South Africa will be called upon to make greater adjustments to black needs than the other way around. This is an essential condition for a shift in white identity in which 'whiteness' can undergo an experiential transformation by absorbing new cultural experiences as an essential condition for achieving a new sense of cultural rootedness. (Ndebele, 2000)*

Between Afro Centric and Euro Centric: Towards a Transitional Paradigm

The increased pride in doing things "the African way" in the post-independence period has meant a "rediscovery" of the so-called traditional ways. Likewise with the concept of *ubuntu:*[4] after the 1994 first democratic elections it has been officially identified as the ideal view of life in South Africa and a solution to contemporary problems. As was commented by Mazwai (in Streak, 1996), editor of Black Enterprise: *" . . . Now that white Western culture is losing its dominance, these values will come to the fore again"* (cf. also Mbiti, 1985: 227).

(my ancestors are)

> *Those who invented neither gunpowder nor compass*
> *those who tamed neither steam nor electricity*
> *those who explored neither sea nor sky*
> *but those who know the humblest corners of the country of suffering*
> *those whose only journeys were uprootings*
> *those who went to sleep on their knees . . .*

My negritude is neither a tower nor a cathedral
It plunges into the red flesh of the earth.

–Césaire, 1969

Dhlomo (1991: 49), however, has a valid point when he states: "... *It is true that we talk about ubuntu, but ... if ubuntu is to be our philosophy of life, then someone needs to provide a theoretical/philosophical framework for it, so that ultimately it can be taught, learned and practiced. This is the only way in the modern world in which we can begin to transmit all the values inherent to ubuntu to future generations of South Africans.* In an effort to operationalize this ethno-philosophy into a workable programme towards moral regeneration and the African Renaissance, we should heed Es'kia Mpahlele's (1982) words: *"African culture has not been static, or preserved in a bottle like a chemical waiting to be analyzed. It has been changing, yielding to new ways, partially disappearing, coming up again and adapting."*

Between Old Gods and New Worlds:
Towards Spirituality and Demythologization

Gogo[5]

We don't eat marogo[6] anymore
We don't drink beer from calabashes anymore

We drive around in BMW's
Lifts with mirrors take us to the next level

We don't listen anymore

Gogo, please plead for us with the badimo[7]
Put meat on their angry graves
Plead for us: Gogo.

–Mayekiso, 1995

The ancestors are considered to be kind towards the community and concerned about their welfare. Since also being close to God, the ancestors are furthermore viewed to be in a position to mediate on behalf of their living relatives to God for his blessings. The very important funeral rituals concerning ancestor worship–even in urbanized communities–are illustrative of the deep roots modern Africa still has in this traditional belief system.

> *A granny is a person to be well treated because she is taken as an ancestor at home.* (Grandson)[8]

Given the before-mentioned belief system, the relationship between people and unfortunate events is, on the other hand, often explained negatively through belief in witchcraft (cf. Niehaus, 2001 for a detailed exploration of this complex phenomenon). Witch-hunting is viewed so seriously that the Commission on Gender Equality called a special conference in September 1998 to consider approaches to traditional beliefs that play out negatively. It featured again as a prominent issue in the *Report of the Ministerial Committee on Abuse, Neglect and Ill-treatment of Older Persons* (2001):

> According to the police (SAPS) in Lebowa, 66 older women have been killed as witches in various villages from 1994 up to 2001. The witch hunters include youths who are committed to "free" people from "supernatural evils." *"If no campaign is launched to eradicate this scourge,"* Khathu Mamaila, a Sowetan journalist, wrote *"the killings are bound to continue from generation to generation."*[9]

The identification of harmful traditional practices and the demystification of mental illness through information and training are of utmost importance and have to feature prominently on the African intergenerational agenda.

I Am Not a Witch[10]

> *I swear God, I am not a witch!*
> *From my inner heart I confess*
> *I am not a witch*
> *I know nothing about his death*
> *and I am not a party*
> *to Mbatia's sudden departure*
> *to the next world*
>
> *I told the crowd*
> *that I was innocent*

even to Lamisi my daughter
my innocence I confessed
I swore all living things under the universe

I beat my chest in agony
to demonstrate my innocence
The crowd was poised
in anger and vengeful stance
in judgement to render
to my innocent soul

With stones, stick and insults
my poor lonely soul was at their mercy.
I cried loud
with hands to heaven
and told my story
over and over again.
Of my innocence

I am not the cause
Mbatia's sudden death
was not my doing
But who will listen?
Damn she who is down
It is the rhythm of the world.

So in far away and hilly Gambaga
I was ostracized
to start a new life
in loneliness in an environment
devoid of love
among colleagues of the same fate.

My heart is sore and bitter
But who will listen?
Even Lamisi my daughter
despised me with the crowd
If I knew fate had this in store for me
I wish I were never born.

Between Continuity and Change: Towards a Translation

Traditional values and practices exist in a paradoxical manner–being inherited and recreated at the same time. They are a means to link the past through present situations with the future: not necessarily a case of going back to the "primitive," but to take the basics forward; not some place we are going to, but something we are creating right now through our actions and the people around us. This asks for a constant and creative hermeneutical process–towards translation, as illustrated in the following vignettes (some more nuanced in their translation than others. . .).

Translation 1

The Irish ambassador officially opened a clinic the other day. Somewhere in one of the deep rural areas of South Africa–blazingly hot and thousands of people. The Ndbele older women danced their traditional dances in traditional attire–but I couldn't help to notice the sunglasses, not to mention the Adidas sneakers. At least they translated an ancient dance into a new look . . . or is it the other way around. . . ? Anyhow, it was the children's turn. And out of the bush . . . three little Michael Jacksons jumped. . . ! Three exact replicas . . .

Translation 2

In an informal way, Moki Cekisani, the founder of the *"Ubuntu Environmental Project"* and Port Elizabeth's citizen of the year (1996), creatively and holistically managed to translate traditional *ubuntuistic* values into practical projects within the desperation of the urban sprawl:

> *Our main objective is to inculcate a sense of caring in the hearts of township people; to conserve and construct their environment to improve their quality of life.*

So he introduced clean-up campaigns and greening projects like *"One shack, one tree!"* (Before this the translation was: *"One settler, one bullet".* . .)

> *Squatter areas are probably going to exist for another 100 years, so we want to make life there as pleasant as possible. We believe that if we can change people's environment, their way of thinking will change. We aim to restore a sense of caring, which people in*

*the townships have lost . . . we want to change the mentality of chil-
dren who throw stones at donkeys . . . if you care more about animals, you will care more about people.*

Translation 3

In their study about contemporary respect relations between Zulu
grandmothers and granddaughters/-sons, Møller and Sotshongaye (1999)
found that grandmothers' teachings with regard to values like respect
are still experienced as instructive, especially if it is reinterpreted/trans-
lated and adapted to the particular context of life in the local township.
The traditional practice of *ukusoma* (sex without penetration), as translated by the grandmothers, is-in view of the HIV/AIDS context–surpris-
ingly well received among the youth in KwaZulu-Natal.

TOWARDS NEW IMAGERIES

The need for a reorientation of both the younger generations and the
older generations at the level of the family and society is a distinct focus
of intergenerational studies in South Africa.

Between the Young Lions and the Old Mothers and Fathers of the Nation

Ramphele (1992) notes, "the Sharpville massacre of 1960 marked the
end of an era in black politics in which young people were beholden to
adult leadership." The struggle by young activists to make the townships ungovernable during the 1980s gave the youth immense power,
freedom and independence from their parents and grandparents.

The situation with regard to education is likewise–older persons (especially black older persons) never had the opportunities their grandchildren have, with the result that the majority of them are functionally
illiterate. The limitations on positive intergenerational exchanges are
self-evident (see "Towards a Developmental Approach" section; cf.
also Cattell, 1994; Campbell, 1994).

*The discourse on respect relations between the generations may
be seen as an attempt to redefine the contract to meet the demands
of global society and South Africa's democratic era.* (Møller &
Sotshongaye, 1999: 19)

Between Respect and Reciprocity

In an interesting study by Van der Geest (1997), *"Between respect and reciprocity: managing old age in rural Ghana,"* he reports about the common occurrence of loneliness and the marginalization of older persons in the southern part of Ghana where some of them actually live in dire poverty and lack adequate help. The younger generation used the principle of reciprocity in their explanation and blamed the elderly for on their turn not having looked after their children when they were young—*"If you were my father and you failed to care for me, I would never visit you, not even when you are sick or old."*

According to this study there seems to be an obvious link between the quality of care in old age and proper care in childhood—respect and dignity are somehow "earned" by the quality of primary relationships.

Otherwise their status will, as the story goes, be like that of the leopard that grew old (Courlander, 1996: 558):

> *When the leopard grew old he became gap-toothed; and he had no means of killing the wild animals or the goats. So he shriveled up with hunger; and while he was cowering, shrunk up in this way, he saw goats roaming near him. But he had no teeth to kill them with, since old age had come upon him; and he remembered the meat, which formerly, when young, he used to eat after killing the goats; and in his sadness he sang this song:*
>
> *'Woe is me! O dark Nali (name of a goat)!*
> *I am too old for the meat of the goat:*
> *The two kidneys, the two arm muscles;*
> *The heart and the dark liver;*
> *A bunch of entrails spread on the rock!'*
>
> *And the goats were mocking at him. And when he had sung this, his soul left him. Now they say as a proverb: 'when the leopard grows old, the goats mock at him.'*

Intergenerational programmes should be instrumental in reconstructing and adding value to the contribution that older persons are making through their pensions to their respective families and communities. Being a pensioner is, on the one hand, often associated with poverty and being a burden to society. On the other hand pensioners should be reminded that although pensions are not fortunes, they are also not nothing! Households with pensioners are, as a matter of fact considered to be better off than those in which there is no pension beneficiary (cf. Møller & Ferreira, 2003).

Older persons should be empowered by adding values like power, prestige and dignity to their role and be made mindful of the fact that pension earnings have contributed to food, clothing, schooling, etc., for children and grandchildren. It seems that in the past both society and older persons themselves have underestimated their value.

On their part grandchildren should be made conscious of the contributions that these older carers have made towards their quality of life. Value should thus be added to the pensioners' role in terms of respect and esteem for the quality they have added to their children and grandchildren's lives.

TOWARDS A DEVELOPMENTAL APPROACH

As the African intergenerational contract is in essence about a traditional social welfare system and thus about survival as well as care and quality of life issues, the developmental outcomes of the programme will determine the relevancy of the particular programme.

Between "Too Much to Die Off" and "To Little to Live Off"

> A few weeks earlier the Tshwane metro had cut off 93-year-old Johanna Mashigoane's electricity and limited her household's access to tap water because she had failed to pay a R9 491 bill.
>
> Close to tears, the old woman told us how she and her four grandchildren battled to survive on her R740-a-month pension.
>
> There was often not enough money to feed the family, not to mention paying for electricity, water and other council services ... Two of Mashigoane's grandchildren are still at school and she is responsible for their school fees. . . . She is just one of many pensioners. . . . (Msomi, 2004: 4)

The vast majority of African pensioners live in poverty stricken *multigenerational households*, and *intergenerational transfers* are a common practice, specifically, the sharing of the non-contributory, means tested state old-age pension[11] as a main source of income for poor households in South Africa. The result, as being shown in one of the key findings in the Møller and Ferreira study (2003), is that none or only a small portion of the pension money is used for the older benefi-ciaries themselves–the major portion or everything goes to the social support of co-residents.

> *The one is at school. I am supposed to see that the school fees are paid, the uniform and everything. He does not have clothes and we are hungry. We cannot educate while we ourselves are hungry. The younger one is staying with me all day because there is no money to take her to the crèche.*

> *They are going to the crèche and sometimes the money gets finished before or without paying the crèche.*

> *I cannot fulfill everything from my pension.*

> *If I could be helped with capital or money to start selling vegeta-bles or anything.*

> *They are emotionally hurt because they are not like other children (do not have things that other children have) because we are not working.*[12]

Between Being a Grandmother and "the Grandmothers' Disease"

The poverty issue is, of course, exacerbated by the HIV/AIDS-pan-demic with an increasing number of skip-generation households where grandmothers have to act as surrogate parents–hence the pandemic be-ing termed as the *"grandmothers' disease."*[13] Programmes to prepare and support older generations to take up the challenges of surrogate parenting as well as the development of income-generating activities are important developmental issues.

> *I do not know nothing . . . I just hear AIDS . . . I myself do not know. I do not know anything.*[14]

> *Looking after orphans is like starting life all over again, because I have to work on the farm, clean the house, feed the children, and buy school uniforms. I thought I would no longer do these things again. I am not sure if I have the energy to cope.*[15]

> *It is difficult! What should I say is the difficulty, because it is just difficult . . .*[16]

> *My mind is standing still and I am confused because I really have a problem.*

I take some of the pension and pay the burial society because I think what if these children die.

If the government could help us because if these children die, it will be difficult because I do not have money to bury them, so if the government could have a plan for funerals.[17]

Between Wisdom and Illiteracy

Although the white population group above sixty shows a functional literacy rate of 87 percent, the literacy rates in other race groups are well below 50 percent, with the proportion among black older persons as low as 17 percent. Intergenerational programmes should focus on basic educational needs as well as expressive learning processes (cf. HSRC, 2003).

Sixteen percent of the 80,000 learners on the University of South Africa Adult Basic Education and Training leg of the South African National Literacy Initiative (SANLI) are sixty years and above.

I never thought that I would ever be able to read my name now I can even write my signature. (Older person)[18]

She is the first person who is able to see everything that does not go well. (Granddaughter)[19]

If they fight with each other, she is able to help them solve their problems. (Granddaughter)[20]

Within the above-mentioned developmental context, the **Grand**mothers **A**gainst **P**overty and **A**ids-project (*G.A.P.A*)[21] is of particular interest. They run:

- *Educational workshops* concentrating on practical topics like for example, Adult Basic Education and Training programmes; nursing skills and HIV/AIDS; tuberculosis; child care; vegetable gardening; nutrition; healthy ageing; household budgeting; business skills and how to access government grants.
- *Support groups:* Peer support groups meet each week where they offer each other advice, friendship and emotional support.
- *Skills training* where they learn skills including sewing, crocheting, knitting and carpet making, etc.

- *Income generation projects:* Older carers are helped to start up their own home-based businesses in order to supplement their income.
- *Educational assistance scholarship program:* Grandmothers could apply for and are assisted to access financial assistance for the schooling of their dependents.
- *G.AP.A. Trading Store:* In May 2002 they opened their first outlet for the goods they are manufacturing. The store that is run by grandmothers sells goods ranging from handmade blankets and quilts to cushions, beadwork and good used clothing.

Between Premodernity and Postmodernity: Towards Confluence

The intergenerational contract is and will, for the time being, be the steering principle of social organization and, for that matter, survival and hope on the continent and in South Africa and should be acknowledged, sustained and harnessed through formal programming. In order to be able to create a relevant framework to institutionalize intergenerational programming within and between different generational networks, we need to establish a comprehensive account of a particular relative social reality. This could be achieved through a dialectical dialogue which will make it possible to accommodate alternatives–it is thus about the participation of programme participants in all aspects of programming.

P.S.

It should be stressed that attending to the subjective accounts of intergenerational experiences is not just of theoretical concern. Liberation from stereotypical/mythical images can indeed help to better adjust intergenerational policies and programmes to the practical needs of people "generationed" together–practicalities (usually taken for granted) like infrastructure, transport, food, etc., should also be considered:

> *. . . The morning before the rally, I fall into a panic of a more practical kind. What does one wear? Jeans, T-shirt and takkies? I'm already aware that the comrades object to the fact that whites who actually have more than enough money, a nice house and two cars always dress down when they come to the townships. As if they don't respect the people. To church or the theatre they wouldn't dress like that, but in the township suddenly they have to show how simply they live. A dress? Silk stockings? I decide on somewhere in between . . ."* (Krog, 2003: 166)

NOTES

1. In analogy of *The Unbearable Lightness of Being* by Kundera, M.

2. Although the intergenerational contract is embedded as a way of living in Africa, the multiple stresses experienced by the extended African family/society necessitate more formal intergenerational programming initiatives and policies.

3. The dichotomies explored are but a few amongst others like familial and institutionalized; communalism and individualism; extended and nuclear; rural and urban, traditional and modernity; humanism and alienation, etc.

4. *Ubuntu* is the Xhosa word for expressing the spirit and ethos of caring and sharing, or mutual support in Africa–"I am because we are."

5. "Zulu" for grandmother.

6. Kind of a spinach

7. Ancestors

8. Møller & Sotshongaye, 1999.

9. South African Department of Social Development, 2001.

10. Ben Pugansoa (Ghana) in African Gerontological Society, 2002; also see Kibuga & Dianga, 2000.

11. South Africa is only one of four countries in Africa with a sustainable non-contributory pension system. The others are: Botswana, Mauritius and Namibia.

12. Different quotes from the Ferreira et al.–study, 2001.

13. Cf. Wilson & Adamchak, 2000.

14. Ferreira, et al.–study, 2001.

15. Agyarko et al.–study, 2002.

16. Different quotes from the Ferreira et al.–study, 2001.

17. Agyarko et al.–study, 2002.

18. Institute for Adult Basic Education & Training, 2003.

19 . Møller & Sotshongaye, 1999.

20 . See note 19.

21. G.A.P.A., 43 Alma Rd, Rosebank, Cape Town, 7700, South Africa Tel: +27 (0) 82 957 3384, *kathbrod@iafrica.com*

REFERENCES

African Gerontological Society. (2002). *Appropriate Strategies for Ageing in Africa: Report on International Workshop on Ageing*. Legon, Accra: (Unpublished).

Agyarko, R. et al. (2002). *Impact of AIDS on Older People in Africa: Zimbabwe Case Study*. WHO: Geneva.

Campbell, C. (1994). Intergenerational conflict in township families: Transforming notions of "respect" and changing power relations. *Southern African Journal of Gerontology*, 3(2): 37-42.

Cattell, M. G. (1994). Intergenerational relations among the Samai of Kenya: Culture and experience. *Southern African Journal of Gerontology*, 3(2): 30-36.

Césaire, A. (1969). *Return to My Native Land*. Harmondsworth: Penguin.

Courlander, H. (1996). *A Treasury of African Folklore: The Oral Literature, Traditions, Myths, Legends, Epics, Tales, Recollections, Wisdom, Sayings and Humor of Africa*. Marlowe & Company: New York.

Ferreira, M. et al. (1992). *Multi-dimensional Survey of Elderly South Africans: Key findings*. Cape Town: HSCR/UCT Centre for Gerontology.

Ferreira, M., Keikelame, M. J. & Mosaval, Y. (2001). *Older Women as Carers to Children and Grandchildren Affected by AIDS: A Study Towards Supporting the Carers*. Cape Town: Institute of Ageing in Africa, University of Cape Town.

HSRC. (2003). *Ageing in South Africa: Report on the Minimum Data Set on Ageing, March 2002*. Pretoria: HSRC Publishers.

Institute for Adult Basic Education & Training. (2003). *ABET-news. SANLI Special Edition*. Pretoria: UNISA.

Kaphagawani, D. N. & Malherbe, J. G. (1998). African epistemology. In: Coetzee, P. H. & Roux, A. P. J. (Eds.). *Philosophy from Africa: A Text with Readings*. Johannesburg: International Thomson Publishing: 205-216.

Kibuga, K. F. & Dianga, A. (2000). Victimization and killing of older women: Witchcraft in Magu district, Tanzania. *Southern African Journal of Gerontology*, 9(2): 29-32.

Krog, A. (2003). *A Change of Tongue*. Johannesburg: Random House.

Kundera, M. (1999). *The Unbearable Lightness of Being*. HarperCollins.

Mayekiso, M. (1995). Ouma. *Tydskrif vir Letterkunde*, 33(3): 44.

Mbiti, J. S. (1985). *African Religions and Philosophy*. London: Heinemann.

Møller, V. & Ferreira, M. (2003). *Getting by . . . Benefits of Non-contributory Pension Income for Older South African Household*. Cape Town: Cape Town University.

Møller, V. & Sotshongaye, A. (1999). "They don't listen": Contemporary respect relations between Zulu grandmothers and granddaughters/-sons. *Southern African Journal of Gerontology*, 8(2): 18-27.

Mphahlele, E. 1982. *African Affirmations*. www.eskiaonline.com.

Msomi, S. (2004). Mbeki brings cheer to granny. *Sunday Times*, April 4.

Ndebele, N. (2000). *'Iph' Indlela? Finding Our Way into the Future.'* First Steve Biko Memorial Lecture: University of the Western Cape.

Niehaus, I. et al. (2001). *Witchcraft, Power and Politics: Exploring the Occult in the South African Lowveld*. London: Pluto Press.

Obee, R. (1999). *Es'kia Mphahlele: Themes of Alienation and African Humanism*. Athens, Ohio: Ohio University Press.

Ramphele, M. (1992). Social disintegration in the black community: Implications for social transformation. In: Everatt, D. & Sisulu, E. (Eds.). *Black Youth in Crisis: Facing the Future*. Johannesburg: Ravan Press.

South African Department of Social Development. (2001). *Report of the Ministerial Committee on Abuse, Neglect and Ill-treatment on Older Persons*. Volume 1. Pretoria.

Streak, D. (1996). Bring back Ubuntu. *Fair Lady*. 06.03.1996: 91-92.

Van der Geest, S. (1997). Between respect and reciprocity: Managing old age in rural Ghana. *Southern African Journal of Gerontology*, 6(2): 20-25.

Watts, J. (1989). *Black Writers from South Africa*. London: Macmillan.

Wilson, A. & Adamchak, D. J. (2000). AIDS in Africa: The grandmothers' disease. *Journal of Age-Related Disorders*, January: 5-6.

SECTION III:
CONCLUDING DISCUSSION

Global Intergenerational Research, Programs and Policy: What Does the Future Hold?

Paul A. Roodin

During the past 3 days of this colloquium we have heard a lively and stimulating set of papers from intergenerational experts across the world. Despite the wide diversity of approaches, frameworks, and rationales adopted for intergenerational practices around the world, there is common ground. Presenters have uniformly argued for the importance of an intergenerational perspective regardless of their culture, the nature of their discipline, or the program model. Whether practitioner, researcher, or theorist, we are all students of this emerging field and committed to the importance of understanding the ties that bind one gene-

Dr. Paul Roodin is Director, Experience Based Education, 138 Rich Hall, SUNY Oswego, Oswego, NY 13126.

[Haworth co-indexing entry note]: "Global Intergenerational Research, Programs and Policy: What Does the Future Hold?" Roodin, Paul A. Co-published simultaneously in *Journal of Intergenerational Relationships* (The Haworth Press, Inc.) Vol. 2, No. 3/4, 2004, pp. 215-219; and: *Intergenerational Relationships: Conversations on Practice and Research Across Cultures* (ed: Elizabeth Larkin et al.) The Haworth Press, Inc., 2004, pp. 215-219. Single or multiple copies of this article are available for a fee from The Haworth Document Delivery Service [1-800-HAWORTH, 9:00 a.m. - 5:00 p.m. (EST). E-mail address: docdelivery@haworthpress.com].

ration to another. There are some unique factors today that have given rise to the focus on intergenerational issues.

An intergenerational perspective is needed to help people in societies all over the world cope with the rapid and dramatic social change that challenges families and communities. Intergenerational programs can strengthen families and communities in response to the emerging threat of HIV and AIDS. AIDS in some African countries ultimately may lead to the destruction of a generation of parents who will leave behind their orphaned children to be raised by grandparents, kin, or even siblings just a few years older (e.g., school age children or adolescents). Without parents, societies will need to create community-based programs to provide for these orphans and for grandparents who help raise their children's children. The challenge is to move from family-based intergenerational responsibilities to developing the social support of the larger community and the willingness of those in need to utilize such support. This encompasses enormous cultural change and will be difficult to accomplish. Developing programs, creating a caring community to meet the needs of these children, and changing the ethos of cultures that have relied exclusively on family support in times of crises is indeed one of the most compelling intergenerational challenges of the next decade in Africa. Thus, some of the current emphasis on intergenerational perspectives has evolved from negative events facing societies today.

From the presentations it is obvious that many cultures already have a high level of intergenerational respect and mutual interdependence. Intergenerational programs may be designed by modeling these positive features of some societies. It has been fascinating to observe the many signs of care and concern that have been developed over many years. These signs of respect, value, and concern for generations are evidence of the importance of intergenerational bonds and mutual exchange. We have noted in presentations markers that include family rituals, cultural customs, stories and cultural myths, gifts, commitment of time, and even style of dress. Intergenerational exchange can highlight dimensions of value in a society. Valued exchanges come from traditional grandparent-grandchild relations, from having elders living longer and playing a larger role in the family and workplace, from new technology such as cell phones, computer e-mail, and telephones, and from having dual income parents who entrust the care of their children to extended kin. We cannot ignore the fact that in many cultures elders are not seen as a burden and a consumer of resources, but a source of strength and productivity with inherent value for all generations.

The presentations have shown the significance of adopting a life-span context when examining intergenerational programs. Just as certain cultures value specific forms of intergenerational exchanges, key points in the lifespan carry special intergenerational significance. We do not want to leave out any of these developmental periods, although it is clear that some are emphasized over others in certain cultures and in certain academic disciplines. Some fields highlight particular transitions in the life span (marriage, in-law relations, birth), while others emphasize other distinct periods (grandparenting, care of aging parents, entry into the workforce). The lifespan context offers a valuable framework for the study of intergenerational relations, and does not over-emphasize one period over another, nor the importance of one field of study over another.

The presentations emphasized the importance of adopting not only a cross-cultural perspective but also interdisciplinary and multidisciplinary perspectives. A diversity of perspectives across the life span is needed to understand the value of intergenerational programs, their structure, and how best to design appropriate research to determine their effectiveness and meaning. It is crucial to note that intergenerational programs and perspectives do not automatically transfer from one culture to another. Programs and perspectives must fit the community, its self-identified needs, and be delivered with sensitivity in concert with community values. One size does not fit all. Intergenerational work requires a life-span perspective, a cross-cultural perspective, an interdisciplinary perspective, and a multidisciplinary perspective in this growing field.

The path to building successful intergenerational programs based on outcomes research is not a simple one. First, we need the support of our international colleagues who are engaged in this type of work. As most in this emerging field have discovered, we often face the challenge of finding respect for the value of what we do from our colleagues, universities, and our communities. Second, we need to find ways of building and sustaining our efforts. Many of our constituents are overwhelmed by what we have learned thus far, and what needs to be done as a consequence. For example, discovering that filial piety in Japanese and Chinese society is largely "idealized" in popular media, and that there is much intergenerational conflict, stress, and role strain, requires a major shift in theory and cultural understanding. Moreover, it is difficult to build the intergenerational resources and programs in the community to address this issue. How can intergenerational specialists assist societies to accept and deal with the reality of rapid social change? What do we offer in the way of assistance to help people adjust to a new social order? Defining intergenerational needs and working beyond traditional assumptions about intergenerational relationships is a challenge for those who want to create *and* sustain programs. This is not a short-term issue, but one that will continue to present a challenge for decades.

All those who work in the intergenerational field must be sensitive to the tension between cultural primacy vs. the homogenization or "flattening" of culture. In essence, it is easy to see the intergenerational field solely from the vantage point of one's own work, one's own culture. This would add depth, but not breadth to the field's growing knowledge base. At the same time, it is misguided to assume that intergenerational work and the importance of generational ties are the same everywhere, no matter what the specific cultural context. Yet, looking at each culture individually would add only breadth, but not depth.

It is easy to ignore these two issues. Building intergenerational programs, of course, requires cultural sensitivity–but how can we guard against this sensitivity and understanding becoming "cultural primacy"? Seeing success in our intergenerational work in one culture seems to suggest that we can transfer our models and success directly to any other culture–without regard to cultural differences. These are both inherent dangers that we must monitor. Certainly intergenerational programs have to be developed and delivered in a way that touches the cultural sensitivities of those with whom we work; it cannot be done in a vacuum. The particular way that a program evolves and its short-term and long-term success depend on understanding and *adapting* the program to cultural realities. One cultural view cannot take precedence over another. Intergenerational programs must be developed and linked to a specific culture and a specific cultural value system. There is no way to short-circuit this process.

However, not all cultures are the same, nor can one cultural view take precedence over others when creating intergenerational programs. Perhaps the best way to represent this tension is recognizing that there is an intergenerational "lens" that colors our view of cultural transmission, family responsibility, and cultural exchange across the generations. Note that we should not be surprised if we fail to find successful outcomes when transferring one program model to another culture, despite agreement about the processes at work. For instance, Dr. Sally Newman suggested that older adults and younger adults share basic developmental and reciprocal needs. Taking her lead from Erik Erikson, she suggests that perhaps there are "universal" needs for each generation that include:

Older Adult Needs	**Children's Needs**
To Nurture	To Be Nurtured
To Teach	To Learn from and About the Past
To Have a Successful Life Review	To Have a Cultural Identity
To Share Cultural Mores	To Have a Positive Role Model
To Leave a Legacy	To Be Connected to Preceding Generations

While these may be considered 'processes' in all intergenerational exchanges between young and old, the specific outcomes for each generation are dependent on context, cultural values, and societal sensitivities. We cannot predict commonalities in outcomes across cultures, despite similarity in intergenerational exchange. Thus, we cannot advocate intergenerational perspectives as a panacea for the multiplicity of social problems in all cultures.

Finally, I wonder if each of the presenters can imagine what the world would look like if indeed the intergenerational programs and perspectives addressed at this colloquium were implemented? What if the advocates of intergenerational programs and views were all extraordinarily successful? What would intergenerational exchanges and reciprocal interactions produce within each of the specific cultures used for illustration? Where would we see benefits–not just for today, but also for many generations to come? *How would our world be changed?* Once we begin to dream of making the world truly intergenerational, it should indeed be a better place for all generations.

Index

A Change of Tongue, 199
AAPI-2. *See* Adult-Adolescent
    Parenting Inventory
    (AAPI-2)
Aborampah, O-M, 23
Abusua mpaninfoo, 36
Achebe, C., 56,57
Acquired immunodeficiency syndrome
    (AIDS). *See* AIDS
Activity theory, in society, 80-82
A-dada, 164,166
Adidas, 205
Adjaye, J.K., 23
Adult-Adolescent Parenting Inventory
    (AAPI-2), 112-113
A-dumbu, 164
Africa
    cross-cultural values in, between
        Black and White, 199-201
    generational relationships in,
        transformations over time,
        171-185
    intergenerational practices in
        between being a grandmother
            and "grandmothers' disease,"
            209-210
        postmodern exploration of,
            197-213
        between premodernity and
            postmodernity, 211
        between respect and reciprocity,
            207-208
        between "too much to die off"
            and "too little to live off,"
            208-209
        between wisdom and illiteracy,
            210-211

intergenerational transmission of
    values in, between Black and
    White, 199-201
transitional paradigm in, between
    Afro centric and Euro centric,
    201-202
African folklore, 57
African society, elders in, 53-61
Age Concern England, 189
Age Concern England Active Age
    Unit, 192
Age Grades, 49
Age-set terms, 164
Aging Well, 85
A-gogo, 164,167,168
Ahoi mata puja, 68
AIDS epidemic, 39,40. *See also* AIDS
    pandemic
AIDS pandemic, in Nigeria
    history of, 43
    intergenerational impact of, 39-52
        interventions for, 48-50
        nature of, 43-45
        social, economic, and emotional
            health impact, 45-46
Akan, of Ghana
    concept of elders, 27-28
    concept of extended family, 28-30
    described, 27-36
    intergenerational cultural
        transmission among, 23-38
        cultural values and, 30-31
        described, 31
        discussion of, 32-35
        gender and, 31-32
        implications of, 35-36
        introduction to, 24-26

mutual assistance in, 30
  study of, methodology in, 26-27
Akuapem, 27
Akwamu, 27
Akyem, 27
Allen, K.R., 18-19
A-mama, 166
Anderson, B., 148,155
Anglin, J., 86
A-nkazi, 166,167
A-pongozi, 167,168
Asante, 27
Asen, 27
Ashanti tale, 56
A-sibweni, 166
Assess Your Stress Scale, 112,113
Asset(s)
  developmental, matching through,
    89-90
  matching through, in society, 87-90
Assimeng, M., 33
Association for the Advancement of
    Health Education, 108
Association of Class Granddads in
    School, 101
Association of Retired Persons, 189
Atchley, 81
Atomism, mosaic, described, 175
Atta, 67
Audit Commission, 193

Barnados, 190
Beauclerk, J., 176
Becker, G., 35
Bengtson, V.L., 13,15,16
Beth Johnson Foundation, Centre for
    Intergenerational Practice at,
    191,194
Better Government for Older People
    (BGOP), 189
BGOP. *See* Better Government for
    Older People (BGOP)
Bhat, A.K., 32,33

Big Brothers and Sisters, matching in,
    87-88
Black Enterprise, 201
Blieszner, R., 13,18-19
Boas, F., 157
Bono, 27
Boström, A-K, 95
Bourdieu, P., 174
Boys and Girls Club, 137
Brahmins of Mysore, 69
Brazelton, 88
Broderick, C., 9
Brubaker, T.H., 13
Burling, R., 160

C4–Contemporary Confluence of
    Cultures on the Continent of
    Africa, 198
Cabral, A., 184
Cain, M., 42
Caldwell, J.C., 25,42
Cattel, M.G., 42
Cauce, A.M., 18
CDC. *See* Centers for Disease Control
    and Prevention (CDC)
CEDEV, 136
Cekisani, M., 205
Center for Gerontology, at University
    of Cape Town, 182
Center for Human Environments, at
    City University of New York
    Graduate Center, 122,124
Center for Social and Urban Research,
    of University of Pittsburgh,
    107
Centers for Disease Control and
    Prevention (CDC), 108
Centre for Intergenerational Practice,
    192
  at Beth Johnson Foundation,
    191,194
Ceremony, Roka, 67
Césaire, 202
Chadha, N.K., 1,63

Chatters, L.M., 12
Childcare, international developments
    related to, 190-191
Children
    Developmental Asset Framework
        for, 89,90
    international developments related
        to, 190
    Nigerian, 41
Children Bill, 190
ChiTumbuka kinship lexicon, 149,150
ChiTumbuka language, 150
Chi-wuya, 166
Chomsky, N., 157
City University of New York Graduate
    Center, Center for Human
    Environments at, 122,124
City-County Building, 132,134
Combinatory, defined, 78
Commission on Gender Equality, 203
Common descent, 160
Community development
    intergenerational engagement and,
        120-121
    intergenerational programming and,
        121-123
Community participation, promotion
    of, intergenerational strategy
    for, 119-146. *See also*
    Futures Festival
"Concept Complexity," 90
Confluence, in intergenerational
    practices in Africa, 211
Counsel and Care, 189
Crago, N., 119
Cross-cultural values, in Africa,
    between Black and White,
    199-201
Cultural reproduction
    described, 174
    in generational relationships in
        Africa, 174-175
Cultural transmission, of
    intergenerational theory in
    society, 82-83

Cultural values, of Akan of Ghana,
    30-31
Culture, high, defined, 179
Cumming, 81
Curriculum 2005, 200

Dade County Public Schools, 122
Dar es Salaam, 60
Daycare Trust, 190
Delhi University, 1
Demythologization, intergenerational
    practices related to, in Africa,
    between old Gods and new
    worlds, 202-203
Denkyira, 27
Department for Education and Science,
    190
Department of Health, 188,190
    Physical, and Recreation Education
        (DHPRE), of University of
        Pittsburgh, 107,108
Descent, common, 160
Descent group, 160
"Design the Ideal Community"
    mural(s), 132
"Design the Ideal Community" Mural
    Painting, 128
Development, community
    intergenerational engagement and,
        120-121
    intergenerational programming and,
        121-123
Developmental asset(s), matching
    through, 89-90
Developmental Asset Framework for
    young children, 89,90
Developmental Asset Framework of
    Search Institute, 89
Dhlomo, 202
DHPRE. *See* Department of Health,
    Physical, and Recreation
    Education (DHPRE)
Dhruvarajan, R., 32,33
Directors for Children's Services, 193

Directors for Older People's Services,
        193
"Disengagement Theory," 81
Diwalii, 68
Dowd, J.J., 34
Duquin, M., 105

ECDAF, 89
Economic impact, of AIDS pandemic
        in Nigeria, 45-46
Economy, social, in Sweden, 99-101
Edos, 177
Education Business Development
        Partnership, 192
Egan, F., 160
Ego, 156-157,157f,163,164,166,
        167-168,169
1884/85 Berlin Conference, 175
Eke, B., 39
Elder(s)
    in African society, 53-61
        folklore view of, 55-56
    Akan concept of, 27-28
Elderly, in India, 64-68
Emory United Methodist Church,
        107,108
Emotional health impact, of AIDS
        pandemic in Nigeria, 45-46
Empowerment, defined, 121
England, population over 60 years in,
        192-193,193f
English perspective, of
        intergenerational
        developments, 187-195. *See
        also* Intergenerational
        developments, English
        perspective of
"Enhancing Global Social Change
        Through Intergenerational
        Initiatives," xi
Epidemic, AIDS, 39,40. *See also* AIDS
        pandemic
Erikson, E., 83,84,85,92,218
Eriksonian theory, 83-85

EU Directive, 190
European Directive on Age
        Discrimination, 189
European Year of Older People 1993,
        98
    Swedish Committee for, 98
Extended family, Akan's concept of,
        28-30

Faith-based intergenerational health
        and wellness program,
        105-118
    described, 107-108
    focus group, 114-116
    results of, 111-116
    typical Saturday schedule, 109-111
*Families: Intergenerational and
        Generational Connections,*
        6,9
Family(ies)
    extended, Akan's concept of, 28-30
    institution of, in India, 64-68
    Nigerian
        children in, 41
        living arrangements of, 41-42
Family studies, 5-22
    described, 7-8
    introduction to, 6
    literature review of, 9-19,10f-11f,14f
Family unit, defined, 151
Fante, 27
Farghal, 178
Fayette County, Penn State
        Cooperative Extension
        Community Development
        Educator in, 127
Fayette County Family Fun Fest, 127,
        129-130,135t
Fayette County Futures Festival,
        127-130,129f,133f,135t
    background of, 127
    outcomes of, 128-129
    process of, 127-128
    reflections on, 129-130

Fayette Enterprise Community/Fayette
    Forward, 127
Federal Enterprise Community, 127
Ferreira, M., 208
Fertility, motive for, "old age
    security," 42
Fetterman, D., 105
"Fiery spirits," in Sweden, 99
Focus class, 161
Folklore, African, 57
Folklore view, of elders in African
    society, 55-56
Folktale(s), Matengo, 56
Freedom of Choice/Older People and
    Public Health, 95,97
Friedlander, D., xii
Fuentes, C., 172
Futures Festival, 119-146
    comparison of, 134-136,135t
    described, 124-127
    evaluation of, 139-140
    Fayette County, 127-130,129f,
        133f, 135t. *See also* Fayette
        County Futures Festival
    Lincoln Place Community Pride
        Festival, 130-134,133f,135t.
        See also Lincoln Place
        Community Pride Festival
    organization of
        "stakeholder analysis" as
            prelude to, 136-139
        background of, 136
        stakeholder groups in,
            identification of, 136-147
        stakeholder interests and
            concerns in, 137-139
    pre- and post-event questionnaire
        tools for, 144-146
    in western Pennsylvania,
        124-136,129f, 135t

GAPA project. *See* Grandmothers
    Against Poverty and Aids
    (GAPA) project

Geertz, C., 150
Gender, in intergenerational cultural
    transmission among Akan of
    Ghana, 31-32
Generation, defined, 155
Generation terms, 164
Generational relationships
    in Africa
        colonial legacy of, 179-180
        concepts of, 173-175
        contemporary transformations
            in, 181-183
        cultural reproduction in,
            174-175
        described, 176-179
        future, construction,
            deconstruction,
            reconstruction, and
            transformation of, 183-184
        introduction to, 162-173
        post-colonial, 180-181
        transformations over time,
            171-185
        scope of, 175-176
    described, 173-174
Generations Together, 107,108
Generativity, in society, 83-85
George, L.K., 16
Ghana, Akan of, intergenerational
    cultural transmission among,
    23-38. *See also* Akan, of
    Ghana, intergenerational
    cultural transmission among
Global intergenerational research,
    programs and policies related
    to, 215-219
God's Bits of Wood, 58,59
Gold, D.T., 16
Goodenough, W.H., 160
Grandchildren, grandparents raising,
    health and wellness issues
    related to, 106-107
Grandmother(s), in intergenerational
    practices in Africa, 209-210

Grandmothers Against Poverty and
    Aids (GAPA) project, 210
"Grandmothers' disease"
    described, 209-210
    in intergenerational practices in
        Africa, 209-210
Grandparent(s), raising grandchildren,
    health and wellness issues
    related to, 106-107
Granville, G., 192
Greengrass, S., 78
Greenspan, 88
Griffin, C.L., 47
Gubrium, J.F., 17
Gush, C., 182

Hagestad, G., 70
Hampaté Ba, A., 54
Handbook on Marriage and the
    Family, 6,9,18
Hanks, R.S., 2,5,16
Hann, D., 18
Hareven, T.K., 13,15,16-17
Haworth Press, Inc., xii
Health
    emotional, impact of AIDS
        pandemic in Nigeria on,
        45-46
    holistic, and wellness, 108-109
Health issues, for grandparents raising
    grandchildren, 106-107
Healthy People 2010,108
Help the Aged, 189
Henry, 81
"Hidden Treasure" Our Heritage–New
    Horizons, 122
Higdon, F., 119
High culture, defined, 179
Hill-Lubin, M., 60
Hirshorn, B., 17
Hoffman, J., 177,180,197
Holistic Health, and wellness, 108-109
Holmstead & Mifflin Township
    Historical Society, 134

"How Spider Obtained the Sky-god's
    Stories," 56
Human Sciences Research Council,
    182-183

I Am Not a Witch, 203-204
ICIP. See International Consortium
    of Intergenerational
    Programmes (ICIP)
Igbo proverb, 59
Illiteracy, in intergenerational practices
    in Africa, 210-211
India
    elderly in, 64-68
    institution of family in, 64-68
    intergenerational relationships in.
        See also Intergenerational
        relationships, in India
Industrial Revolution, 13
Intergenerational cultural transmission,
    among Akan of Ghana,
    23-38. See also Akan, of
    Ghana, intergenerational
    cultural transmission among
Intergenerational developments
    English perspective of, 187-195
        activities, 191-192
        childcare and, 190-191
        children and, 190
        future directions in,
            192-194,193f
        introduction to, 187-188
        NGOs and, 190
Intergenerational Directory, 191
Intergenerational engagement, and
    community development,
    120-121
Intergenerational Family Studies
    Research in the 1960s, 9
Intergenerational Family Studies
    Research in the 1970s,
    9-12,10f-11f

Intergenerational Family Studies Research in the 1980s, 12-13

Intergenerational Family Studies Research in the 1990s, 18-19

Intergenerational health and wellness program, faith-based, 105-118. *See also* Faith-based intergenerational health and wellness program

Intergenerational initiatives, in Sweden, 95-103
described, 98-99
"fiery spirits" and, 99
financial support for, 101-102
future of, 102-103
historical perspective of, 97-98
introduction to, 96-97
social economy and, 99-101

Intergenerational practices, in Africa
between being a grandmother and "grandmothers' disease," 209-210
developmental approach to, 208-211
new imageries in, 206-208
postmodern exploration of, 197-213
between premodernity and postmodernity, 211
between respect and reciprocity, 207-208
between "too much to die off" and "too little to live off," 208-209
towards spirituality and demythologization, 202-203
translation-related, between continuity and change, 205-206
transmission of values, 199-206
between Black and White, 199-201

transitional paradigm, 201-202
between wisdom and illiteracy, 210-211

Intergenerational programmes
and community development, 121-123
English perspective of, developments in, 191-192
rationale for, 120-121
roots of, 120-121

Intergenerational relationships
among Tumbuka of northern Malawi, 147-170,151t, 153f,153t,157f. *See also* Tumbuka, of northern Malawi, intergenerational relations among
changing pattern of, in Nigeria, 42-43
in India, 63-73
binding factors in, 69-71
changes in, 68-69
traditional Nigerian patterns of, 40-42

Intergenerational research, global, programs and policies related to, 215-219

Intergenerational studies, 5-22
described, 8-9
introduction to, 6

Intergenerational theory, in society, 75-94
activity theory, 80-82
combinatory aspects of, 78-80
concepts for, 78-80
cultural transmission of, 82-83
generativity, 83-85
life span theory, 83-85
matching through needs and assets, 87-90
reciprocal transformation, 86-87
relating to, 86
trends in, 77-78

Intergenerational transfers, 208

International Consortium of
	Intergenerational
	Programmes (ICIP), 1,120

Jenks, C., 174,179,181
Joseph, S., 184
*Journal of Intergenerational
	Relationships*, xi, 8
Journal of Marriage and the Family,
	6,9

Kaphagawani, D.N., 198
Kaplan, M.S., 119,126,178
Keita, F., 59
Kids Club Network, 190
Kim, T-C, 84
Kinship
	among Tumbuka of northern
		Malawi, 157-161,159f
	defined, 155
Kinship terminology, of Tumbuka of
		northern Malawi, semantic
		analysis of, 161,163-169,
		166t-168t
Kivett, V.R., 17
Komter, A.E., 25
Kotre, 85
Krog, A., 199
Kwawu, 27

Language, ChiTumbuka, 150
Larkin, E., xii, 3
Lawton, L., 18
Lee, G.R., 12
Lerner, R., 76,77
Levi-Strauss, 150,160
Lewis, E., 12
Life span theory, in society, 83-85
"Life-Time Intergenerational
		Exchange/Wealth Flow"
		model, 42

Lincoln Place Community Pride
		Festival, 130-134,133f, 135t
	background of, 130-131
	outcomes of, 132-134,133f
	process of, 131-132
	reflections on, 134
Lincoln Place Presbyterian Church,
		131,134
Longevity revolution, defined, 121
Lounsbury, F.G., 160,161
Lusophone, 176

Malawi, northern, Tumbuka of,
		intergenerational relations
		among, 147-170,151t,153f,
		153t,157f. *See also*
		Tumbuka, of northern
		Malawi, intergenerational
		relations among
Malinowski, B., 174
Mamaila, K., 203
Mambo Leo, 58
Mancini, J.A., 13
Mande, 59,60
Mantra, 67,68
Marriage, among Tumbuka of northern
		Malawi, 157-161,159f
Marshall, Gen. G.C., 128
Marshall Park, 128
Matching
	in Big Brothers and Sisters, 87-88
	described, 87-88
	developmental assets in, 89-90
	through needs and assets, in society,
		87-90
Matengo folktale, 56
Mayekiso, 202
Mazwai, 201
Mbele, J., 53
Mbiti, J.S., 198
McAdams, D., 84
McCrea, J., 105
McLoyd, V.C., 18

Mende of Sierra Leone, "Poro" secret
society of, 54
Mersey Valley Housing Programme, 192
Moetlo, 45
Moller, V., 206,208
Monongahela River, 136
Mosaic atomism, described, 175
Mpahlele, E., 202
Mphande clan, 151-152,151t
Mphande, L., 147
Mpumalanga Department of
Education, 200
Mu-chekulu, 166
Mu-dumbu, 166,167,169
Mu-lamu, 167,168
Mu-lolokazi, 166
Multigenerational households, 208
Multigenerational relationships, in
society, 90-91
Muntu, 166
Mu-nyane, 165
Mu-pwa, 167
Mu-sweni, 165
Mu-vyala, 168,169
Mu-woli, 165
Mu-zukulu, 164,165,167

NAPA. *See* National Association for
the Providers of Activities
(NAPA)
Narby, J., 176
Nash, S., 105
National Association for the Providers
of Activities (NAPA) for
Older People, 192
National Council on Family Relations,
5,7
National Pensioners' Convention, 189
National Service Framework for Older
People, 188,189
Ndbele, 205
Need(s), matching through, 88-89
in society, 87-90

Neighborhoods-2000,122
Netherlands Institute of Care and
Welfare, 142
Newman, S., xii, 76,77,194,218
NGOs. *See* Non-governmental
organizations (NGOs)
NHS, 188,189
Niakoro, 59
Nigeria
AIDS pandemic in,
intergenerational impact of,
39-52. *See also* AIDS
pandemic, in Nigeria,
intergenerational impact of
family living arrangements in,
41-42
intergenerational relationships in,
changing pattern of, 42-43
Nigerian families, children in, 41
Nigerian patterns of intergenerational
relationships, traditional,
40-42
*1987 Handbook on Marriage and
the Family,* 13-15,14f
*1999 Handbook on Marriage and
the Family,* 18
Nobel Peace Prize, 128
Non-governmental organizations
(NGOs), 189-190
intergenerational developments and,
190
older people and, 189-190

Obi, G.L.O., 46
Obierika, 56,57
Oduaran, A., 171,173
Oduaran, C., 171
Ohadike, D.C., 54
Oklahoma State University, 122
Okonkwo, 57
"Old age security" motive for fertility,
42
Older people

NGOs and, 189-190
    policies relating to, 188-189
Onyenechere, E., 46-47
Onyisi, 54
Ousmane, S., 58

Panchayati Raj system, 70
Pandemic, AIDS, in Nigeria,
    intergenerational impact of,
    39-52. *See also* AIDS
    pandemic, in Nigeria,
    intergenerational impact of
Parental Stress Center, Inc., 107-108
Parish Nurses of Mercy Hospital, of
    Pittsburgh, 107
Penn State Cooperative Extension,
    124,131,136
Penn State Cooperative Extension
    Community Development
    Educator, in Fayette County, 127
Penn State McKeesport Campus,
    University Center for
    Community Engagement and
    Partnership at, 124
Penn State McKeesport–UCCEP, 131
Penn State University, 124
Pennsylvania, western, Futures
    Festival in, 124-136,129f,
    135t. *See also* Futures
    Festival
Peterson, G.W., 15,18
Pfeifer, S.P., 9
Pharas, 67
Pittsburgh Council for International
    Volunteers, xii
Ponzetti, J.J., Jr., 2,5
Popular Movements Council for Rural
    Development, 101
"Poro" secret society, of Mende of
    Sierra Leone, 54
Post-colonial generational
    relationships, in Africa,
    180-181

Postmodernity, in intergenerational
    practices in Africa, 211
Premodernity, in intergenerational
    practices in Africa, 211
PRO. *See* Swedish Pensioners
    National Organization
    (PRO)
Programme(s), intergenerational,
    English perspective of,
    developments in, 191-192
Programming, intergenerational, and
    community development,
    121-123
Proverb(s), Igbo, 59
Puja, 68

Ramphele, M., 206
Rappaport, J., 121
Raynes, N., 187
Reality, social, relative, 198,199
Reciprocal transformation, in society,
    86-87
Reciprocity
    defined, 165
    in intergenerational practices in
    Africa, 207-208
Red Cross, 101
Redevelopment Authority of the City
    of Uniontown, 127
Relationship(s)
    activity theory and, 80-82
    centrality of, 80-82
    intergenerational. *See*
    Intergenerational
    relationships
    multigenerational, in society, 90-91
Relative social reality, 198,199
*Report of the Ministerial Committee
    on Abuse, Neglect and
    Ill-Treatment of Older
    Persons*, 203
Reproduction, cultural
    described, 174

in generational relationships in
Africa, 174-175
Research, global intergenerational,
programs and policies related
to, 215-219
Respect, in intergenerational practices
in Africa, 207-208
Richards, L.N., 16
Rites of passage, phases of, 155
Rittman, M.R., 17
Robbins, L., 119
Roberto, K., 18-19
Roberts, R.E., 16
Roka, 67
Roka ceremony, 67
Rollins, B.C., 15
Ronström, O., 96
Roodin, P.A., 215

Sagan, 67
SANLI. *See* South African National
Literacy Initiative (SANLI)
Sapir, 154
SASC. *See* Swedish Association for
Senior Citizens (SASC)
Save the Children Fund, 190
Schonpflug, U., 35
Second Chance, Inc., 107
Secret society, "Poro," of Mende of
Sierra Leone, 54
Semantic analysis, of kinship
terminology of Tumbuka of
northern Malawi, 161,
163-169,166t-168t
Senior 2005,98,99,100
Sentinel Survey, 43
Shaadi, 67
Sharpville massacre, 206
Silvers, J., 44
Simple class, 161
Smith, B., 194
Smith, T., 76,77
Social economy, in Sweden, 99-101

Social impact, of AIDS pandemic in
Nigeria, 45-46
Social reality, relative, 198,199
Social Service Agencies, 137
Society
intergenerational theory in, 75-94.
See also Intergenerational
theory, in society
multigenerational relationships in,
90-91
Sotshongaye, A., 206
South African Community Agency for
Social Enquiry, 182
South African National Literacy
Initiative (SANLI), 210
Spiritual Well-Being Scale (SWBS),
112,114
Spirituality, intergenerational practices
related to, in Africa, between
old Gods and new worlds,
202-203
Sprey, J., 17
Srinivas, M.N., 69
St. Aubin, E., 84
Stakeholder analysis
in Futures Festival organization,
136
as prelude to organization of
Futures Festival, 136-139
Stakeholder groups, in organization of
Futures Festival,
identification of, 136-147
Sussman, M.B., 9,15-16
Swahili, 55,58
SWBS. *See* Spiritual Well-Being
Scale (SWBS)
Sweden, intergenerational initiatives
in, 95-103. *See also*
Intergenerational
initiatives, in Sweden
Swedish Association for Senior
Citizens (SASC), 101
Swedish Committee for the European
Year of Older People, 98
Swedish Government, 96

Swedish Pensioners National
    Organization (PRO), 101

Taboo, 154
Taylor, R.J., 12
Tekeuchi, D., 18
"Test Your Knowledge" Quiz Show,
    128
"Test Your Knowledge" trivia game, 141
Things Fall Apart, 56,57,59
Thomas Coram Foundation, 190
Thoza, 151
Tikka, 68
"Too little to live off," in
    intergenerational practices in
    Africa, 208-209
"Too much to die off," in
    intergenerational practices in
    Africa, 208-209
Tower Hamlets London, 192
Townsend, J., 176
Trafford, 192
Trans Age action programme, 192
Transformation(s)
    in generational relationships in
        Africa, 171-185. *See also*
        Generational relationships,
        in Africa, transformations
        over time
    reciprocal, in society, 86-87
Transitional paradigm, in Africa,
        between Afro centric and
        Euro centric, 201-202
Translation, intergenerational
        practices and, in Africa,
        205-206
Treas, J., 15,18
Troll, L., 9,12
Tucker, M.B., 12
Tumbuka, of northern Malawi
    history of, 150-151
    intergenerational·relations among,
        147-170,151t,153f,153t,157f

terms of classification of,
        161,162f-163f
    semantic analysis of, 161,
        163-169,166t-168t
    kinship among, 157-161,159f
    marriage among, 157-161,159f
2003 Colloquium, Pittsburgh, 2
Twifo, 27

"Ubuntu Environmental Project," 205
UCCEP. *See* University Center for
        Community Engagement
        and Partnership (UCCEP)
Uchendu, 56
UNAIDS, 49
Unanka, G.O., 42
Uniontown Downtown Business
        District Authority, 127
University Center for Community
        Engagement and Partnership
        (UCCEP), at Penn State
        McKeesport Campus,
        124,136,137
University of Cape Town, Center for
        Gerontology at, 182
University of Pittsburgh, xi
    Center for Social and Urban
        Research of, 107
    DHPRE of, 107,108
University of South Africa Adult Basic
        Education and Training, 210
University of South Florida, xii
Unoka, 56,57
Urhobos, 177,178-179

Vaillant, G., 85,88
Value(s)
    cross-cultural
        in Africa, between Black and
            White, 199-201
        intergenerational transmission
            of, in Africa, 199-201

cultural, of Akan of Ghana, 30-31
intergenerational transmission of, in
    Africa, 199-206
Van der Geest, S., 207
VanderVen, K., 2,75,77
Vollebergh, W., 25

Walters, J., 12
Walters, L.H., 12
Ward, C., 77
Wasa, 27
Wellness, holistic health and, 108-109
Wellness issues, for grandparents
    raising grandchildren,
    106-107
Western Pennsylvania, Futures
    Festival in, 124-136,129f,
    135t. *See also* Futures
    Festival

"Where Is This Place?", 128-129,129f
Whorf, B.L., 154
Wijkström, F., 101
Wilson, L., 18
Wisdom, in intergenerational practices
    in Africa, 210-211
Witbank Society for the Aged, 200
WWW Federation, 132

Yoruba, 176
Young, Rev. C., 149,150
"Youth and Elderly Against Crime"
    program, 122
YWCA, 137

Zulus, 177

BOOK ORDER FORM!

Order a copy of this book with this form or online at:
http://www.haworthpress.com/store/product.asp?sku=5514

Intergenerational Relationships
Conversations on Practice and Research Across Cultures

____ in softbound at $34.95 (ISBN: 0-7890-2626-0)
____ in hardbound at $59.95 (ISBN: 0-7890-2625-2)

COST OF BOOKS _____

POSTAGE & HANDLING _____
US: $4.00 for first book & $1.50
for each additional book
Outside US: $5.00 for first book
& $2.00 for each additional book.

SUBTOTAL _____

In Canada: add 7% GST _____

STATE TAX _____
CA, IL, IN, MN, NJ, NY, OH & SD residents
please add appropriate local sales tax.

FINAL TOTAL _____

If paying in Canadian funds, convert
using the current exchange rate,
UNESCO coupons welcome.

❏BILL ME LATER:
Bill-me option is good on US/Canada/
Mexico orders only; not good to jobbers,
wholesalers, or subscription agencies.

❏ Signature _____

❏ Payment Enclosed: $ _____

❏ PLEASE CHARGE TO MY CREDIT CARD:

❏ Visa ❏ MasterCard ❏ AmEx ❏ Discover
❏ Diner's Club ❏ Eurocard ❏ JCB

Account # _____

Exp Date _____

Signature _____
(Prices in US dollars and subject to change without notice.)

PLEASE PRINT ALL INFORMATION OR ATTACH YOUR BUSINESS CARD

Name

Address

City   State/Province   Zip/Postal Code

Country

Tel   Fax

E-Mail

May we use your e-mail address for confirmations and other types of information? ❏ Yes ❏ No We appreciate receiving
your e-mail address. Haworth would like to e-mail special discount offers to you, as a preferred customer.
We will never share, rent, or exchange your e-mail address. We regard such actions as an invasion of your privacy.

Order From Your **Local Bookstore** or Directly From
The Haworth Press, Inc. 10 Alice Street, Binghamton, New York 13904-1580 • USA
Call Our toll-free number (1-800-429-6784) / Outside US/Canada: (607) 722-5857
Fax: 1-800-895-0582 / Outside US/Canada: (607) 771-0012
E-mail your order to us: orders@haworthpress.com

For orders outside US and Canada, you may wish to order through your local
sales representative, distributor, or bookseller.
For information, see http://haworthpress.com/distributors

(Discounts are available for individual orders in US and Canada only, not booksellers/distributors.)

Please photocopy this form for your personal use.
www.HaworthPress.com

BOF04